PUBLICATIONS OF THE
STATE HISTORICAL SOCIETY OF WISCONSIN

EDITED BY

JOSEPH SCHAFER

SUPERINTENDENT OF THE SOCIETY

———————

CARL SCHURZ

MILITANT LIBERAL

WISCONSIN BIOGRAPHY SERIES

VOLUME I

Date Due

CARL SCHURZ ABOUT 1904

CARL SCHURZ
MILITANT LIBERAL

BY

JOSEPH SCHAFER

SUPERINTENDENT OF THE STATE HISTORICAL SOCIETY
OF WISCONSIN

THE ANTES PRESS
EVANSVILLE, WISCONSIN

TO

LILY ABBOTT SCHAFER

INTRODUCTION

Carl Schurz in his essay on Abraham Lincoln defined the dangers which beset the biographer, whose relations to the subject of his work have been personal and sympathetic. 'We are,' he wrote, 'inclined to idealize that which we love—a state of mind very unfavorable to sober, critical judgment.'

Mr. Joseph Schafer has struck the keynote of his biography of Carl Schurz when he characterizes him in his subtitle as militant. He has labored under no disadvantage arising from personal friendship or even personal acquaintance, and the result of his objective judgment is a very virile portrait of the statesman.

It is at the author's request, made after the biography had been written and set up for printing, that this introduction is penned by one who realizes there were depths in the character of Carl Schurz with which only the members of his family could be familiar and of which they alone could fully know the antecedents.[1] There were, indeed, sharp contrasts in his character which only his intimates and those who loved him could well understand, contrasts which made him all the more lovable. In endeavoring to tell of these the writer of these paragraphs finds herself beset by the very pitfalls which Carl Schurz found threatening him when he wrote of Abraham Lincoln.

To the readers of this volume who are not familiar with Carl Schurz's *Reminiscences* it will be of interest to read what he himself says regarding his childhood

[1] The writer of this foreword, Marie Jüssen Monroe, is a daughter of Antonie Schurz Jüssen, Carl Schurz's youngest sister, and of his cousin, Edmund Jüssen.

and the early influences which moulded his later life.
They will realize that his sympathy for the so-called
'common people,' his appreciation of the simple
pleasures of life, his insistence that the purest and most
enduring joys are those which have not to do with
money or worldly possessions, were a heritage from his
parents that exercised a controlling influence over his
entire career.

Those of his grandchildren who recall Christian
Schurz, Carl Schurz's father, as a white-haired, blue-
eyed old man, removed from all practical duties of life,
think of him always as busy among his flowers and
birds, or in his primitive chemical laboratory, or as
roaming the near-by woods in search of botanical specimens, or, again, as seated on the piazza of his home in
his dressing gown and skull-cap, smoking his meer-
schaum pipe and discussing the latest astronomical or
chemical discoveries with the one scholarly friend whom
he found in the little town in Illinois where he spent the
last ten years of his life. They remember, too, the keen-
eyed, practical-minded old lady, with the soft, wavy
auburn hair framing her strong features, who was so-
licitous that her grandchildren should behave properly
and whose interest in public affairs was ever active and
intelligent.

Here is what Carl Schurz wrote of his father.
'Much I owed to the instruction which my father gave
me at home. I had frequented the village school hardly a
year when my father resigned his position as schoolmas-
ter. The salary, about ninety dollars a year, was too pit-
ably small to support the family, to which in the meantime two little girls had been added. My father, like all
who feel within themselves a yearning for knowledge
with few opportunities for satisfying it, had the earnest

ambition to give his children the education that fate had denied to him. With this object in view he made a start in a new direction and opened a hardware shop, . . . hoping that the business would gradually yield an income sufficient for the family needs. In me he believed that he had discovered an aptitude for study. He therefore decided that at the proper age I should go to the "gymnasium" and later to the university, to be fitted for one of the learned professions. For the time being I continued to attend the village school, but the instruction I received there was early supplemented in various directions. It was my father's especial wish that all his children study music. To this end, when I was about six years old, a queer little piano was procured which had neither pedals nor damper, and possessed several peculiarities incident to old age. But it served well for my first finger exercises and to me the instrument was very beautiful.'

For some time the village organist was the boy's music teacher until he himself admitted his inability to teach his pupil anything further. From that time on Carl walked four miles twice a week to the neighboring town of Brühl, where he received musical instruction from a well equipped organist and his first instruction in Latin from the parish priest. In describing his father's interest in literature and history and his desire that his family might share that interest, he writes: 'The low, whitewashed walls of the small, modestly furnished living room of our house, in which we also took our meals, were hung with the portraits of Schiller, Goethe, Wieland, Koerner, Tasso and Shakespeare; for poets, historians and scientists were my father's heroes, and he early told me of their creations and achievements. He read every book he could lay his hands upon and had collected a few of his own, among them Becker's *Universal History,* some German classics and some translations from Voltaire and Rousseau.'

Christian Schurz had all the qualities peculiar to the student who craves knowledge for its own sake. By practical people he was counted a dreamer. His speculative mind frequently dwelt on some abstract or scientific theory which sent it wool-gathering to the detriment of his material interests. He was not qualified to meet the competitive conditions of his life in a striving young American community and he confined his business efforts in America to the management of the fields and gardens of his son's farm at Watertown, until he retired from all active labors to the home of his elder daughter.

The mother, Marianne Jüssen Schurz, was of a different mould. Her son writes of her: 'My mother's opportunities for cultivation had never extended beyond the parish school and intercourse with relatives and friends. But she was a woman of excellent mental qualities—in a high degree sensible, of easy and clear perception and discernment, and apt to take a lively interest in everything deserving it. But the chief strength of her character lay in her moral nature. I know of no virtue that my mother did not possess. . . . Of literature she knew little, and with grammar and style she had never been troubled. But many of her letters written to me at different times and in different situations of life were not only filled with noble thought and sentiment, but possessed a rare poetic beauty of expression; the unconscious greatness of her soul found its own language. Her very being exercised a constantly elevating and stimulating influence, although she could aid her children but little in the acquisition of what is commonly called knowledge.'

All of these influences remained with Carl Schurz throughout the changing and absorbing experiences of his eventful life. Many a happy hour he spent with his sisters, who were members of his family during a long succession of summers at Lake George, recalling the early days in the little German village and later days at Watertown, Wisconsin, where the family had found congenial spirits among the German immigrants, many of whom were counted impractical idealists. To have known him in these later years is to have known a man whose dominant traits were a love for nature and humanity alike, one whose militant spirit was not bowed but softened and controlled by a large minded and matured estimate of life.

George McAneny, his friend and aid through the strenuous years of work in the interest of Civil Service reform, honored the memory of Carl Schurz in a commemorative speech on the occasion of the centenary celebration held in New York in March of last year. He said in part, in speaking of his love for the German language and literature and the arts: 'These qualities of mind, with his own love of beauty, whether expressed in reflective writing or in music, or in any other fashion, ran all through his being. He was himself a master of music and often the music in his heart ran through his fingers into a rare composition of his own.

'The story is told—and it is true—of an evening during Lincoln's most troubled times, when the President, tired to exhaustion lay on a couch in his White House sitting-room, unable, literally, to get to sleep; of his beloved young German quietly coming in, sensing it all, and beginning softly to play from Beethoven; of the distressed Mrs. Lincoln sitting watchfully by until the touch of Schurz's magic closed the President's eyes and there fell upon him the first long and restful sleep he had known for days.

'The quality of his soul was well shown, too, in his love of the out-of-doors and of the beautiful lake where, for a quarter of a century in the summer time, he "worked and played, rested and created." The woods about the home he knew there are of surpassing loveliness, and kept in the fashion that springs from German appreciation of the forest. We were neighbors at Lake George, and it happened to be my good fortune to share with him there many of his days and many of his walks and to listen to his dissertations upon the stirring times and events through which he had passed. It was there, too, that he wrote his memoirs. He had names for the great trees. "Old Abe" was the finest of them all. He had names for the rocks and rills,—the rocks of "Brunhilde" and of the "Walküre," the spring of "Bimini." The densest grove of pines was to him the "Schwarzwald." Everywhere among the woods and paths, and about the lake itself, he had found things worthy of these names, sprung from his memory of German legendry and from his own beautiful fancy.

'I doubt whether Schurz could have played the great part that he did in public affairs had not his nature also held the greatness of this simplicity of which I tell you. He could not have done in the field or in the forum or, in his many messages to the people, what he did had he not been the Schurz who loved the God that the abundance of nature revealed to him.'

If the measure of man's character be in his capacity for bearing sorrow and a like capacity for appreciating the joys of the passing hours, Carl Schurz had more

than the average of strength and force of character.
Those of us who watched his silent soul-struggle after
the death of his brilliant, promising, young son Herbert,
marveled at the ability for concentrated mental effort
in which he found the best panacea for his grief. To
have seen him emerge from that sore trial, retaining his
joy in life and with unimpaired appreciation of the
blessings still left to him, was to have learned an un-
forgetable lesson.

There were still other trials, growing out of his attitude toward national problems. His support, in 1900,
of William J. Bryan as the opponent of imperialism, in
spite of the fact that he felt Bryan lacking in many of
the qualities of statemanship, under the conviction that
even Bryan in the presidential chair would be less of a
misfortune for the country than imperialism, furnished
a marked example of this. He knew that by throwing
his influence toward the election of the man whom he had
bitterly opposed in former campaigns, he was certain to
forfeit the approval and even the confidence of many
of his friends and followers, and both approval and confidence, whether given him by personal friends or by the
public at large, were very dear to his heart. Often he
discussed that trying situation with his neighbor, Dr.
Abraham Jacobi, a friend so honest and loyal that he
could not desist from pointing out again and again the
perils of such a course. In the solitude of the woodland,
to which he invariably turned when his mind was
troubled, he made his decision upon this vexing problem
and acted as his conscience dictated, well aware of its
probable consequences, which did not fail to fulfill the
fears and prophecies of his friends. He suffered more
from the misunderstanding of his position in this critical situation than he had ever done throughout his long

public career for to be misjudged caused him profound sorrow.

But such dark days were few and far between, and for us, who shared many of the summers preceding the close of that unusually active and happy life, the highlights in it are many and the shadows few.

The frontispiece of this volume, selected by me at Doctor Schafer's request, is a reproduction of a photograph made by Marianne Schurz, Carl's youngest daughter, at a moment when he had returned from one of his walks through the woods and was resting on the piazza of his cottage. The date is about 1904—two years before his death.

MARIE JÜSSEN MONROE

Milwaukee, Wisconsin
January 11, 1930

PREFACE

An early interest in Carl Schurz was derived from my father and mother, both natives of the Rhineland, the one reared in the Mosel Valley, the other at Euskirchen. Although much older settlers in Wisconsin than Schurz, they greeted joyfully the advent of their brilliant *Landsmann* into the political life of the state and remained his devoted admirers to the end of their days. They knew the story of his dramatic experiences in Germany and familiarized their children with it.

The present work had its inception in plans adopted three years ago by the State Historical Society of Wisconsin to honor the memory of Carl Schurz on the occasion of the centenary of his birth, March 2, 1929. For that purpose I prepared under legislative encouragement, a volume of Schurz's *Intimate Letters,* translated from the German, which was published by the Society in February 1929. A sketch of his career had already been written by me and published in the *Wisconsin Magazine of History,* xi, 373-394.

These and other preliminary studies suggested the desirability of preparing an adequate biography of this puissant character, who passed out from among us nearly a quarter of a century ago, and a survey of available materials seemed to justify the undertaking. Among these, the letters to Schurz, deposited in the Congressional Library, the letters by Schurz lent this Society by the Schurz family,[1] the letters printed by Georg Reimer of Berlin in *Lebenserinnerungen,* iii, 1912, and the material printed in *Speeches, Corres-*

[1] See *Intimate Letters,* State Historical Society of Wisconsin, *Collections,* xxx, Preface.

pondence, and **Political Papers,** Frederick Bancroft editor, 6 volumes, 1913, constituted the principal primary sources. A large number of Schurz's later letters remain to be segregated from the collections of his American correspondents, but the main interpreting activities of his career are reasonably well illustrated by those which have been made accessible.

In addition, we have much supplementary material in the newspapers, both those he edited and others which carried speeches and articles of his not otherwise published. One important document, his contemporaneous account of the capture of Rastatt, which had been lost for eighty years, I had the good fortune to discover in Bonn, Germany. The notes on the text will convey to the critical reader necessary detailed information about the sources used. I had at my command the newspaper and book collections of the State Historical Library, and also the German historical and literary works of the University Library. Numerous individuals provided personal items about my subject, but I am under special obligation in this respect to Marie Jüssen Monroe of Milwaukee, Wisconsin, a daughter of Schurz's sister Antonie and of his cousin Edmund Jüssen, who is now nearest of kin to Carl Schurz. At my eleventh hour request, Mrs. Monroe consented to prepare the introduction for this book.

The steadfast and generous support of the Executive Committee of the State Historical Society of Wisconsin and the administrative aid of the Assistant Superintendent, Annie A. Nunns, have contributed in no small measure to the early completion of the book.

JOSEPH SCHAFER

Madison, Wisconsin
November, 1929

CONTENTS

LIST OF ILLUSTRATIONS

CARL SCHURZ
MILITANT LIBERAL

CHAPTER I

THE BACKGROUND

CARL SCHURZ was born March second, 1829, in
Liblar, a small village near the left bank of the
Rhine some dozen miles above the city of Cologne. The
place lies in the southern segment of the great river
plain which, beginning at the point where the Rhine
emerges from the highlands, a short distance above
Bonn, stretches north past Crefeld to unite with the
tide flats of Holland. Westward in a line from near
Düren to Euskirchen, the Eifel range shuts off the
view, while the *Drachenfels* and other members of the
Sieben-Gebirge (seven mountains) stand guard over
the region at the south and east. Taking the river as
one boundary, and drawing lines from Cologne and
Bonn to Düren and Euskirchen respectively, we enclose
a district mainly agricultural which supports a score
or more of rural villages, all easily accessible to one another, to the commercial capital Cologne, to the Saar
with its rich mines of coal, and to Bonn the university
city. Liblar lies near the northeast angle of the indicated area, but its people, a century ago, as now, circulated freely among the villages of the plain within our
lines and to some extent beyond these boundaries, especially to the north. The river, also, stemmed by
steamboats, invited to travel and traffic in the opposite
direction, as far at least as Frankfort where were held
the great annual fairs. Such was the geographical background of Carl Schurz's early life.

The chosen ones of earth rather than its obtrusive
nonentities are our real 'self-made' men. The greater

the soul the more it owes to personal endeavor, the less relatively to parental nurture, heredity, or early surroundings. Genius seems to be independent of a family tree, save for purposes of decoration; independent likewise of the character of its environment. Poverty or riches, crudity or culture are almost matters of indifference to one who in some way gains the impulse to self development and possesses a spirit that compels him to carry on. Nevertheless, when we look for the origin of the self-culture quest or what we call ambition, and for the driving force we call will, it quickly appears that the great soul is tethered to the earth as well as linked with the stars. His family and home community are therefore lights by which to study the beginnings of his career.

The stock from which Carl Schurz sprung was sound but undistinguished. His father, Christian Schurz, grew up at Duisdorf, near Bonn, an orphaned peasant boy about whose intimate circumstances tradition is silent. He was born in 1797 and was eighteen at the time of Napoleon's expulsion from Europe, which freed the Rhineland from the French domination. Like other sensitive youths, young Schurz absorbed the stories of wars and politics in this era of magical change, retaining them throughout life as his individual record of two decades which to a saddened but hopeful Europe meant as much as the previous thousand years. A man who had personally witnessed the endless fanfare of Rhineland recruiting; whose eyes opened wide at sight of a defeated French army returning from the east; who had once seen the conquering Napoleon and later joined a regiment for Waterloo in the hope of bearing aid to Napoleon's conquerors, stood in no need of books to stimulate his interest in modern history. Experienced with much feeling, for Christian Schurz was an emotional soul, the memories of those years never forsook him but supplied ample resources for the story-telling of which he was extremely fond and by which he initiated his son into the romance and politics of modern history.

On leaving the army, where he seems to have gained the rank of corporal without encountering active fighting, Christian entered a training school at Brühl to prepare for teaching, and on completing his course, accepted the post of school master in Liblar which he retained for some ten years, until the growth of his family dwarfed his meager, inelastic salary. He was the type of man who can be depended upon to make the practice of his profession a kind of religion. While not exceptional or especially effective outside, in the schoolroom he was a rigorous but kindly autocrat who knew what was necessary to induce children to learn. His knowledge of the subjects taught was more than equal to the demands of his position, and he had in addition certain intellectual fads like chemistry and botany in which he dabbled persistently for many years. These, together with his interest in remembered history and in public affairs marked him off from the average pedagogue and probably gained him more credit for learning than he really deserved.

In truth Christian Schurz was a man of only moderate gifts. Ambition was strong in him but he lacked both the steadiness of purpose and the mental keenness to win high success. Yet he sometimes surprised those who knew him best, as when he rose in a public meeting and made a political campaign speech. He was amiable but what is called 'homely' in appearance (save for a pair of fine, twinkling blue eyes). His stature was medium, frame robust, temperament active.

He had a passion for gardening, floriculture, fruit-growing, and was excessively fond of birds, of which he always kept an assortment about him. He was a good man, tender and true, but of a dreamy, unpractical turn and generally 'down on his luck.' One feels that if nature had granted Christian Schurz just a little more vital energy, had put a slightly better cutting edge upon his mind, or implanted in him a more imperious will, he might have accomplished large and useful things. As it was, despite many admirable qualities, his life was a partial failure.

One piece of good fortune, however, came to Christian Schurz at the age of thirty when, through his singing school, he attracted Marianne Jüssen, whom he married in 1827. Mrs. Schurz was a slender, comely woman, with wavy golden hair. While technically uneducated beyond the rudiments of learning, she was in all essential respects the reverse of ordinary. She was a splendid housekeeper and manager of family affairs, had a head for business, which her husband had not, and was gifted in understanding children. Her moral penetration equalled the practical. She had no need of a theory of ethics, for instinct enabled her to classify actions unerringly as either right or wrong. She lived a simple, sincerely pious life, with no touch of the prevalent skepticism yet with large Christian tolerance for those who, like her good man, failed to measure up to her standard of faith and practice. She is said to have shown much originality in speech and her distinguished son ascribed to her a vein of poetry and eloquence. 'I know no virtue,' he wrote, 'that my mother did not possess. . . . The customs and forms of the great world were of course unknown to her, but she possessed the rare grace of noble naturalness which goes far to supply a deficiency in social training. . . . The unconscious greatness of her soul found its own language. Her very being exercised a constantly elevating and stimulating influence although she could aid her children little in the acquisition of what is usually called knowledge.'

The one section of Carl Schurz's charmingly written *Reminiscences* which reveals in him a strain of the hero-worshipper refers neither to his father nor to his mother. It is the story of his grandsire, Heribert Jüssen, the giant *Burghalfen* of Count Wolf Metternich's seigniory at Liblar. A *Halfen* was a tenant who cultivated land on halves and since Jüssen was a large scale cultivator and utilized the old *Burg,* or castle, for living house and farm operations, he was called *Burghalfen.* He would rank socially with the English yeomen, though he was not a free-holder. Or, he might have been called a great peasant to distinguish him from the lesser peasants. At all events he enjoyed a high prestige among his fellows, and the sincere friendship of the count and the count's family.

But what won him the admiring reverence of his grandson was certain personal qualities that set him off from common men: a magnificent and handsome person, locally unequalled physical strength, a reputation for performing feats which no one else was able to duplicate, an imperious temper and dominating will that made him a virtual ruler over a community of peasants; lastly, a dramatic gift which set him up the observed of all at the *Kirmesses* (carnivals) and church parades.

At the time of Carl's birth, his parents were still living in the old castle with his mother's parents where they made their home at the time of their marriage. They continued to reside there until the child was four years of age, and as long as he remained at home in

Liblar he frequented the castle and court yard, accompanied his grandfather as he went about his farm work, watched him direct and discipline his men, or visit condign punishment upon some community wrongdoer; for in such cases Jüssen was self-appointed judge, jury, and executioner, all with the tacit approval of the neighborhood.

The old castle yard was separated by a bridged moat from the grounds of the new castle, where the count's family resided in summer, where distinguished personages assembled in full view of the *Burg* folk, and where the exciting preparations for hunting the wild boar in the adjacent forest must have thrilled the hearts of eager children watching big-eyed from the opposite bank. That was particularly true in Carl Schurz's case because, by invitation of Count Metternich, his grandfather, father, and uncles often participated in the chase on equal terms with the lords and gentlemen.

It would be hard to say whether the boy inherited from his grandfather anything aside from his splendid physique. Certainly the *Burghalfen* bequeathed to him neither his handsome countenance nor his business aptitude. Nevertheless this early association with a masterful personality, under surroundings in which pomp and pageantry played no inconsiderable rôle, left an indelible impress upon the child's character. Heribert Jüssen was one of the men who, in a world ruled by caste, 'stood erect in his own boots;' his spirit recognized no social superiors. The child who watched him with loving veneration became himself a militant democrat,[1] at first in his own country, by way of protest against conditions as they were, and then in the land of supposedly

[1] Socially, not politically.

equal opportunity. Jüssen was accustomed to impose his own will upon others. The child whose heart throbbed in unison with his would later manifest the same urge to dominate over his fellows. Grandsire and grandson were alike haters of wrongdoers and righters of wrongs, though the primitive methods of the one had no place in the enlightened polity of the other. There was, in old Europe as elsewhere, a 'master' spirit, sharply opposed to its correlative the 'servant' spirit. Carl Schurz, despite his humble birth and the relative poverty of his family was as clearly representative of the 'master' spirit as was John C. Calhoun. The explanation, unless we are prepared to ascribe everything to heredity, must be sought in the Liblar background of his earliest years, which we have here described.

CHAPTER II

BOYHOOD TRAITS AND HABITS

MOTHERS of noted men have not often been diarists. Hence the biographer is denied an accurate knowledge of those unusual experiences of childhood which, like the bent twig, might explain how his subject's character was given particular twists and directions. In Carl Schurz's case a very slight substitute for such a record can be found in the few incidents of earliest years which he describes, from memory or tradition, in his delightful personal story. One of these he calls 'a very exciting love affair.' It occurred when he was not quite four years of age, the other party being Marie, a beautiful young lady, daughter of the house of Metternich, who lived in the new castle across the moat from the *Burg*. Marie had been so good to the lively, interesting little Carl that he fell over ears in love with her and boldly announced that he intended to marry her. The idea that she could harbor any other plan, since by his own decision she belonged to him, never crossed the mind of this precocious 'cave boy.' So, when one day he espied Marie fishing for carp at the moat alongside of a young gentleman who obviously had a tender interest in the girl, Carl flew into a towering rage. He screamed at the young suitor to go away and called on the bystanders to throw him into the water. His outcries attracted a crowd, none of whom took his tantrum as other than amusing, which only added fire to his fury. At last the Metternich housekeeper had the good sense to coax him into the kitchen with the promise of a jar of quince jelly, when peace descended once more on

THE *BURG* AT LIBLAR IN WHICH CARL SCHURZ
WAS BORN MARCH 2, 1829

courtyard and carp pond. Presumably Marie and her
grown up lover continued their fishing. Another of his
recollections is of sitting on his grandfather's knee and
telling him marvelous stories of imaginary hunting ex-
peditions in which, with manifold strange adventures,
he had bagged both big and little game. As a variation
from his own story telling, he made his grandfather tell
him anecdotes of the French time, of the invasion of the
Rhineland by the Cossacks, and other stirring incidents.
A blazing temper, exuberant fancy, and a gift for talk
—these qualities were well defined in Carl Schurz before he reached his fifth year.

Carl's school career, which began when he was between five and six years old, was more than commonly
diversified. The village of Liblar afforded only the elementary grades, taught during his first school year by
Christian Schurz. There his formal start was made,
but since his father was bent on having him study music
in addition and there was no suitable teacher at home,
he walked to Brühl, four miles, twice a week to receive
instruction from the church organist there. A little
later his younger brother, Heribert, went with him to
take music lessons and during Heribert's hour with the
organist Carl was receiving a Latin lesson from the
priest. This regimen must have continued for a number
of months. Later, Carl was placed at Brühl in a model
school attached to the teacher's seminary, and at the age
of ten he entered the Jesuit gymnasium in Cologne to
prepare for the university.

There is in Carl Schurz's case, no evidence of that
startling precocity which we meet with in the stories of
men like John Stuart Mill, but like Webster he confesses he does not remember how or when he learned to
read. His father, of course, had taught him at home in

order that he might start more than even with the school classes. From the first, the father expected him to lead his fellows in learning and to be perfect in every school task. Proving himself both apt and ambitious, the Schurz family promptly decided that Carl, their eldest, the pride and hope of the whole connection, must have his chance to become a learned man. But this meant redoubled pressure upon him to excel in his school work. His love of applause enticed him to do his best, so that for the most part, he seems to have endured stoically his father's nagging urgency. But occasionally the boy's nerves became overtaxed and then a miniature rebellion was apt to break out.

Occasionally, also, Christian Schurz felt called upon to administer such reproof as, for cases of negligence in study, parental tradition has made and provided. This Carl Schurz frankly confesses in *Reminiscences*, but we need not depend for the fact upon his memory alone, excellent as that would naturally be on such a point. The earliest letter to Schurz that we possess was written by his mother when he was twelve years old.[2] In it she urges him 'to be industrious in all subjects,' the school report to which she refers in the same letter evidently pointing out laxness in some branch. Nearly three years later we have another and most pathetic letter from his mother to him. She says:[3]

> Dear Carl: Your departure today was very hard for me. I shed many tears and have not got myself in hand yet. Was it your father's letter, which I found yesterday; or is it a presentiment about the future? Dear Carl, you shall want for nothing, not a single thing. You see how hard it is for me when your dear father is a little severe with you. Give us pleasure; let it

[2] *Intimate Letters of Carl Schurz.* J. Schafer, (ed.) State Historical Society of Wisconsin, *Collections,* xxx, 1. Citations hereafter giving only the dates of letters all refer to this book.
[3] **Letter of January 3, 1844.**

be your whole purpose to make yourself and us happy. It depends solely on your industry and deportment; you have talent. Your father, indeed, can sometimes be hard, but you are also his pride; he is truly fond of you. Where will you find a father who needs his money so much and who is spending and has already spent so much on his child! Think of your poor little sisters. I hope therefore you will do everything to give your parents and sisters happiness. You will do that gladly, won't you? Also, dear Carl, gladden us frequently with a letter that has some significance. It is dreadful to hear from a child: "I shall write no more at all because you let others read my letter." That is a cold-hearted excuse. Children must not conceal anything from their parents. . . . Do not forget your prayers; think often of the dear God. Then he will not forsake you. Keep well and cheerful and study with pleasure.

At the date of this letter Carl was about half way through the gymnasium curriculum. Being nearly fifteen, he was probably showing some of the emotional disturbances characteristic of the adolescent period. His father was not an expert in the psychology of youth and could see but one explanation of the boy's failure to obtain a rating of perfect in every subject carried. That explanation, in view of his known ability, was willful neglect of his work. Then, too, Carl was displaying an unwonted streak of perversity in protesting against having his clever letters handed around to friends and acquaintances. This was wholly unlike him. Ordinarily he was not at all displeased at being talked about and praised; he could endure much adulation, though sometimes he pretended that it wearied him.

The reason for his low grades is not far to seek. His was a selective mind, not a machine for grinding Euclid and Horace into the same fine meal for the soul's sustenance. Carl Schurz by nature was a humanist. The Latin and Greek classics fairly inspired him, history was a never ending delight, and German composition, because it led him to test his powers of writing both in prose and verse, monopolized every available moment of his time. On the other hand, he felt little need for or interest in the mathematics and natural sciences to which, accordingly, he devoted time only grudgingly and because he was required to 'pass' them.

At the gymnasium Carl encountered two remarkable teachers whose admirable instruction confirmed an early ambition in him to excel in the ancient languages, composition, and history. The first of these was Heinrich Bone under whom he studied Latin and German during the first three years at Cologne, the other Professor Pütz, who, at a later stage of the course, opened up to him entrancing vistas of world affairs. In his *Reminiscences* Schurz describes the methods used by these two stimulating teachers. Professor Bone seems to have hit on a single general rule for composition which was not unlike Lincoln's self-discovered rule, namely: Take a subject about which you have or can acquire some real knowledge, think out every point to perfect clearness, and write in a simple, direct way. Carl caught the idea promptly, some of his descriptive compositions pleasing the teacher so much that they were read to the class as examples of what might be done with the subject in hand. The Latin texts, Caesar, Nepos, Cicero's Orations, were treated as if they were living productions of a living people about whose situation and doings much information was gathered as a background for the reading. The history was taught by the oral narrative method, to which Carl was accustomed from the story telling of his father and grandfather. But Professor Pütz required his pupils to be prepared to recite to him each day what he had related to them the day before. For text-book the boys used merely a dry syllabus.

At about the age of eighteen Schurz wrote a novel, *Richard Wanderer*[4], which was never published but still exists in manuscript. The background of his hero's story obviously is based upon his own early experiences which at that time lay only a few years behind him. Extracts from it may, with proper caution, be used to piece out the meager details we have about his boyhood and early youth. Thus we infer that he was a cheerful boy, as 'I dug and planted after school, and sang with my brother whom I loved like my own soul.' He recalls 'the joy when I took first place in school and with great erudition, tried to impart to my brother what I knew and he did not.' His father's talks with the *Burgemeister* about America and the revolution, and about the Napoleonic campaigns held him spellbound. The return home at Christmas from the gymnasium where he had lived through the first homesick term was an event never to be erased from his memory. Then he exhibited 'vast knowledge of declination and conjugation, the Latin exercise and German composition. And my father, in his pride, had a velvet coat made for me in which I paraded as the first student.'

The final touch in the quotation above may be fanciful, but possibly the velvet coat was a reality, for his father's pride was capable of leading him into any extravagance. There follows the story of his first verses, and at greater length, an account of his first play, written to be presented to his father on his nameday. It was so good, in his own opinion, that he had no doubt it would be performed on the stage. 'I heard myself called out,' he says, 'saw the curtain rise, and heard the endless cheering. I even considered the speech I would make at the supper which would follow the presenta-

[4] The *Richard Wanderer* has recently been printed under Professor Julius Goebel's editorship.

tion.' That his father, 'in silent ecstasy,' carried the
playlet around with him, and that the people to whom
he showed it 'were mightily surprised that a young boy
should have written it all,' was perfectly in character
and apparently gave him no offense. But then these
things all happened before he was thirteen, when the
emotional complexes were less uncertain in their re-
actions than they became in later adolescence.

The death of his brother Heribert at the age of eight
was a real tragedy to Carl, for the two boys had been
all in all to one another. Carl describes how his father
came to Brühl, and in tearful broken words told him the
sad story of Heribert's short illness and swift passing.
Then the two walked home the four miles, hand in hand,
each trying to comfort the other, their hearts all but
breaking.

To partly compensate for this loss Carl had many
cousins living scattered among the towns and villages
of the plain, whom he visited at the *Kirmess* seasons and
with whom he enjoyed many a memorable frolic. It is
related—but not by Carl—that on their frequent excur-
sions riding in the Jüssen donkey cart he had a way of
slipping out of the seat just before the destination was
reached, mounting the donkey, and making the grand
entry as the observed of all observers. We have here
the early emergence of a trait which proved, like his intellectual precocity and sympathetic spirit, a permanent
character element.

CHAPTER III

WOOING THE MUSES

CARL spent at the gymnasium the seven years from 1839 to 1846, absolving the remaining one year by an examination for which he had prepared privately. His parents having removed to Bonn, he lived at home and, until the gymnasium record could be cleared, studied at the university as an irregular student. His candidature for the doctorate began in 1847 and lacked one year of being completed when he left the university in 1849.

This period of advanced study covered almost exactly the second decade of Carl's life and witnessed the acquirement by him of those intellectual habits and interests which were destined to shape his career. The main influences coöperating toward his education were, perhaps not in the order stated, the opportunities he had, at Cologne and Bonn, for self-training, the stimulation received from fellow students, the lectures of great scholars, and his intimate association with literary men and politicians, especially Gottfried Kinkel.

From the day he learned to read, Carl was always a lover of books. He tells us of the joy he experienced as a young child in reading folklore tales like *Robinson Crusoe* and the *Landwehrmann,* and of the grim determination with which he plodded through Klopstock's *Messiah* because his father had unwisely given him that tedious poem to read on his way to and from Brühl. As he grew in mental grace, libraries that he could range through unhampered were always more significant to him than the formal lessons and lectures of the schools.

At the gymnasium Carl became intimate with two natives of Cologne, Theodore Petrasch and Ludwig von Weise, whose friendship contributed both to his enjoyment and to his intellectual growth. Petrasch was a charming fellow two years Carl's senior, bright, handsome, dashing, with considerable information and a flair for literature. He was an admirable spur to Carl, for his mind worked rapidly, he was opinionated, and ready with a plausible judgment whatever the subject under discussion. His self-confidence and candor while often refreshing, not infrequently goaded Carl into vigorous argumentation, either defensive or offensive. Nevertheless, Petrasch was 'like a brother,' which probably explains the downright way the two had of mutually exposing one another's weaknesses. But it also led Petrasch to take the younger boy's part against others and to help him to get his bearings in new and trying situations. Carl later, with pardonable exaggeration, thanked Petrasch as the first person who had shown him that he was not commonplace, and for aid in overcoming a disposition to bashfulness!

Von Weise, as the prefix to his surname implies, belonged to an old aristocratic family. He was not as quick-witted a man as Petrasch but was also bright, interested, and earnest. Both of them must be ranked far below Schurz in a final summary of achievements, yet for a time at the gymnasium and later at Bonn they were his recognized leaders. Petrasch came to America in 1863 bringing many of Carl's early letters with him, which enabled the Schurz family later to assemble an interesting collection of them for publication.[5] They have a unique value for the biographer on account of the glimpses they afford of the young man's teeming

---

[5] See *Intimate Letters*. Preface and 293-294.

mind in the years of its maturing, from 1845 to 1849, and they also throw light on the intellectual interests of himself and his group as they met to discuss such things in general as appealed to all.

The Cologne gymnasium during these years had a reputation for political conservatism, religious bigotry, and obscurantism. But Carl was already liberated religiously, through his home influences,[6] and being a voracious reader, for whom the presence of a library was a challenge to enter the tempting fields of literature and history, he became reasonably independent intellectually also. At seventeen he is already able to write, with gentle sarcasm, about the philosophy teaching to which, at the gymnasium, he doubtless had to pay homage. It was 'positively a comedy,' he said, the way Vosen, 'cuts loose on Spinoza, Hegel, and Schelling.'[7] Carl was interested in philosophy, though not Vosen's kind, and read rather widely, especially in the domain of ethics. But his affections were fixed upon literature in which during the last years at Cologne, and the first years at Bonn, he fairly steeped himself.

In his private reading Schurz was inclined to hold a particular subject long enough to gain more than a smattering acquaintance with it, but he also had enough of that genial desultoriness to insure his discovering new literary interests from time to time. Thus in one letter of 1845[8] he writes a somewhat crude critique of Byron, after having read *Beppo, A Vision of Judgment, The Siege of Corinth, Parisina, Mazeppa* among the poems, and also *Manfred* and several others of the dramas. All those works, save *Manfred,* he finds 'de-

[6] He tells us that he lost interest in formal religion soon after being confirmed.

[7] Letter of January 27, 1846.

[8] Letter of November 17, 1845.

ficient in prose content.' Besides, in his opinion they
suffer 'from extremely heavy wit.' About the same time
he hears a performance of *Hamlet,* of course in German,
which grips him so powerfully that he decides forthwith
to become a dramatist, if possible. With that object in
view he reads with feverish eagerness in the history of
Anglo-Saxon England, finally taking King Edwy as
the hero of his proposed play. But in less than a month
he has abandoned the attempt, having come to see that
'my powers were too weak for the task, my versatility
too little developed, and that I must study much more.'
He had turned the search-light in upon himself in an
effort to discover his true bent and for the moment was
discouraged about his literary future. A mere 'quill-
driver' he did not want to be, yet he could not claim to
have achieved anything of consequence thus far in
either prose or verse. The best of his many poems, he
thought, was a six-line phantasy entitled *Melancholy,*[9]
which can be rendered in English as follows:

> Oppressive fall the burning rays
> Upon the weary valley's ways.
> The brooklet creeps, and mute the breezes all;
> Upon their stems the blossoms droop and fall.
> A single rose, all withered, faint, and frail,
> Looks yearning tow'rd the sky's mysterious,
> darksome pale.

The character of this and other specimens of his
poetry, the quest for a mediaeval dramatic theme, and
a strong partiality he showed for legends as a form of
poetic expression, suggest that Schurz had not freed
himself from the romanticism with which the Cologne
literary atmosphere was still charged. His novel,
Richard Wanderer, already referred to, confirms the

[9] Translation by Prof. B. Q. Morgan. For the original German see
Intimate Letters, 8.

impression. It was his most ambitious venture of the
gymnasium period. The manuscript as we have it
would make a book of some thirty thousand words, but
having been rewritten after his settlement in Bonn we
cannot be sure about its original form. The effort he
put into the work made the writing of the novel an epoch
in his life. While engaged upon it he said: 'I am full
of material, penetrate it, and reproduce in a way that
gives me joy.' 'But,'—he adds—'I often rise from my
page with a feeling that the thing is all wrong from the
foundation up.'[10] That feeling passed into conviction
when, through the growth of artistic taste, he came to
realize that he had produced an impossible story about
impossible characters. The original design had been to
show the contrast 'between the ideal world in the mind
of a young poet, and the crass prose of everyday life.'
It turned out to be a sentimental, melodramatic performance the sight of which, in his riper years, must
have given Schurz many a qualm.

We have a record in *Reminiscences* of another pre-
tentious work upon which Schurz was engaged in February, 1848, when news of the Paris revolution came to
Bonn. This was a drama, based upon the history of the
reformation, for which he had taken Ulrich von Hutten
as the hero. Since it was never completed, nor the un-
finished fragment saved, no comparison can be made
with his novel. He gives us to understand that it was
the outgrowth of a new and profound historical interest
developed at the university where he was studying to
become a professor of history and where he had every
encouragement to do thorough and significant work.

The University of Bonn in the period 1846-49
was in its second bloom. Founded in 1818 to be a

[10] Letter of April 3, 1847.

'spiritual fortress' of Prussia in the Rhineland, some of
the greatest scholars of Germany accepted places on
its faculties. Among them were Niebuhr, Fr. Schlegel,
Hüllmann, Georg Hermes, G. W. Freytag, and the re-
nowned historian, poet, and traveler, Ernst Moritz
Arndt. The beginnings were so hopeful and stimulating that initial obstacles, though many and serious, were
successfully overcome and Bonn, by the end of its first
decade, ranked as one of the leading German univer-
sities. A variety of causes now conspired to produce
not only stagnation but retrogression. The Prussian
government during the reaction after Napoleon's fall
being keenly on the hunt for 'demagogues,' scented
radical doctrine in some of Arndt's writings and forbade
him to teach. Some of the leading professors died,
some others found congenial situations elsewhere. A
violent dispute over the theological teaching of Hermes
disrupted the Catholic theological faculty and injured
the university's standing with the people of the Rhineland.

These conditions prevailed, with varying intensity,
through the 1830's, but at the accession of Frederick
William IV in 1840 a new era began. The theological
schism was healed, and liberals the world over rejoiced
when Arndt, after more than twenty years of enforced
silence, was permitted to resume his lectures in history.
A group of promising young men came in as docents,
among them Von Sybel, one of the founders of the historical seminary. Several scholars of marked distinction
were added to the faculties. In the department to which
Schurz was attached as a student the most influential
new professor was Friedrich Christoph Dahlmann, a
great historian who was officially designated for the
chair of economics and politics. Dahlmann's lectures

are said to have been so popular, partly on account of his subjects, for he dealt with both the English Revolution and the French Revolution, and partly on account of his power as a speaker, that although he used the largest assembly hall on the campus no seat was ever vacant.

The university soon began to attract larger numbers of students, and it became the fashion for noblemen and princes to send their sons to Bonn. Albert of Coburg, shortly before he became prince consort of Queen Victoria, was a Bonn student, he and his brother Ernst spending eighteen months there in 1837-38.

Schurz almost certainly came under the influence of both Dahlmann and Arndt, as he did that of Ritschl in philology, but in his impatience to describe the exciting incidents of the revolutionary days, he neglects to tell us anything whatever about the teaching of these men or even to name the first two. Inferentially we may credit to Dahlmann a good share of Schurz's unusual interest in and grasp of the principles underlying the French Revolution, while his absorption in the reformation history may have been due to Arndt's lectures, or to the noteworthy *History of the Reformation* by Leopold von Ranke published about that time. As a patriot pledged to the unification of Germany, Schurz undoubtedly sang with the multitude Arndt's inspiring national hymn: *What is the German's Fatherland?*

Another influence, the potency of which he recognized fully, was his close association with a group of brilliant, scholarly young men with whom he was affiliated in *Burschenschaft Franconia,* one of the leading student societies at Bonn. To be brought into competition with minds like Johannes Overbeck, Carl Otto Weber,

Julius Schmidt, Ludwig Meyer, and Adolf Strodtmann, all of whom attained distinction in the scholarly
and literary worlds, was the acid test for Schurz. He
was too proud and ambitious willingly to be second if
there was even a remote chance for him to be first. Notwithstanding his professed bashfulness, he was re-
strained by no inferiority complex and, thanks to his
father, he had the habit of scholastic leadership. His
first public appearance in *Franconia,* as editor of the
Beer-Zeitung, or *Lampoon,* was an extraordinary
triumph which at once established his prestige. By the
summer of 1848 he was regarded as one of the outstanding men, possibly the most prominent man, among the
nearly one thousand students of the university.

But the strongest single influence of the Bonn period
upon Schurz's immediate career unquestionably was
Gottfried Kinkel, a lecturer on art history and in-
structor in public speaking. Kinkel was thirty-two
years of age when Schurz encountered him in the speech
department and, by his brilliant handling of the first as-
signment, captivated the young master. The picture of
Kinkel given us by Schurz and others is that of a wholly
unusual man. He was physically imposing but graceful, with handsome features, vibrant, finely modulated
voice of exceptional tone register, and the air of a conquering prince. His eloquence, tested in many a crisis,
was among the rarest, and with all these gifts he united
a jovial Rhenish disposition and a love of fun which was
irresistible particularly to the young. He was a native
of the Rhineland, born at Ober Kassel east of Bonn, and
had been educated for the evangelical ministry, his
father also being a pastor. His original appointment
at the university was as professor of church history, but

his marriage with Johanna Mockel, a divorced Catholic, caused complications which were finally adjusted by attaching him to the philosophical faculty as lecturer on the history of art. The speech work, which may appear to be an intruder in that department, could be justified logically as being one of the fine arts about whose history some knowledge was desirable, but the practical consideration was Kinkel's unique qualifications for imbuing his hearers with the ambition and the taste to succeed in the art of speaking.

In this one instance Schurz gives us a hint as to the professor's method. Kinkel asked him to discuss Mark Antony's oration over the dead body of Caesar. He had to explain, in detail, how the orator produced his effects upon the Roman rabble, at the same time warily guarding against compromising himself with the senatorial party. After the discussion he was required to declaim the entire speech. This performance brought him an invitation to Kinkel's house.

Mrs. Kinkel, a highly endowed woman and an accomplished musician, gave her brilliant husband the most perfect support in his social and intellectual relationships and their evenings at home in the old *Poppelsdorf Schloss* at Bonn became known for the animated gatherings of poets, students, burghers, workingmen, professional men, artists, and sometimes princes who rejoiced in the Kinkels' hospitality. Their home was also the place where, each spring, the *Maikäfer Bund* held its annual festival.[11] This was a literary organization started by Kinkel, Johanna, and some of their poetical friends. Begun as a dramatic club for the reading of Shakespeare's plays, it soon developed into a society

[11] The *Maikäfer* is the insect we call the June bug.

for stimulating literary and artistic creation. Prizes were awarded, the ceremony of crowning the victor, copied from the Greek games, was instituted and so many gifted men and women received from it the impulse to produce that it can be said to have exerted an important influence on the poetry of the Rhineland. Aside from Kinkel, who occupies a secure place in the German literary pantheon, particularly on account of his epic *Otto der Schütz* which went through fifty editions, the *Maikäfers* included, at various times, Karl Simrock, editor and translator of the Nibelungen cycle and other early Germanic works; Alexander Kaufmann, whose 'rich fancy strewed songs like a rain of spring blossoms,' as Johanna Kinkel wrote; Arnold Schlönbach, poet and humorist; Jacob Burkhardt, the historian of the Italian Renaissance, and many others. The *Maikäfers* came and went as occasion served, but those who lived in Bonn met periodically at Kinkel's house to read their newest works, to talk, and to enjoy Johanna's superb musical entertainments. Their last annual festival was the one held in the early summer of 1847. Before the time for the next one came around the revolution, with its myriad distractions, had wrested sovereignty from the muses at *Poppelsdorf Schloss* even as the people had wrenched it from the hands of the German princes.

Schurz began visiting at Kinkel's house in the winter of 1847-48, whether as a participant in the *Maikäfer* evenings we do not know, though his dominant interests, down to the outbreak of the February revolution, continued to lie in the literary field. There is evidence that as late as August, 1846 he cared but little for politics, and when a bloody riot took place in Cologne resulting

in a number of deaths, many injuries and great loss of
property, he wrote about it with epigram and jest, a
thing those who knew him at a later time would hardly
understand.   It means that, in his eighteenth year,
Schurz had not yet become the politically-minded and
deadly serious man the world knows.   Now the signs
portended a rapid and violent change.

CHAPTER IV

HISTORIAN OR POLITICIAN

THE Kinkel who read, in thrilling cadences, before the *Maikäfer Bund* his epic *Otto der Schütz,* was an authentic literary artist. But there was another and a very different Kinkel with whom the student of Carl Schurz ought to become acquainted, the politician, publicist, and revolutionist. This character can be discovered in his poetry, for Kinkel's literary affections, vagrant at first and attracted by many and diverse objects, tended to focalize in the German life of his own day and to be motivated by current politics. He wrote in 1842:[12]

> Nun ist mir längst vorbei die Zeit
> Romantisch zu phantasiren,
> Und wo ich hinaus in die Welt nur seh,
> Muss ich politisieren.

In prose English:

> The Time is long past when I was
> content romantically to "phantasyize,"
> and now, wherever I look out upon the world,
> I am compelled to "politicise."

He was a true child of the War of Liberation, born August 11, 1815, less than two months after Waterloo. With the generation that cradled him, he longed for a united Fatherland and the dowering of his people with all the rights and liberties that belonged to men in the century following the French Revolution. Kinkel had hoped much from Frederick William IV, who in some

---

[12] Poem *Die Sieben Berge,* see Dr. Joesten, *Literarisches Leben am Rhein* (Leipzig, 1899), 76.

respects desired to be known as a liberal ruler, but the reforms expected at his hands failing to materialize, a settled distrust of kings took possession of his mind and he began to look forward to a revolution.[12] This, of course, must come from the West. When it did come in February, 1848, no one in Bonn hailed it with greater enthusiasm or labored with more pertinacity to win scope for its successful operation in Germany.

But he did not wait for the arrival of the revolution before beginning to discuss it or the need for it with his friends, and there is no doubt that those who gathered at the *Schloss* during the winter of 1847-48 heard much of their host's positive and somewhat radical political philosophy. Being both a versatile scholar and a keen, witty conversationalist, he was ideally fitted to lead in discussing current topics. It would be incorrect to say that he succeeded in divorcing his young disciple from his love for polite literature, but if we are right in inferring that Schurz, on arriving at the university, was still a romanticist in his literary bent, and comparatively indifferent to politics, the contact with Kinkel soon gave him a new trend as a writer and a shift in interest toward public affairs. Kinkel's influence combined with the lessons impressed during the next two years in the practical school of life made Schurz an ardent devotee of politics for the remainder of his days.

Kinkel was an agitator, but an agitator of the highest type, ready at all times to make personal sacrifices for the cause on which his heart was set. A united Germany being the object of his passionate desire, the news from Paris announcing the revolution which substituted for Louis Philippe 'Citizen King' a republic headed by

[12] See De Jonge, Alfred, *Gottfried Kinkel as a Political and Social Thinker*. Columbia University Press (New York, 1926).

Louis Napoleon gave him the glad hope that at last the
union might be attainable. For a new French Revolution, like the one of 1789, contained the threat of war
and war clouds lowering from the west had a particularly disturbing appearance to people in the Rhineland.
Was that fruitful region to be once more torn from the
cultural entity called Germany, as had been the case a
little more than half a century before? Could reactionary Prussia unaided defend her western province
against a resurgent France, exalted by the success of
the new revolution and confident in the power of Napoleon's name to work miracles! German unity, it
seemed, must come as a condition of Germany's independence.

At that time Kinkel was not the most distinguished
of the Bonn patriots, for a united and free Germany
was the ideal of practically all of the professors, and
men like Arndt and Dahlmann had a wider reputation
and higher prestige than he. Accordingly, in the first
weeks following the news from Paris these men took the
lead, their objectives being first, democratic reform in
Prussia, and second, the unification of the German
states, which were being rapidly revolutionized, under a
Prussian hegemony. An address to the King of Prussia drawn up by Dahlmann was adopted by the university faculties on the eighth of March, two weeks after
the Paris news arrived. It begged the monarch to consider that only a united and internally satisfied people
could withstand the danger which was threatening from
France, and therefore the hopes of all Prussians for a
representative assembly and freedom of the press (reforms already promised by his father) must be fulfilled.
For the carrying out of his father's promise, the king
had only to give the word and all Prussians would throw

up their hats. This act would fit Prussia for the headship of Germany. A national parliament, 'under the
exalted leadership of your Kingly Majesty,' the peti-
tioners say, 'will complete the unification of the empire,
proving to the whole world that true popular liberty is
attainable elsewhere as well as in the British Isles. It is
the ardent desire of the people throughout Germany to
honor, in the person of your Kingly Majesty, the guide
and defender of Germany's future, and thus to see
Prussia ascend to a plane of importance to which even
the eagle eye of the Great Frederick could not attain.'
All but three of the professors signed this address,
Kinkel among the rest.[14]

Frederick William IV was being bombarded with
similar addresses from many quarters, as were the rulers
of other German states, usually with apparent success.
But the Rhineland, by reason of its critical situation,
was especially active in trying to make political unification a reality as quickly as possible. The king received
delegations, heard their appeals, and gave them such
satisfaction as he pleased, which sometimes was very
little. To a Cologne committee, however, he announced
in effect: 'Let there be a federal system created out of
the confederacy; I will place myself at its head.' When
the news of this promise reached Bonn both town and
university went wild. A great parade was organized
on March twentieth. Dahlmann and Arndt were fetched
from their homes as honored guests of the occasion,
while Kinkel bore the black-red-gold banner at the head
of the column and, in the market place, delivered it into
the hands of the mayor in a speech which electrified his
hearers. 'And thus I unfurl thee, thou German Banner!' he cried, 'Thou shalt assemble underneath thy

[14] Hansen, J. (ed.),*Die Rhein Provinz*, 1815-1915, ii, 127-128.

folds all tribes of our own race. . . . May the words
come true which the King has spoken: "Let a federal
state be born out of the confederacy of states!" I lift
this flag and call, long live the great, the everlasting
German Reich, sacred through our union!' The black-
red-gold banner was the emblem used in the German
War of Liberation, the colors symbolizing night, blood,
day—'out of the night, through blood, into the light.'[15]

Up to this point the university had been remarkably
unanimous, the town heartily supporting it and it the
town. A citizen guard was formed in which both students and professors participated, and when the election to the National Parliament took place seven or
eight of the latter were chosen to seats in it, others being elected to the Prussian Diet. Kinkel apparently
was not a candidate for either assembly in 1848, but in
March, 1849 he was sent, by the Democratic party of the
Bonn district, to the lower house of the Prussian Diet.
His rise to popular influence was due in no small measure to his standing with the leaders of the student body,
men like Schurz receiving a hearty welcome as speakers
by the surrounding peasantry, and partly to his editorship of the *Neue Bonner Zeitung* assumed in August,
1848.

By that time the course of King Frederick William
IV had come to be pretty clearly foreshadowed. He
promised reforms when the political situation seemed
to demand such promises, as in March, 1848, when he
agreed to give Prussia a popular constitution, and for-
got them when the exigency passed. Kinkel was convinced that the other German states, practically all of
which had secured constitutions during the March days,

---

[15] De Jonge, Alfred, *Gottfried Kinkel as Political and Social Thinker*,
17. See also note 44, 16. Hansen says, (ii, 128) he 'hailed the brotherli-
ness of all classes and the unity and freedom of Germany.'

would refuse to come into a federal union under an un-
reformed Prussia. Prussia must make herself an example to Germany by granting the 'rights of man' as
the whole world had come to understand them, a free,
representative law-making body, a responsible ministry,
freedom of speech, of the press, of assembly, freedom
to bear arms. The sovereignty of the people, in short,
was the controlling principle. To Kinkel it seemed clear
that, in extracting from the king of Prussia the promise
of a constitution, the people had actually effected a revolution which it was now their duty to complete.

Political differences soon declared themselves. The
Democratic party, aside from the main body made up of
earnest believers in thoroughgoing democratic reforms
such as Kinkel stood for, included on the one hand the
less radical socialists, on the other the more radical constitutionalists. Karl Marx and Engels, the great socialist organizers, and their followers wanted a workers'
Rhenish republic which was to be confederated with
similar republics throughout the world. The conservative constitutionalists wanted mild reforms with national
unity, and a ministry responsible to the majority in the
parliament. Most of them stood for unity under Prussian leadership, and stressed their loyalty to the Hohen-
zollern house. On the other hand, a large body of
Catholics, who acted with the conservative constitutionalists on most points, favored an Austrian headship of
the Catholic church, but were willing to let Prussia execute the decrees of the National Parliament. This
duality in the program of the constitutionalists weak-
ened the party's influence and gave the Democrats a
logical advantage in their propaganda.

The alignment of parties being what it was, there
could be little question about the political inclinations of

zealous and informed patriots like Carl Schurz. Obviously, the sane radicalism of the Democratic party would attract him because it was in harmony with the teaching of history and with common sense. He worked in closest agreement with Kinkel for the success of that party in the state, while in the university he took up with enthusiasm the plan of organizing the student societies into a general confederation, and in developing a 'universal union of associated students,' such as had existed after the War of Liberation and had been dissolved when the reaction came through Vienna. 'The best spirit,' Schurz writes, 'prevails in our party and we radicals stand unqualifiedly at the head. Von Weise and I enjoy a very extended popularity. . . .'[16] A month later we find him 'provisional president' of the student union, an office which affected his scholarly life adversely. 'But—Good God—who defends himself against the Devil when he comes in so flattering a disguise?' With Kinkel he attended the early autumn convention of the Democratic societies in Cologne, they having been named as delegates by the Bonn society. At that meeting Schurz followed the, to him, unusual course of remaining a quiet observer. It was there he saw and heard the socialist leader Karl Marx, for whose personality he conceived a strong aversion.

When Kinkel took the editorship of the *Bonner Zeitung,* in August, Schurz became his journalistic aide, but in September he made his first long trip, to Eisenach, to attend the assembly of the student organizations of all Germany. This experience made a profound impression upon his mind as the *Reminiscences* testify. The delightful acquaintanceships formed, the proof he discovered that German university men were all zealous

[16] Letter of May 29, 1848.

for a United Fatherland, the hopeful leadership for the national cause which the student groups represented, and no doubt the feeling within himself that he was fitted to be a leader among these coming leaders of the great German nation, sent him back to the university a different man from the one who had sailed up the Rhine two weeks earlier.

This was the first general congress of the student organizations since the meeting at the Wartburg in 1817 which had been followed by acts leading to their suppression. Now it looked as if a similar exhibition of political radicalism might result in a similar catastrophy. For, after the business of the congress was over and a large share of the delegates had gone home, there was a night of festivity at the same old Wartburg, the students being joined by many townspeople and by soldiers from the Eisenach garrison. Of course, there was a flow of oratory, which, through the ardor of youth, patriotism, and wine took on by degrees a radical tone. The soldiers' imaginations were captivated by it to such an extent that they cheered the idea of a republic, refused to obey their officers, and volunteered to be at the service of the impassioned young politicians. To cause a mutiny in the army was disquieting, but the students succeeded in persuading the soldiers to go back to their regiment and also prevailed on the officers to overlook the technical violation of military law. Now someone suggested that an address to the German nation be adopted, which was forthwith drawn up in a highly dictatorial tone and with a king-baiting comment on the reactionary political tendencies of the time. Schurz was one of the signers of this document and on his way down the Rhine, reflecting that it might be taken seriously by the Prussian government, wondered if it would get him into real trouble. Fortunately, however, it attracted little notice.

Meantime Schurz's activities as student leader grew ever more strenuous until he felt justified in describing himself as a sadly overworked man. The general union of students on the campus was perfected, the university authorities setting aside the great music hall for their meetings, and listening with respectful attention, if not with trepidation, to the resolutions on university affairs which the student leaders were presenting in a spirit of mounting imperiousness. Schurz no doubt continued to attend lectures, but his writing had now departed from its earlier literary paths and was centered upon questions of the moment. Many of the editorials in the *Neue Bonner Zeitung* seem to be marked by his facile pen but being unsigned they cannot be identified with certainty. During Kinkel's absence in Berlin, from March to May, 1849, Schurz suggested changes in the form and content of the paper which show that he possessed business insight; and he was quite as ready to give advice to Kinkel as he would be later to give advice to Lincoln.[17]

There is no better way to summarize the change which came over this ambitious young author, in the space of two years, than by quoting from two of his letters. February 6, 1846, he chides Petrasch with laxness in pursuing the literary aims toward which they were both striving. He was not producing lyrics, sonnets, epics fast enough. 'I should like to urge you to productiveness again,' says Schurz, 'to the will-to-do. Time is too glorious and youth too fleeting. With it [youth] the heaven-aspiring flame sinks, sinks murkily down into the ashes. Truly, a man can extend his youth, ex-

---

[17] Letter of March 20, 1849.

tend it very much (as Goethe indicated) but not to use
does not mean to lengthen it.' This is the language of
one who believes his life to be dedicated to the muses,
and it should be contrasted with what he wrote on the
twenty-sixth of June, 1848. 'In connection with our
great political happenings the thought has come to me
over and over how petty a thing it is to withdraw out of
the big, free, mighty, stormy world into the conditions
of academic life.' There spake the young politician.

CHAPTER V

A RHENISH RUBICON

THE word 'revolution,' spoken in quiet times to men who are habitually law-abiding, causes a shock not unlike that induced by the sudden apparition of a blood-curdling spectacle. On the other hand, the word 'politics' suggests respectable lawful activity in the management of associational life. While there are many similarities in the methods used by politicians and by revolutionists to bring about their results, both seeking to mold the social mind, in their attitude toward established authority they are at opposite poles. In the Rhineland of 1849, however, the contrast in that respect was not so sharp. Many things were happening which blurred the distinction between politics and revolution and the moment came when, through the confounding of loyalties, it practically disappeared.

The March uprisings, resulting in such a joyous smashing of prerogatives and substitution of liberal constitutions as to merit the appellation of 'people's springtime,' subsided quickly, the agitated masses quietly settling back into their customary activities. In most cases they failed to create safeguards guaranteeing the permanence of their reformatory work. They put faith in the honor of princes and too often their confidence was betrayed. But at all events the March days brought the prospect of that 'liberty' which, ever since the War of Liberation, had been the first of the patriots' two fundamental demands as they contemplated the future of their Fatherland.

The National Parliament, initiated by a small consultative group in Heidelberg, but recognized by all the states, had come into being as the appropriate means of fulfilling the other demand for German unity. To complete the program it would be necessary only to prepare and adopt a constitution for a free and united Germany, and to select a national executive. The principles of liberty demanded by the revolutionists in all the states, and which had been promised by the rulers, it was assumed, would be put in operation without undue loss of time. The train, therefore, was laid for a full realization of the age old German hope, so glowingly acclaimed during the War of Liberation and so wistfully adhered to by the generation which succeeded the liberators.

The people, however, abdicated too soon and reaction, under the guidance of Austria, quickly set in. Her objectives were mainly two: to hinder the general adoption of democratic reforms; and to prevent unification of Germany on a German basis, which would have reduced the importance of Austria in the union by keeping out her thirty million non-Germans. With this situation the National Parliament, meeting at Frankfort-on-the-Main, seat of the old confederation diet, was obliged to cope. The problem was so perplexing and difficult that it may have been asking too much to expect either a *Professors' Parliament,* as this body has been called, or any other type of constituent assembly to solve it. But the manner in which the parliamentary craft was wrecked in the passage between Austrian and Prussian absolutism can be indicated, and this will help to explain how it happened that Carl Schurz became a revolutionist.

When Schurz, in September, 1848 passed up the Rhine on his way to Eisenach, he broke his journey at

Mainz in order to pay a visit to the parliament city. He arrived at Frankfort at a moment big with tragedy to all friends of freedom and unity. The Parliament had passed a seemingly innocuous resolution ratifying Prussia's treaty with Sweden, called the Truce of Malmö, virtually concluding the war over Schleswig-Holstein. This truce would leave German Schleswig to be incorporated permanently in non-German Sweden, contrary to the wishes of the people of that duchy who, on the principle of self-determination, desired union with Germany. The Parliament strongly sympathized with the Schleswig people, and ardently desired their attachment to the German political system, but it felt too weak to rebuke Prussia or to run the risk of alienating her support. Thus the ratification was purely for policy's sake.

This vote was carried by a very small majority, and hardly had it been announced when a tumult was raised by the Frankfort populace, the meeting place was invaded, indignities put upon members, and as a crowning outrage, Prince Felix Lichnowski, deputy from Silesia, and his friend General von Auerswald were brutally murdered by the mob. Soldiers were summoned, but the rioters having thrown barricades across the streets, a fight ensued and a number of men were killed before quiet could be restored. Schurz arrived just after the battle, saw the blood-stained pavements, the barricades, and gazed with mixed emotions on the dejected countenances of the parliamentarians. With several friends he discussed, on the scene of the disaster itself, the probable meaning to Germany of the Parliament's loss of prestige. Then he proceeded on his way to the students' congress where Prussia's 'treason' in negotiating the truce with Sweden, the Parliament's self stultification in ratifying, and its consequent exposure to popular hatred and distrust became the principal theme of student conversation, conference, and oratory.

The parliamentary body, however, recovered some of their lost popularity through the soundly democratic imperial constitution which they published not long after these events. Austria's relation to the empire, one of the two most critical problems, they settled—on paper—by providing that the constitution should apply only to German states; but they appointed diplomatic agents to negotiate with Austria about another union, which was designed to care for all problems of common interest to her empire and the new German Reich. Austria's reply was to withdraw her delegates and indulge in muttered threats. Then came the supreme question of the imperial executive, which caused grave difficulty. Finally, by a very narrow majority, it was agreed to offer the hereditary imperial dignity to King Frederick William IV, but with only a suspensive veto over legislation. This noteworthy act, which many believed would complete the union of the Fatherland, was received with the ringing of bells, impromptu parades, oratory, and the blare of music. The twenty-eighth of March, 1849, it was thought would be one of the great days of German history.

So it would have been had not April third supervened to rob it of its glorious possibilities. On the last named day the parliamentary committee, dispatched to Berlin for the purpose, made a formal tender to the king of the headship of the German nation. It was a test he was not strong enough to endure. Despite earlier averments of his readiness to settle the German question if necessary 'against Austria,' he now proved unwilling to face the prospect of a war with that power.

Besides, he loathed the democratic features of the constitution, felt insulted by the withholding from him of the full veto power, was reluctant to coöperate with the kind of democratic Parliament which the constitution called for, (having created for Prussia a diet based partly on numbers and partly on wealth), and he wanted to have the princes overhaul the Parliament's draft. Some have suspected that the king was verging toward insanity but, while he was reduced to that condition later, there seems no conclusive evidence that at this time he was other than his own perverse, vacillating, fundamentally absolutist self.

The king's ingrained inconsistency now became the Parliament's and the nation's hope. Since he had not, in set terms, rejected the imperial dignity, there was still a chance that he might reconsider and accept it. At all events, the Parliament was nearly at the end of its resources; so it resolved to adhere to the constitution as drawn up, despite the king's objections, and to hope for his final submission to the popular demand for Prussia's leadership.

The king, however, proceeded on a plan of his own for the creation of a new German confederation of which Prussia was to be the head. On April twenty-eighth he formally and definitely refused the offer made by the Parliament, and that body, on May fourth, adopted an address appealing to the 'governments, the legislative bodies, the communities in the several states and to the whole German people to stand up for the recognition and the introduction of the national constitution.'[18] They provided, at the same time, that elections to the first legislative diet of the empire (*Reichstag*) should be held July fifteenth and that the

---

[18] Quoted in Schurz *Reminiscences*, i, 167-168.

new diet should meet August twenty-second. Until
such time as Prussia should adopt the constitution, the
sovereign of the largest coöperating state was to be the
executive head or regent.

So the plans of Prussia and those of the Parliament
clashed. But what about their jurisdictions? In Prussian territory would the act of Parliament be the supreme law of the land, or was Parliament acting on the
suffrance of the powerful northern sovereign who had a
large and well drilled army at his back? How far
would Prussia carry her opposition to the Parliament's
plans to obtain the ratification and adoption of the constitution by the several German states? What heed
would her sovereign pay to the diet of his own creation,
the lower more popular branch of which had voted to
adopt the national constitution?

All of these questions, at that moment, could be
answered only on the theory of probabilities. Nobody,
outside of the Prussian ministry, knew with certainty
what to expect, but the matter would not remain long
in doubt. All the smaller states, save Bavaria and
Baden adopted the constitution, but in Saxony there
had been a mild revolution which was now promptly
put down by Prussian bayonets. Two days prior to
Parliament's decree of May fourth, the Rhine Palatinate, which since Napoleon's fall had been attached to
Bavaria as the Rhine Province had been made a part of
Prussia, revolted in the hope of forcing the Bavarian
government to accept the constitution. In the neighboring Baden a rising occurred on May tenth and these
two movements coalesced under a common provisional
government. At the same time rebellious outbreaks of
workingmen and peasants, led by men of the higher
classes, took place in most of the Rhenish cities. The

Prussian government had ordered the reserves (*Land-wehr*) to assemble for regimentation and this hateful order the men were inclined to resist with violence. But everywhere in the Rhineland these risings were easily suppressed.

It was at this precise moment, May tenth, the very day of the Baden uprising, that Carl Schurz became a revolutionist. The *Landwehr* of the Bonn district had been ordered to concentrate at the Siegburg, a fortress a few miles northeast of Bonn on the east side of the Rhine which was used as an armory. The men were restless, sullen, rebellious, their ugly mood due in part to the anti-Prussian propaganda of Kinkel, who had but just returned from the session of the Prussian lower house where the constitution had been enthusiastically ratified. Arguing that the lower chamber of the diet, elected by popular suffrage, had given the true expression of Prussia's will, Kinkel now hit upon the plan of leading an armed force, by night, to the Siegburg, seizing the place, and arming the *Landwehr* with Prussian guns. From the standpoint of Prussia's governing authority this of course was the crassest kind of rebellion. Yet Kinkel later, in his clever and eloquent defense plea, convinced a Cologne jury that it was not merely a patriotic but a lawful proceeding in view of his loyalty both to the will of the people of his state and to the Parliament which had claimed the support of all true Germans.

Schurz describes for us the Siegburg fiasco: how the students cared for the *Landwehr* and others as they collected in the city of Bonn, the suppressed excitement during the day, the speech of Kinkel who appeared before his followers musket in hand, the organization for the attack which was in charge of Fritz

Anneke of Cologne. He also tells us of his hurried call at the house to take leave of his parents and sisters, the visit to his own room and the view he had from the window over the glorious Rhenish landscape with its *Sieben Gebirge* in the foreground. All this he was now to leave, perhaps forever.

Then at night came the actual operation. Their company, pitifully small as compared with the numbers who had shown unlimited heroism so long as daylight lasted, crossed the Rhine by the ferry and started down the Siegburg road. Schurz had been detailed to manage the ferry, and it occurred to him—afterwards—that it might have been a good military precaution to render it useless after their men had landed. But he allowed it to return to Bonn which afforded the Prussian cavalry a perfectly convenient means of crossing in pursuit. The storming party had not marched many miles when the sound of galloping hoofs caused a scattering into the cornfields. The few Prussian horsemen passed on to the Siegburg; no one was molested on either side; the attact failed to come off but participants in the attempt had become liable to apprehension and trial for treason.

Schurz accordingly did not return home, but went soon up the Rhine as far as St. Goarshausen where dwelt Nathan, an inn-keeper whose kindness to university students was proverbial. Having had practically no rest for four days and nights, he first of all took a much needed long sound sleep. After that he decided on his future course, which was to join the revolutionary movement in the Palatinate and Baden. Several student friends had remained with him to that point. Now they resolved to turn back and take the consequences of their acts. He could not do so. While it gave him a 'singularly uncomfortable feeling' to reflect that he 'was running away' from the authorities, a much more hideous thought followed, 'that I could not be proud of the act to which I owed my outlawry, although its purpose had been patriotic.' . . . 'And now farewell to the beautiful student life and its precious friendships, its ideal endeavors and hopes, its glorious youthful dreams!' Carl Schurz, accustomed till then to sail only on safe waters, had permitted himself to be swept into the vortex of revolution.

CHAPTER VI

CAPTURE AND ESCAPE

GERMAN historians are fond of insisting that the revolutionary risings in the Palatinate and Baden were 'meaningless' and that Kinkel's attempt upon the Siegburg was 'crazy.' But these judgments are too sweeping and probably colored by lights reflected back upon this period from a more brilliant epoch in Prussian history. To the democratic leaders in the Rhineland immersed in the events of 1849, the *Landwehr's* bitter opposition to being used by this government, against the partisans of the National Parliament, must have given more than a ray of hope that the reaction might now be arrested and perhaps ultimately rolled back. The people, by moving directly in the matter, as Kinkel and others urged, might yet save the constitution. There was inflammable material enough at hand to make a terrific holocaust if zeal for the new constitution should prove to be as widespread and as genuine as it seemed to be, and if the reserves of emotional energy, after a year of agitation, were not too greatly depleted. Workingmen in the manufacturing towns, suffering from maladjustments of the new industrialism, were clamoring for steadier employment, peasants were restless because harvests had been scant and prices low. The educated classes felt deeply outraged by Prussia's obsequiousness to Austria and by her treason to the ideals of freedom and unity.

At the moment there was doubt also about the soldiers. The Baden revolution actually began with a mutiny among the troops at Carlsruhe and Rastatt. If

the armies of the other states were similarly disaffected
the sovereigns might suddenly find themselves whirling
in mid air, all supports being rudely withdrawn from
under their feet. The Palatinate and Baden revolutionists quickly assembled a force of near fifty thousand
men, most of them military insurrectionists. They were
over confident about reinforcements coming to them
spontaneously from near and far, but they did, in fact,
accept the services of many foreigners including a Ger-
man-Polish legion. Had the business been better managed, on a broader basis of organization and with proper
attention to money and supplies, failure need not have
been the foregone conclusion it now seems to many
writers.[19]

The Siegburg attempt, one of a number of half-
hearted risings in the Rhineland, deserves special attention because it was the means of wrenching Schurz loose
from his social moorings. Unquestionably the affair
was badly managed. Kinkel was the type of man
whose mind was brilliant and logical so long as it was
permitted to function along theoretical lines, he was
not, however, fitted to direct critical activities of a practical nature. The plan of attacking the Siegburg was
presumably his own, yet according to Schurz the democratic committee was busy with the arrangements all
day. This shows that he distinguished not at all between
the requirements of a military problem and those of the
ordinary political questions coming before a party's
managing council. The openness with which recruiting
was conducted rendered pursuit a virtual certainty, yet
no precautions were taken either to prevent the Prussian cavalry from crossing the Rhine or to stop them on

---

[19] Schurz in *Reminiscences* points out what he deemed the mistakes
of the revolutionary committee. He thinks a general rising in support of
the revolution in Baden might have been produced by effective work.

the other side. In a word, the attempt was, what Schurz in his *Reminiscences* and in his contemporaneous letters calls it, a 'fiasco' or a 'farce.' He seems to blame Anneke for the outcome more than Kinkel, but the latter was no doubt responsible for giving Anneke military charge of the expedition and ought to have assured himself in advance that it would be conducted with at least ordinary prudence. None of the eventualities which might have been predicted having been provided against, the cornfield was necessarily the last refuge of the bewildered and frightened marchers when the danger of an attack became imminent.

Speculations about what might have happened had something else not occurred are rarely fruitful. Nevertheless, there is reason to question whether, without the impulse which the Siegburg project gave him, Carl Schurz would have swung himself into the revolution at all. Late in life his memory fixed upon this incident and the fiasco with which it ended as the main force impelling him forward on the path of doubt and danger. Fortunately that testimony does not stand unsupported, for in a letter from Rastatt to the home folks dated July twenty-first (1849), written in the belief that he was about to be shot by the Prussians, Schurz says he had for some time wished to fight for his principles and since 'the first attempt in that direction ended in a farce' he was 'irresistably urged into the struggle' as if he had 'to expiate a sin there.' The same idea emerges in a second letter from Rastatt written two days later to his university friends. Speaking of the circumstances which, up to a certain point, had kept him by force 'on the right track,' he adds: 'Then I did a ridiculous thing which at the same time involved an act of treason; this marks a break in my life course.' There follows the story of his going into the Palatinate and joining the revolutionary forces.[20]

From these statements it is a fair inference that if it had not been for 'the ridiculous thing' which Kinkel's ineptitude led him into, Schurz would have kept away from the disturbed area, at least for a time. But time was of the essence of his personal problem. Changes were taking place with such kaleidoscopic suddenness that a few days would have sufficed radically to alter his views of the general situation. It was on the twentieth of May, ten days after the Siegburg fiasco and the Baden military revolt, that the National Parliament began to disintegrate. On that day sixty-five of the most substantial members including such pivotal men as Gagern, Dahlmann, and Arndt, seceded in a body because they were unwilling to cut the last bonds uniting the Parliament with Prussia and plunge Germany into political chaos. Their withdrawal left the 'rump' virtually a revolutionary committee which could exert no real leadership in German national affairs and which soon found itself driven from pillar to post.

This parliamentary break-up was an event well calculated to steady an intelligent patriot like Schurz and it was quickly followed by other impressive incidents. By the end of the month Prussia had completed her diplomatic arrangements with Grand Duke Leopold of Baden which, on June twelfth, started two Prussian army corps south under the command of the King's brother, the later Emperor William I. This was the force which was destined to bring the revolution to a bloody end.

Schurz was too prudent to risk his life without some equivalent gain, either for society or for himself, and he

[20] In his letter, April 19, 1852, to Adolf Meyer he says: 'I found myself compromised in the United Germany movement on the Rhine, had to leave my home, was in the Palatinate and Baden, . . . &c.'

was under the most solemn obligations not to waste it. The parents were poor; they had sacrificed much in order to give him a chance to become a professor, a status he could hope to attain only after completing the work for his degree in 1850. The education of his two sisters had had to be neglected on his account and he was anxious to become established in order to be able to help them as well as to relieve his father and mother. Though profoundly patriotic, he was generally under the dominion of common sense and, after May twentieth and especially after June twelfth, common sense warned loudly against participation in a movement which the Prussian government condemned as treasonable. But having become implicated prematurely in the Siegburg business, Schurz's pride goaded him on to imperil his life without the assurance that any good would result from the sacrifice.

The 'sin' he had to expiate, after the tenth of May was a sin against his own personality, in plain terms a humiliation. For Schurz was sensitively proud, and a miserable failure to which his utterly unmilitary management of the ferry contributed, was a torment to his soul. The news that this valiant company of one hundred and twenty students and workers went into hiding at the approach of thirty Prussian horsemen, would be sure to cause much levity in Bonn where party spirit was running high and conservatives were losing no opportunity to score against their democratic opponents. Schurz had been conducting his democratic propaganda in a somewhat arrogant spirit and, while respected and admired by most, he had then, as he always would have, plenty of rivals, critics, and detractors. Should he return to the city he would be sure to encounter amused smiles, contemptuous or scornful looks, and words fraught with double meanings. Without taking into account the chances of arrest and trial on the charge of treason, or the prospect of clearing himself of the charge, the 'ridiculous thing' of which he certainly had been guilty would be fatal to his acquired prestige. On the other hand, by going forward rather than back, he would at least have a chance to redeem his military character and to add to his reputation as a radical politician. Of course there was risk in the forward movement, but the backward look was too horrible to contemplate. He preferred to confront the certain dangers of war afield rather than to have his military honor and bravery impeached at home. Carl Schurz could be more easily daunted by sneers than by grapeshot.

It was about the fifteenth of May when Schurz sought employment at the hands of the revolutionary committee and for several weeks the work he was given to do might be described as political rather than military. But, on June twenty-third, he was in the skirmish at Bruchsal where he 'rode in the first line,' the 'bullets, grape and canister whizzing around' him. He had never, he says, felt so happy or so purified as when experiencing this first 'baptism of fire.' It redeemed him from the Siegburg disgrace. A little later, when the main Prussian force appeared he was in much of the fighting that took place around the walls of Rastatt, particularly the battle on the Murg River June twenty-eighth to June thirtieth. There he stood up to the Prussians and 'gave them blow for blow.' Thus he saved his honor 'from the mockery and revilings' of his adversaries, words almost certainly referring to the situation created by the Siegburg episode which did not easily pass out of his mind.

It was on the last day of the Murg battle, June thirtieth, that Schurz, acting as messenger for Colonel Anneke, entered the fortress of Rastatt. His mission performed, he was about to ride back to camp when, to his amazement and horror, he learned that the Prussian siege lines had been completed and every avenue of escape from the fortress city cut off. Profoundly dispirited by this surprise move against him in the game he was playing with fate, he accepted a place on Governor Tiedemann's staff and performed such service as was assigned him during the twenty-three days that were left before the garrison was forced to surrender, 'at discretion,' to the Prince of Prussia. Some of his activities of this period he describes from memory in *Reminiscences*. Others can now be gleaned from a report he wrote on the *Last Days in Rastatt* which was published in a Bonn newspaper beginning one month after the surrender.[21] This document proves he was not too closely engaged to prevent his observing all significant movements that took place in the fort, the effects of the enemy's bombardment, which began on the night of July sixth to seventh, the sortie of July eighth, directed against the enemy's siege guns, the demoralization of citizens and soldiers under the fear of the ultimate surrender of the place, the capitulation of the garrison. He had kept a diary painstakingly 'and in extended manner,' from the time he entered on his revolutionary career. The portion relating to the capture of Rastatt he considered especially authentic

[21] *Ein Tag in Rastatt*, the first three of a series of eight installments, printed in *Neue Bonner Zeitung* for August 22, 29, and September 5, deals with incidents of July 8 when a sortie was made against the besiegers. *Unsre drei letzten Tage in Rastatt*, five installments, explains itself. The entire document translated by the present writer, who found it in Bonn, November 3, 1928, is reprinted in *Wisconsin Magazine of History*, xii, 239-270.

because, being constantly in touch with Tiedemann, he was informed about every move, offensive and defensive. That diary, later lost, was the basis of the narrative just described, which he sent home from Zurich, Switzerland, on the eighteenth of August.

Unfortunately, the narrative does not cover the incidents connected with Schurz's escape from Rastatt. For that story we are forced to depend on his memory of fifty years later as recorded in *Reminiscences*. But, although recollections are a poor substitute for contemporaneous evidence, they in turn vary as the circumstances under which the original experiences were gotten, and the particulars of the way he cheated death in one of its most ignominious forms are not likely ever to have become so blurred in Schurz's mind as to make a clear and substantially accurate narrative of them impossible. A few slight errors, especially in chronology, we are able to detect, but in the main the story of the escape as he wrote it can be taken as trustworthy.

The chief means of Schurz's self rescue was a big, uncompleted sewer or drain tube nearly man high inside and lined with brick, one end of which was in the fortress, the other in a cornfield north of the city in the general direction of Steinmauren, a village three miles away near the bank of the Rhine. The fortress end was somewhat hidden by ditch and hedge, but he had noted it on one of his tours of observation and had feared the enemy might send spies in through that opening. Happening to recall it at the critical hour when, on the afternoon of July twenty-third, the garrison was assembling for the final act of capitulation, Schurz together with his attendant Adam (surname unknown) and an artillery officer named Neustädter, dropped out of the rear ranks and slunk into the sewer. Their plan was

to walk through about midnight, emerge in the cornfield, and pick their way to the Rhine where they hoped
to find a boat in which to escape across the river to
French soil. In this they were foiled, for on nearing the
end of the sewer they distinctly heard the Prussian
guard which was evidently set in double line, making
escape impossible. They could not remain longer in the
sewer, because, due to heavy downpours of rain, it had
become a roaring torrent carrying down live rats and
other beasties which swirled around the men's legs.

They therefore concluded to risk the upper air once
more and by good fortune Adam recalled that a cousin
of his lived near the fortress end of the sewer in a house
which might be reached safely by crossing a succession
of garden hedges. They went to the stable belonging
to this house proposing to sleep in the hay. But when
Adam spoke to his cousin she came out in great alarm,
announced that some Prussian cavalrymen were to be
billeted at her house that morning and would doubtless
visit the stable to look for horse fodder. She insisted on
the refugees leaving her premises. For some hours they
secreted themselves in a hollow square formed by ricks
of stovewood. The rain, however, was falling so heavily
that some shelter had to be found. Now, Schurz knew
that laboring people generally sympathized with the
revolution, so, on seeing a man with a saw pass by he
threw a chip, attracted his attention, and asked him to
find them a refuge and some food; for in the past
twenty-four hours they had had nothing but a loaf of
bread, some sausages, and two bottles of wine. The
workman pointed out a small low shed built as a lean-to
against the end of a large shed or barracks. The lower
part of this housed workmen's tools, but under the low

sloping roof was a loft just large enough for three men
to lie on their backs in dust 'inches deep.'

Here they lay unrelieved, cramped, wet, cold, and
stiff from Tuesday afternoon till late Thursday night.
Their friend had promised to bring them food but failed
to come. Hunger and thirst were becoming unendur-
able, but what could be done with the adjoining barracks
full of Prussians and a watchful guard all around
them? At one time they heard firing and thought that
the fusillades had begun. This gave them sensations of
the most doleful character. As a matter of history the
execution of Tiedemann and twelve of his officers occurred some time after this. If Carl had been in the
fortress when the garrison surrendered, he would probably have suffered death by the same means.

Suddenly Schurz recalled having seen a workman's
home so near the ricks of wood that, by careful maneu-
vering, a man might slip out, gain the house, and possibly secure succor for all. Neustädter made the attempt
and met with success. He brought a piece of bread and
a green apple, but better than this, the man promised to
scout the cornfield and the Steinmauren road and bring
them word if the way of escape seemed clear; also, he
agreed to bring food. Next day he came with a generous basket of provisions, reporting that the guard had
been withdrawn from the outside end of the sewer, and
that the way to the Rhine was open. He was instructed
to find a boatman, have him ready at a definite point on
the river bank near Steinmauren the following night
at midnight, to meet the refugees near the sewer end in
the cornfield and guide them to the boat. On Friday
night, after the Prussians in the shed, wearied with
dancing and befuddled with beer, had settled into a
noisy sleep, the three men emerged from their hiding

place in the loft, partook of a famous midnight supper
prepared by the workman's wife, and then slipped past
the sentry into the sewer. On reaching the field end
they gave a low whistle. It was answered and now their
guide, whose name was Loeffler, led them to the bank
of the German Rhine, which to them at the moment
was doubly dear because it was not 'German' exclu-
sively.

A man lay sleeping in a skiff. He was quickly
aroused and told these were the men he was to put
across. After making his bargain with them, he proceeded but landed them on an island near the left bank
and returned to Steinmauren. However, they were
able, after daylight, to attract the notice of French customs officers who brought them away. When they at
last felt themselves safe on French soil the first thing
they did was to shout long, loudly, and repeatedly.
Then they walked to the inn at Selz, a nearby Alsatian
village, procured food, a hot bath, and a bed. They slept
undisturbed for twenty-four hours. On Sunday afternoon, Adam having left them, Schurz and Neustädter
walked to Strasburg, and the following day, July
thirtieth, just a week after the capitulation of Rastatt,
they crossed the Swiss border. Here they separated and
Schurz rested for a few days at the village of Dornachbruck some miles from the boundary near the city of
Basel. It was from there, not from Selz, as he later remembered the matter, that he wrote the joyful news of
his rescue to his distressed family.

Why he should have delayed a single moment after
reaching the left bank of the Rhine seems almost inex-
plicable. He did not suppose the letter he wrote before
the surrender of Rastatt would have been sent to Bonn
so soon and without it his people would know nothing
about his presence in the doomed fortress. Still, the

uncertainty about his fate, in view of all that had happened must have caused the sharpest anguish. Possibly some obstacle to safe communication with Bonn constrained him to defer writing until he should reach a safe refuge in Switzerland.[22] The letter from Rastatt, however, reached Boon soon after the surrender and Christian Schurz started immediately for the captured fortress in the hope of once more seeing his son alive, or at least learning his fate. He called on the Prussian commandant, who naturally was unable to find Carl's name on the list of prisoners. But he gave Christian a pass permitting him to visit the casemates, which he did, anxiously scanning the huddled groups of men fearing yet hoping to discover the supposedly luckless boy. In one prison hole he saw Kinkel who was cut to the heart on learning that Carl, too, was probably a captive, subject to the same fate which awaited himself, and this through his own ineffectual revolutionary activities.

The fact that Carl was not in the captured stronghold gave the distracted father a certain dubious satisfaction, and on crossing the river to Selz he learned, at the inn, that he had made his escape and was then on his way southward. Almost beside himself with joy, Christian Schurz hurried back to carry the news to his grief-stricken wife and daughters. But Carl's letter from Dornachbruck had anticipated his arrival in Bonn where he found everyone rejoicing in the young man's miraculous luck.

[22] The letter from Dornachbruck, dated July 31, 1849, opens with these words: 'At last I find a moment of quiet to let you know that I am rescued and free. . . . I wrote you the last lines in the comfortless anticipation of falling into the hands of my most embittered enemies. Fate changed this and I was given back my life after having already looked death in the eye. I do not know if you received my last letter from Rastatt. If you did, it went off sooner than I had intended,' and so on. Tradition says the Rastatt letter, when received at Bonn, was wadded up, wrapped round with worsted yarn, and in that way dispatched by the hand of Carl's youngest sister, Tony, to the several relatives in the neighborhood.

CHAPTER VII

THE FREEING OF KINKEL

IT IS possible to follow in fancy the jubilation among the relatives and friends of our young revolutionist over the fact of his physical safety. By an unheard of good fortune, he had preserved his life when others of similar military rank and guilt, trapped in the fortress of Rastatt, had been doomed to face the daybreak firing squads. As a Prussian engaged in rebellion he would have been subject to the full penalty prescribed for traitors, and being known as an agitator, little mercy could have been expected. At the best, life long imprisonment would have been his portion. Yet here he was in the neutral land of Switzerland, weary unto death to be sure, but wanting only sleep, food, and a little leisure to bring back, in surging flood, all his magnificent powers of body and mind.

Personally Schurz examined his case in a somewhat different perspective. He, too, thanked fate for preserving him against a terrible menace but that was only one element in his luck. The experience of ten weeks duration in the thick of a revolution had been fruitful in knowledge far beyond his expectations. At the university his program had included a very careful reading in the literature of the French Revolution and similar social cataclysms and in hearing lectures upon them. Now he had been able, in human nature's own laboratory, to test acquired facts and principles. He had 'traversed the revolution as a nature student traverses a mountain range,' gaining new insights at every step. It proved to be a school of social science many times more effective than the one he had deserted so cavalierly on the tenth of May.[23]

Another advantage, to which allusion has already been made, was his gain in reputation among the common people who were so largely democratic in their political sympathies. Schurz recognized gleefully that his 'popularity and standing' had risen on account of his participation in the revolution and he was sensitively careful to do nothing to forfeit what he had gained. Looking forward, as all revolutionists did, to a new movement which he believed must come to complete the interrupted work of reforming and unifying Germany, his position would be one of high distinction and wide influence as compared with that which he occupied in the recent upheaval. His father believed it might be possible for him to obtain an individual amnesty, but Carl was exceedingly wary about jeopardizing this new reputation and when the question of the amnesty arose, though he desired it intensely, he indicated how impossible it would be for him to accept favors from the existing Prussian government since by doing so he would lose all the prestige his recent experience had won for him.[24]

The principal loss suffered lay in the interruption of his studies and in the impossibility of resuming them at Bonn. But he might be able to make amends for that. At first he thought of going to French Switzerland and taking up his historical program at the university of Geneva. But for some reason which the letters fail to explain, possible anxiety to greet revolution-

[23] Letter of July 23, 1848.
[24] Letter of October 3, 1849. If the amnesty were to be secured at all it must be done by his friends, not by himself. He was glad to suggest the mode of procedure but he must not be known to have knowledge of what was done. He even cautioned 'destroy this letter.'

ary friends who had crossed the border, this plan was changed on the arrival at Dornachbruck of Adolf Strodtmann with letters and supplies from the family and with money raised for him by his friends of *Franconia*. The very next day after Strodtmann found him, the two men started on the long walk across country to Zurich which became Schurz's home during his seven months sojourn in Switzerland. Zurich also had a university, though its department of history was very weak, and here he thought of completing his preparation for the doctoral examination, which might have been accomplished in a single year. He believed he could thereafter gain an appointment to lecture as docent in history. There was talk in Zurich about founding an institution for the training of refugees which also might yield some advantages.

Still, the situation in Switzerland, though pleasant in many respects, was precarious: rumors about designs against the refugees chased one another continually. It was widely believed that Austria would find means to compel the Swiss governments to withdraw their protection from them, and it was already observable that the Zurich police eyed them askance. So he endured a period of enforced 'watchful waiting' while working unremittingly upon his program of studies, and writing occasionally for liberal German newspapers as a support to his slender purse.

At Zurich Schurz found Colonel Fritz Anneke and many other refugees from the army of Baden. Among them was the great composer Richard Wagner, a casualty of the earlier Saxon revolt. Here were joyful greetings, excited and interesting talk, but Schurz had little time or inclination to cultivate the class to which most of these men belonged. The professional revolutionist, he soon discovered, could not hold himself to any productive or improving work, but preferred to waste his days speculating on the time and circumstances of the next convulsion, and the place he would have in it according to his deserts, quarreling with his fellows, gaming, and drinking. Schurz promptly renounced most of his acquaintances of these early days and devoted himself unreservedly to serious study. Of course, he had dreams; dreams of getting back to his glorious Rhineland. Dreams of settling in Belgium as near Bonn as possible; dreams of residence and study in Paris. Fate, however, which had a way of settling Schurz's personal problems with scant reference to plans of his own, soon found a solution which his reflections do not seem to have forecast. This was by sending him off on a new enterprise, more dangerous in some respects than that from which he had just escaped, but calculated to win for him literally a world wide fame.

His beloved mentor, Kinkel, had had even stronger reasons than himself for precipitate flight after the Siegburg fiasco because he had been the instigator and responsible leader of the proposed attack on the Prussian armory. Like Schurz, he passed into the Palatinate and procured employment as secretary to the revolutionary committee. Later, when the Prussians came down in force, he took his musket and joined a company as a common soldier. At the battle on the Murg he was wounded in the head, rendered helpless, captured, and clapped into prison. After the capitulation of Rastatt he was brought to trial before the court martial, along with the revolutionary officers.[25] Kinkel conducted his

[25] Corvin, in his *Erinnerungen,* gives a tragic picture of Kinkel and himself, carried from the prison to the court on a cart which suggested the 'tumbrils' used in Paris during the revolution to carry victims to the guillotine.

own defense, making so eloquent and ingenious a plea
that the military court refused to order him shot, as the
Prussian government desired. Instead, they sentenced
him to life imprisonment in a fortress! This meant
that his person would be free, that he could devote his
time to study and writing, or spend it as he liked otherwise; he would be a prisoner but a prisoner with honor.
The government overruled the court. They could not
condemn Kinkel to death, but they changed the verdict
to imprisonment in a civil prison. Here he would be
put in stripes, given a number, placed in a cell, and provided with compulsory work. This, it was probably
felt, would quickly reduce a proud spirited man like
him, bringing on premature decay and death.

He was kept until October in the prison at Bruchsal,
was then taken to Naugard in Pomerania where he was
in close confinement till April, 1850, when they brought
him to trial at Cologne for the Siegburg conspiracy. At
Cologne, again, as before his military judges, Kinkel
rose to heights of oratory and argument to which forensic history offers few parallels. As his judges were a
jury of burghers, he was even more successful, winning
a verdict of 'not guilty' both for himself and for those
arraigned with him, some of whom, Schurz among the
number, being tried in absentia. The Prussian government's reason for the trial of Kinkel at Cologne could
have been nothing other than the hope of bringing him
to the guillotine; for he had already been condemned to
penal servitude for life because of his participation in
the Palatinate-Baden revolution. The people felt he
was being subjected to persecution. At Cologne there
was such a tremendous popular demonstration in his
behalf that the officials decided to place him in a prison
far removed from his native Rhineland, at Spandau,

near Berlin. While being transported thither Kinkel
attempted to escape but through a mishap failed. Soon
the prison doors closed on him, his task of spinning wool
was allotted daily, with other menial labors, and there
he was to be left to wear his soul away.[26]

Early in the year 1850 Schurz was brought into the
Kinkel case through a letter from Mrs. Kinkel which
reached him at Zurich. In this letter Johanna presented Kinkel's situation and his family's misery with
all the tragic power of which her gifted pen was capable,
and she resolutely insisted that some brave soul must be
found who would undertake the complicated and dangerous task of releasing him from prison. She did not,
in terms, ask Schurz to take upon himself the rôle of
deliverer, but he inferred from her language that she
was seriously thinking of him for the part. This idea
gave him some restless days and nights. Reflecting
upon his duty in the matter, balancing the chances of
success and failure, considering also the danger he
might court in entering Prussian territory, he finally
decided to make the attempt.

The first step in preparation was to procure through
his people at Bonn a passport issued in favor of his
cousin, Heribert Jüssen, who resembled him strikingly
in appearance. Armed with this document, he returned
home, visited his parents, saw some of his university
friends, and had conferences with Mrs. Kinkel about
plans of procedure.

This was apparently in March, 1850, while Kinkel
was still at Naugard. On the third of March a notice
appeared in the *Neue Bonner Zeitung* calling upon all
friends and well wishers to come to the aid of Kinkel,

---

[26] Adolf Strodtmann wrote a ballad, *The Spinners' Song*, about Kinkel
in prison, and was promptly expelled from the university of Bonn in consequence.

evidently implying the need of funds. This and other similar appeals netted a considerable sum of money which Mrs. Kinkel now placed unreservedly at Schurz's disposal. He then went to Paris, where he remained till the trial at Cologne was over, and Kinkel had been in Spandau long enough to let the excitement attending his trial and removal quiet down. Then he passed to Berlin, traveling as Heribert Jüssen, and from there managed the delicate work he had in hand.

It was a detective's job Schurz had taken. The problem was to find some jailer or turnkey who, for an adequate compensation, would agree to get Kinkel out of his cell and down into the court of the prison. Much time was lost and many clues followed and abandoned before such a man could be found and there was constant danger of betrayal while the search was in progress. Finally, a strong reliable jail attendant named Brune was secured as turnkey accomplice, other confederates to assist on the street being already in hand. A plan of operations was now adopted, and the project set for the night of November fifth to sixth. Against that time Schurz made his other arrangements, which included several relays of teams to carry Kinkel and himself to the sea coast. At the coast were trusty friends who would hurry them out to sea.

On the night agreed upon everything was in readiness to carry out the conspiracy. Word had been smuggled to Kinkel warning him to be ready at the stroke of twelve. Brune had received his money in advance. Schurz, his heart pounding with excitement, was waiting in the street below. His friend Hensel, with a swift pair of horses attached to a light wagon was ready to begin the long drive to Rostock in Mecklenburg. Two faithful confederates were on guard to prevent interference from the police. A nearby innkeeper, Krueger, who was the first and most pivotal of Schurz's aids, was prepared to assist in every appropriate way, and the relays of teams stood ready on the road at the stations agreed upon.

But the hour for the jail delivery passed with no sign of jailer or prisoner. At last the man came with downcast, gloomy countenance, and offered to return his money. Something had gone wrong. A key, which was absolutely indispensable to the success of the operation and which had always been left by the warden in a certain place accessible to the turnkeys, had inadvertently been carried away. Thus all the labor, all the detailed planning and plotting seemed to have gone for naught.

Was this the end of the great enterprise? For a moment it seemed to Schurz that the rehabilitation of his plan would be impossible. There were too many filaments to be kept in hand, too many extraordinary adjustments to permit the hope that nothing would happen in the meantime to expose the conspiracy to the authorities. A terribly gloomy day was passed by him in notifying his relays of the misadventure. But next night on asking his faithful Brune if he thought there would be a chance to get Kinkel out later, he was told that if he could keep the way of escape to the north open and if Kinkel were brave enough to descend from a dormer window tied to a rope, it might be accomplished the same night, because, through the illness of one of the guards, he, Brune, had been detailed for that night also.

Difficult as the arrangement was, Schurz found that Hensel, the gentleman who had agreed to drive the first relay, was willing to spend his splendid span on the venture, driving till the horses should fall exhausted. So the plan was tried. At midnight of the sixth to seventh of November, 1850, confederates stationed at the street ends of the jail were grimly ready to ward off any intruding watchman, using force if necessary. Schurz stood in partial concealment, where he could see the designated dormer window and detect the signal light to which, when it came, he would reply with sparks from flint and steel. Hensel was ready, seated in his wagon, to drive rapidly, rumbling over the cobble stones, in order to drown the noise of falling bricks that might loosen above when the heavy man should be let down. Krueger, at the inn hard by, was entertaining a group of Kinkel's jailers with a special brand of punch which made them unusually jolly and carefree.

Just after midnight the thing happened. Slowly, the form of Kinkel descended, to be received by Schurz on the pavement, driven in Hensel's wagon to the inn, refreshed with some of the punch prepared for his jailers, and then hurried with Hensel's fast team toward Rostock after feigning to follow the Hamburg road. A drive of two nights brought them to the sea-coast at the harbor of Warnemünde. Here a democratic merchant friend freighted one of his own vessels the *Little Anna* with wheat, and instructed his skipper to sail, with all despatch, to England or Scotland. The vessel got under weigh November seventeenth, 1850, the two men having lived in the interim quiet and undisturbed in the house of their benefactor. Police authorities issued proclamations right and left, while all the newspapers were filled with stories of Kinkel's escape, and with diverting reports prepared by democratic friends about his having sailed to England from Bremen, about his having been seen in Switzerland, and being fêted in

Paris, where he delivered a speech which they pretended to quote.

The *Little Anna* was buffeted by storms on the North Sea, as might be supposed, she being a vessel of only forty tons, but the two fugitives suffered no harm and, the winds failing to permit her to reach the English port of Newcastle, she put in at Leith the harbor of Edinburgh. The day of landing was Sunday, the twenty-eighth of November, 1850. Schurz describes for us how he and Kinkel walked the Edinburgh streets all day in search of a restaurant which might be open for business on the Sabbath and when they found one, just at nightfall, they discovered that between them they knew only three English words which applied to the business in hand. But these words, 'beefsteak,' 'sherry,' and 'pudding,' reinforced by a judicious exhibition of gold coins, brought them an ample repast.

During their sea voyage Kinkel wrote a letter to Christian Schurz, as the father of 'my [his] rescuer.' In the most unreserved manner he acclaims Carl as the person responsible for his release, and predicts that the gratitude he will receive from Kinkel's partisans, and from a multitude of others who sympathized with his suffering, would enable the young man to win a high goal for himself. Indeed, when Carl's name became associated in the public mind with the rescue of Kinkel, his place in the affections of democracy all over Europe was established. He had entered the revolution to redeem his own character. Through it, and this corollary to his revolutionary service, he had become a hero to a considerable portion of mankind.

THE AGED GOTTFRIED KINKEL

CHAPTER VIII

REMOTER EXILE

THE time devoted by Schurz to the Kinkel rescue, some two thirds of a year, counting from the date of his departure from Zurich, in the long run proved a more profitable investment than the three months spent in the revolution. At the moment of triumph, however, he felt it as another interruption of his studies and proposed a prompt return to Paris in order to prosecute his work. He would not soon again abandon 'the safe soil of a neutral land. A quiet scholarly activity' he hoped would furnish scope and means for himself, and also serve as a support to his parents and sisters.

The sojourn with Kinkel in the British Isles was brief. He soon settled in Paris, taking a cheap suite containing among its furnishings a piano, one of the luxuries Schurz hardly knew how to dispense with because music had become a necessity to him and performing on that instrument was destined to be a solace to him all his life. He studied hard, wrote some articles for the Liberal German press, and hobnobbed with revolutionists from various European countries, especially such as were gifted in music, art, or literature. Paris to him epitomized modern history. The 'variagated affairs of Europe' could be read 'upon the windows of the Tuileries, in the Luxembourg Gardens, and in the courts of Versailles.' Every pillar, every plaster cast, seemed to preach the 'glorious memories of the Revolution, the national pride in the Empire.'

There was, however, another aspect to the French capital which excited less enthusiasm namely, the sur-

veillance over foreigners exercised by the Paris police.
Schurz had already passed half a year in quiet study
and observation when, one day on the street, he was
placed under arrest and clapped into jail as cell mate of
a common thief. Outraged beyond measure by the in-
dignity put upon him Schurz opened his mind to the
police authorities in written communications couched in
faultless French and breathing the fiercest spirit of
independence. He demanded to know on what charge
he was being held but his petition in this respect gained
little heed. Finally, after four days, he was taken before the police commissioner who proved to be a Frenchman of model courtesy who complimented Schurz on the
perfect French in which his petition had been couched,
explained that there really was no charge against him,
hinted at orders from higher sources, and suggested the
desirability at his early convenience of shifting his residence from Paris to some other country.

This suited Schurz, who had been strongly urged by
Kinkel to come to London and was about ready to
make the move when the arrest occurred. Kinkel had
settled with his family in a house in St. John's Wood,
London, which was at that time a refugees' quarter of
the city. Germans, Russians, Italians, French, Hungar-
ians, and in fact nationals of most of the countries of
Europe lived in that community. Kinkel was a distinguished leader and his home, somewhat like the
Schloss at Bonn, became an important social center for
the revolutionist group. Tradition tells us how the
Kinkels entertained men of European note, like Maz-
zini, along with refugees of lower grades of revolutionary significance. They had prevailed upon the Schurz
family to let them give Carl's sister Antonie [Tony]
instruction in music and pedagogy to fit her for school

teaching. Tony therefore spent the year 1851 in the Kinkel household and it is her recollections, passed on to her children, even more than Schurz's *Reminiscences,* upon which we rely for information respecting these gatherings.

The refugee group in London, during the summer of 1851, signalized its importance by developing a grandiose scheme for financing a new revolution. This was the so-called German National Loan. The idea was to induce friends of freedom and unity throughout the world, and particularly in America, to subscribe to a fund of some millions which was to be made available for carrying on the next revolution and might be repaid within a certain number of years after the union of Germany should have been achieved. Apparently monies paid in advance might be put at interest by the London committee or lent for the support of movements deemed contributory to the uprising destined to rejuvenate the Fatherland.

Schurz believes this project was too chimerical to receive Kinkel's unreserved approval. He, himself, with the optimism of youth, gave it enthusiastic support and was prepared to help carry it into successful operation. His services were soon called for. The London committee, fired with zeal for the cause, decided to unite in it the revolutionists of all Europe and, since a large number of refugees were in Switzerland, Schurz was commissioned to visit them for the purpose of recruiting their support. Also, he was to make observations on the development of revolutionary sentiment in France. Schurz went to Switzerland in late summer, was received with the acclaim due to a knight errant on account of his freeing of Kinkel, pledged the leading refugees to the support of the National Loan, and then enjoyed a glorious vacation among the high Alps. With several friends he 'climbed around in the snow, saw an avalanche, heard glaciers thunder' and spent a night above the clouds. What he learned about sentiment among the French people convinced him that a new revolution was about due and he looked for the explosion in 1852.[27]

Shortly after Schurz crossed over to the continent, Kinkel sailed for America to engage in the campaign for raising the Loan. The committee considered him their strategic man for the purpose, the story of his condemnation, imprisonment, and rescue having penetrated to the remotest abodes of Germans and being known also to millions of others all over the world. Besides, Kinkel was an orator of such drawing power that men would go to hear him not only out of curiosity but also for what he had to say. When Schurz got back to London in October, he lived at Kinkel's house, managed the correspondence, furnished the American press with material calculated to keep the campaign at a proper temperature, and received reports from the field of activities. Kinkel's lectures aroused tremendous interest in the cities, especially those canvassed first, Philadelphia and Baltimore. He later went to Cincinnati, and other German centers as far west as Milwaukee, continuing active till the spring of 1852.

The results of this canvass have never been revealed in detail. If the enthusiasm aroused by Kinkel personally could have been coined into double-eagles, it would have netted a generous war chest for the next revolution. Unfortunately, most of the Germans then in America were as yet poor and the resources of the well-to-do minority were deeply pledged to the support

[27] Letter of October 17, 1851.

of enterprises much nearer to them than a hoped for national rising in the Fatherland.[28] Subscriptions could be secured to some extent, probably on the understanding that their collection was as dubious as the revolution itself, but the agitation yielded little cash. One statement has it that Kinkel received ten thousand dollars; another that he paid over to Kossuth at Cincinnati, in February, 1852, the sum of sixty thousand dollars; and there are still other estimates.[29] Whatever the exact amount it would be but a drop in the bucket when it should come to the carrying on of a war.

America was not yet saturated with gold, despite the recent tapping of the treasures of California. Besides, there quickly developed political objections to the propaganda which first Kinkel, then Kossuth, carried on. American newspapers reminded these European emissaries that America was a neutral country and that it was hardly good taste for them to come here with the purpose of meddling in our affairs. Both Kinkel and Kossuth hoped for governmental sympathy in America and both were disappointed.[30]

In Schurz's view, the German and the Hungarian agitator were both illogical in continuing their campaign after the adversary had dug in. Unlike most of the professional revolutionists, he was disposed to recognize facts and the Napoleonic *coup d'ètat* of December second, 1851, was an incident affecting revolutionary programs the world over. It had come upon Schurz as

[28] Schurz, letter to Kinkel, April 12, 1853.
[29] De Jonge, Alfred, *Gottfried Kinkel &c.*, p. xiii note 5 and p. 31 note 87. See also the bitter comments on Kinkel of Karl Heinzen in *Deutscher Radikalismus in Amerika*, 63-67.
[30] An illustration of one type of error in Schurz's *Reminiscences* is his statement i, 388: 'Before Kossuth began his agitation in America, Kinkel had returned from there.' The two men were lecturing contemporaneously during several months.

a great surprise, for as late as October twenty-fifth he considered 'a most fortunate outcome' of the crisis in France as 'not at all doubtful.' Now, after thinking the subject through, he agreed with Louis Blanc, whom he accidentally encountered seated on the same bench with himself in Hyde Park, when the Frenchman exclaimed, referring to Louis Napoleon's triumph: *'C'est fini, n'est ce pas? C'est fini!'* Reaction had now fortified itself and it might be many years before Europe would see a successful new revolution. Thus reasoned our young politician.

Schurz's decision, in view of this probability, was characteristic. He would not wear away his life waiting for something to happen in Europe, but would go to America and help to bring things to pass. Germany was closed to him, England gave him sanctuary as an exile but no encouragement to become a citizen. In America the principles for which he had contended at home were established and hopefully developing. If he could not become a citizen of a 'free Germany' he would at least be a 'citizen of free America.'[31] 'I formed my resolution on the spot,' he says. 'I would stay but a short time longer in England and then—off for America.'

As in most cases involving important changes in life plans, the actual process of decision was less simple than the above statement implies. Schurz's parents, no less than himself, were experiencing a crisis in their affairs. The evil reputation Schurz gained for himself among the Prussian officials, civil and military, by his agency in freeing Kinkel, recoiled upon the heads of his family in Bonn. Their petty business of feeding students was practically ruined. Garrison soldiers entered

---

[31] *Reminiscences,* i, 400 and letter to Adolf Meyer, April 19, 1852.

the house and 'with naked swords' committed frightful devastation for which they received the commendation of their officers. Things went so far that in the spring of 1852 the Schurz family were threatened with eviction from their home.[32] Now it happened that one of Carl's cousins, Edmund Jüssen, had pioneered a way in company with an uncle, to America, settling in Wisconsin where he was later joined by the older members of his family. The Schurzs desired to join those relatives in America and it was the plan for Carl to live there with his parents.

Nevertheless, one cannot fail to gain from Schurz's letters of 1852, the impression that he was going to America in order to find scope for the political activity which had come to be necessary to his happiness. 'Our great hopes'—for the revolution—'have come to nothing or they have receded into the indefinite distance.' 'I am tired of the futile doings of the refugees.' 'I require close, definite objects, and I am going where I can find them. I want to make the period of my exile fruitful.' The above are some of the crisp reasons Schurz gave his friend Althaus for the project of going to America. He wanted to be fully occupied in public activities such as America afforded. Yet, he did not want to be counted out when European affairs should become interesting once more. A most significant expression is this: 'I am saying farewell to Europe with the certainty of being back again at the right time.'[33]

At the moment of writing the above letter all arrangements had been made for the voyage to New York. The item of greatest importance was Schurz's marriage, July tenth, 1852, in London to Margarethe

[32] Letter of March 7, 1851.
[33] Letter to Frederick Althaus, August 4, 1852.

Meyer of Hamburg, a beautiful and accomplished young woman of excellent family who was then not quite nineteen years of age. Her father, Heinrich Meyer, had been a prosperous manufacturer-merchant and a liberal in politics. As such he entertained at his home a certain Johannes Ronge, an ex-priest who had become conspicuous by bearding his bishop in one of the church quarrels of the day, had renounced the priesthood and for a time attracted considerable notice as the hero of a rebellion against episcopal tyranny and as a founder of the so-called German Catholic church.

One of the Meyer daughters fell in love with Ronge, and against her father's wishes, married him, which resulted in her permanent alienation from the family in Hamburg. Ronge became a revolutionist and a refugee, was obliged to go to London where his wife, a trained Froebelian kindergartner helped to make a living by maintaining a small school for the young children of refugees and others. In 1852, however, Mrs. Ronge was taken seriously ill. Her father had died ten years earlier, the head of the family now being the eldest brother Adolf Meyer, while a younger brother Henry was a partner in the business. Their young sister Margarethe had just completed her high school studies. Pity for the distressed sister in London induced Margarethe to go to her aid. She, too, had learned the system of Froebel, which enabled her to keep the little kindergarten running while Mrs. Ronge was convalescing from her illness. She has been credited with having opened, at Watertown, Wisconsin, in 1856, the first kindergarten in America.

It was at Ronge's house, where he went on business, that Carl Schurz met Margarethe. He found her not only a lovely girl but an intelligent and earnest woman

of fine social sympathies and an ambition for service.
Her knowledge of and eager interest in Carl's heroic
rescue of Kinkel established a bond between them and
it was not long before they were betrothed.

Now came the delicate problem of gaining the consent of Adolf Meyer to their marriage and removal to
America. The Meyer family had lost one daughter to
a revolutionary adventurer and Adolf, who was anything but a revolutionist, would be slow to approve of
his young ward marrying a man of similar character
and antecedents, even without the corollary of their
migration beyond the Atlantic. He therefore pointedly
asked Schurz to tell him how he expected to support a
wife—which Schurz did with an effectiveness that removed all obstacles to the union.

But the plan to sail in July was rudely interfered
with by a violent attack of scarlet fever which brought
Schurz to death's door and made necessary a sojourn of
several weeks duration at the Malvern water cure.
Finally, toward the end of August, they sailed and on
the morning of September seventeenth, with the 'buoy-
ant hopefulness of young hearts' 'saluted the New
World.'

CHAPTER IX

BEGINNINGS IN AMERICA

CARL SCHURZ, at the time of their arrival in America, was in his twenty-fourth year, in perfect health and what he was apt to call good fighting trim. Tradition asserts that the recent illness, scarlet fever, had induced in him an abnormal growth and there is some evidence to confirm it. At all events Schurz later described himself as 'well over six feet' and it has been stated that he was six feet one inch in height. In March, 1849, however, he wrote Kinkel that the examination for military fitness made him 5′8″3‴ tall, or five feet, eight tenths and three hundredths of a foot. This of course, was by the Rhenish measure wherein the foot is slightly longer than the English foot, making his height at that time approximately five feet eleven and a half inches. Anatomists find it a rare thing for men to grow half an inch after the age of twenty, yet Schurz must have grown at least one and a half inches.

He weighed not more than one hundred and thirty-five pounds, such was the grey-hound leanness of his body, but he was muscular, strong, and resilient. Like his grandfather Jüssen, his body expanded above the waist line, arching out into a broad but not deep chest, topped by capable shoulders and a massive head. His limbs were long and straight ('Apollonian' he once called them in jest), gait rapid and graceful, all bodily movements quick and nervous. He had large, penetrating brown eyes and a wealth of wavy brown hair. But for his peaked, irregular countenance, he would have been regarded as a handsome man. At this time

he wore a short mustache which by 1860 had been ex-
changed for a long and straggling one imparting—
with his unshorn locks and somber aspect—a peculiarly
wistful cast to his countenance. In middle life, after
adopting the full beard which then was fashionable and
which effectually screened the peculiar imperfections of
the lower portion of his face, Schurz was a fine looking
man. We are dealing with him, however, as a lithe
graceful boyish figure, keen and eager of aspect, who
loved walking, riding, hunting, music; who was intellectually alert, voluble in speech, a great reader, a student, a devotee of politics.

The question of where they were to live in America
was not decided in advance by this young pair. Schurz
believed he was prepared to encounter any phase of
western life, however crude, but he was not sure that
Margarethe, brought up in luxury in a refined home
and cultured environment, would have been willing at
once to become a pioneer. She was enchanted by the
first view of New York, but she became ill at the hotel
in that city when lonesomeness and homesickness drove
them to seek the neighborhood of friends. Adolf
Strodtmann was temporarily settled with his wife in
Philadelphia where lived also a relative of the ill-starred
Governor Tiedemann, Schurz's commander at Rastatt.
This gentleman, Henry Tiedemann, was practising
medicine. He and his family became warm friends of
the Schurzs, frequently entertaining them in their house,
and affording Margarethe and the children a home on
a farm he owned near Philadelphia for long periods during the Civil War, when Carl was at the front.

At Philadelphia the Schurzs at first lived in hired
rooms and later, on the arrival from Germany in the
spring of 1853 of Carl's family, they took a house which

was presided over by the elder Mrs. Schurz, the daughters finding employment in a millinery store. Margarethe's first child was born during that year, which made release from household cares a necessity for her.

But what work of importance engaged Carl? Before leaving London he had written of his plans, pointing out that he expected to begin by giving lectures in the principal cities on subjects connected with his studies, and particularly on the period of French history from 1789 to 1851. The December reaction (1851) being in his view the most significant event of recent times, would constitute the natural climax of his discussion. Schurz was impressed with a certain duality in French history between the people's love of liberty and their acceptance of strong government—a contrast which he found running all through the period he would treat. It was expressed later in the title of his lecture, *Democracy and Despotism in France*.

From his vantage ground as revolutionist and hero, Schurz had canvassed the opportunities for a lecturing career in America before coming to the country and had found them good. Yet it is all but certain that during the two and a half years spent in Philadelphia he did not enter regularly upon the lecturing business. Had he traveled as a lecturer we would have letters written to his wife, whereas, except for those written in the spring of 1854 from Washington, there are no letters to her for two full years or until he made his first trip West in September and October 1854. Besides, Schurz's letters to Kinkel, his old master of public speaking, have nothing to say about lecturing, and the newspapers, so far as they have been examined, are also silent.

That Schurz should have thought of lecturing as a means of support is interesting as showing that he understood perfectly the advertising value of his revolutionary experience and particularly his freeing of Kinkel. But the same argument would apply in the field of authorship into which we know he tried to enter. Writing to Kinkel in April, 1853, he speaks of their quiet winter and of the fact that he had 'got a book ready' which would be sent to Germany, of course, for publication. It was not merely an account of the French Revolution, which he calls the old plan; he had 'broadened the scope and drawn in the most recent history,' briefly summarizing the details. So, the lecture he had contemplated had been writ large in the form of a book, a not unusual experience for a student whose mind is too full of his theme to permit the necessary compression.

The book was not published, for as late as October, 1858, Schurz asked his brother-in-law to return the manuscript since he wanted to make from it a couple of essays for which he 'could get very good pay.' Nor do we find evidence that Schurz succeeded in another plan, broached to Kinkel, of writing a new kind of book on America. Certain essays on Wisconsin we find him writing in the spring of 1856 but, though he sent these to London magazines, we have not found them in print. Thus it does not appear that his concentration upon study and writing, during the first three years in America, produced anything in the way of a pecuniary income.

A portion of his time was devoted to the very practical object of mastering the English language, a task he performed with such distinguished success that some account of his method of study becomes necessary. Schurz describes his procedure in *Reminiscences*. It was, fundamentally, the composition method, the same he had employed in Paris when engaged in learning French. The first step was to acquire something of a vocabulary, and for this he read English newspapers as well as he could, including the advertisements where the meanings of words are often to be inferred from the accompanying illustrations. Having gained some command of words he next wrote brief compositions, translating from English into German and back again, comparing with the original, correcting, and revising. After a time he undertook to read English novels, beginning with Goldsmith's *Vicar of Wakefield,* and following with Scott, Dickens, Thackeray. Later he read Macaulay's historical essays, then portions of Blackstone's *Commentaries*; and, as the most onerous task of all, because of the enormous and complicated vocabulary employed, Shakespeare's plays. He 'thumbed his dictionary conscientiously' but never used a grammar. Having failed to take up the study of English while living in London, the work he did in Philadelphia was his first introduction to a language and literature of which Schurz in a few years became an ornament. Of his progress he says in less than six months he was able 'to carry on a conversation in English on subjects not requiring a wide knowledge of technical terms, and write a decent letter.'

The stage of proficiency he described had certainly been attained long before he visited Washington, in March, 1854, since he participated there in a series of interviews with prominent American politicians including President Pierce and Secretary of War Jefferson Davis. But the study of English went forward uninterruptedly. In 1857, when Schurz was nominated for lieutenant governor in Wisconsin, he told John Gregory, who was amazed at his command of English, that

he had read the works of Edmund Burke and other
classical English writers. He accounted for his mastery
of an idiomatic style by saying it was his invariable
habit to note down on slips of paper all peculiar words
and phrases met with in his reading. These he would
carry in his pockets. By way of illustration he then and
there emptied one of his pockets, turning up the most
heterogeneous collection imaginable of scribbled over
scraps of paper, such as blank corners of newspaper
pages. At odd moments he would con these over until
their contents became an organic part of his language
equipment, serviceable under any conditions.

It is a commentary on the indefiniteness of Schurz's
plans, at the time of his arrival in the United States,
that although one of his announced purposes had been
to settle his parents and sisters in Wisconsin, two years
were allowed to slip away before he even made a
journey into the West. And when he did so the object
was a wholly different one although, by a natural chain
of circumstances, it led to the removal of the family to
Watertown the following year. It appears probable
that Margarethe vetoed for a time the pioneering plan.
'You know,' wrote Schurz, 'how she imagined this wild
America would be.'[34] She had lived a sheltered life,
surrounded by conveniences and luxuries. As Carl
bluntly told her brother, before his marriage to her, she
had had too few problems to solve. Margarethe had expected to find everything crude in America and had
even been agreeably surprised to discover beauty, comfort, and convenience in the sea-port cities of New York
and Philadelphia. But she set her face against the
western adventure and had to be persuaded to it by degrees, and with some subtlety.

[34] Letter to Charlotte Voss, October 20, 1852. *Speeches &c.*, i. 1.

One consideration urged upon her by Schurz, was that the western states would afford the opportunity for political preferment which she coveted for him, and another was that the chances of making profitable investments were fabulously good in that region. When he went West, in September, 1854, he had two fairly definite objects in view, aside from a mere tour of inspection. First, he wanted to see the old Baden revolutionist, Frederick Hecker, who lived on a farm near Belleville in southern Illinois, not far from St. Louis. Hecker had been in the country since 1849, three years longer than Schurz, was a keen politician, and it seems probable that in view of the new alignment which the Nebraska Act was causing, Schurz was anxious to confer with him on the future of politics in America, particularly the attitude to be taken by German leaders. He also wanted to go hunting with Hecker, but this object was not of critical importance. Second (and this may have been a mere incident) Schurz bore a commission to enter upon a negotiation in Indianapolis in regard to a gas business.

The literary result of the trip was a series of four remarkable letters dated from Indianapolis, St. Louis, and Watertown, in September and October, 1854. With the exception of the Washington letters of March in the same year, these are the first of the long series of Schurz's letters to his wife from whom he had evidently not been separated at all during their first two years except by the length of his short stay in Washington. The letters from the West were obviously designed to engage Margarethe's sympathetic interest in the continental regions of America. He gave her several brilliant word pictures of scenery, he described (not from observation but from some book he had read) the primitive log cabin

life of the frontier, and dilated upon the magnificence
and marvelous growth of the cities, especially Chicago.
'Assuredly,' he says, 'you must sometime make this
journey with me and see everything that I have seen.'
There was so much of the grand and beautiful that a
visitor was amply repaid for the expenditure of time,
money, and comfort required for seeing it. 'I believe,'
he says, 'you would quickly lose your opposition to the
West if you could once see it. I will not say that in
beauty this country surpasses the East. On the contrary, the tremendous plains on both sides of the Mississippi are not of durable interest. But an endlessly
fresh spirit surges through this land. Whithersoever
you direct your gaze something great can be seen developing. Grandeur is the characteristic of the whole
western life. It seems charged with hopefulness, and
the war against obstacles opposing civilization is carried on in the serenest confidence of victory.'

In the above account of Schurz's life, prior to his
settlement in the West, we find nothing to indicate that
he had an income, either regular or irregular. His books
did not sell and lecturing was deferred to a later time.
Some have speculated as to whether or not at this
period he may have been in the employ of revolutionary
societies abroad which financed him. That he was deeply
interested in persuading the American government open-
ly to favor a liberal movement in Europe, and especially in Germany, is clear from several statements in his
letters.[35] It is also clear that, in a quiet way, he was doing some organizing among the Germans in this country
designed to bring pressure to bear upon the government.
But that is precisely the kind of activity in which Schurz

[35] See especially the letter to Kinkel, of April 12, 1853, the one of
January 23, 1855, and the letters to Mrs. Schurz from Washington, March
23, 1854. The last two named are in *Speeches &c.*, i, 14; 11-14.

could never avoid engaging whenever his heart was in a
movement, and there is no reason to suppose that he was
acting in other than a private capacity. The most likely
revolutionary source from which he might have drawn
was the fund raised by Kinkel during his lecturing tour
in America in 1851 and 1852 under the London refugees' plan for the German National Loan. But the
correspondence with Kinkel, so far as we have it, fails
entirely to show that Schurz was receiving any of those
monies, to which he might have urged a good moral
claim, since he had had a definite part in raising them as
Kinkel's business manager in London during the latter's
American tour.

Schurz's personal financial situation at the end of
May, 1852, is indicated by the fact that he had just sent
to his parents all the money he had, except a few pounds
not yet collected of which he hoped to send them a part.
July tenth he was married and took a house in London.
His earnings in six weeks could not have exceeded two
hundred dollars and were probably much less. But
whatever the amount it was the last of his personal income before sailing for America. Then came a
couple of weeks at Malvern and a cabin passage
for himself and wife on the *City of London,* one of the
best trans-Atlantic packets. It is clear, therefore, that
he could not have depended on his own means even to
get to America, much less to live there after his arrival.

Wire-drawn speculations about Carl's source of pecuniary supply are all the more beside the mark when it is
recalled that, in accordance with his usual luck, he
had married not only a beautiful, charming, and tal-
ented woman, but an heiress. We do not know the exact
amount of Margarethe's original inheritance, but it is
believed to have been twelve or fifteen thousand dollars.

Neither do we know in what manner it came to her, whether all in a lump or in several installments. But there is no real doubt that this was the money which enabled Schurz to spend practically four idyllic years, including parts of one year abroad, before being forced into the sordid business of making a living.[36]

We have called Philadelphia Schurz's first American home and it is true that during the period October, 1852, to March, 1855, he gives no other address. Carl and Margarethe, however, moved about somewhat and it is certain that in the summer of 1854 they passed a certain period in the pleasant Moravian village of Bethlehem, perhaps merely as summer vacationists. The time was spent in a variety of diverting activities, including horse-back riding, pistol practise, and especially the reading of Dickens.[37] Whether or not they were able, at that season, to enjoy the music provided by the Bethlehem Philharmonic Society, we cannot be sure.[38] But Carl and Margarethe were both deeply interested in all musical activities.

[36] A portion of the Meyer estate consisted originally of unproductive lands lying outside the city of Hamburg. This was left undivided by the heirs, it is said, until it was later taken into the city and became very valuable. The Schurz children were made well-to-do through their inheritance of their mother's share of this 'second' estate. Interview with Marie Jüssen Monroe.

[37] See Schurz's letter of September 17, 1860.

[38] Bethlehem was for several decades the virtual musical capital of America. Löwe's *Seven Sleepers* and Haydn's *Creation* had been presented before 1840. Grider, Rufus A., *Historical Notes on Music in Bethlehem.*

CHAPTER X

BREAD-WORRYING

MARGARETHE'S fortune, unlike the divinely blessed widow's cruse, had this characteristic of merely earthly treasuries that it tended to become depleted with enjoyment and use. Had it been more ample, it would have provided for more years of happy family association, intensive application to study and writing, quiet urban and rural enjoyments. But by the latter part of the year 1854 it appears the Schurzs had come to a decision about the need of providing against the future by means of profitable investments of the balance, and by laying the foundations for a business or professional income.

The idea of making money was on Schurz's mind when he undertook his first trip West in September, 1854, for as already mentioned he visited Indianapolis with a definite mission which he referred to as the 'gas business.' At Indianapolis he interviewed Nathaniel Bolton, a prominent man of affairs and husband of the poetess Sarah Bolton whom he had met at Washington in March; he called on Governor Wright and perhaps others among the men of importance. He found the auspices good but we do not know the result. Street lighting by means of gas began in Indianapolis about the time of Schurz's visit or a little later. But the gas company, which held a non-exclusive charter, was in disfavor among the citizens and it seems probable that he was representing Philadelphia capitalists who wanted a chance to compete with that company in the hope of driving it to the wall.

Various passages in his letters testify to the money-making motive of the trip to the West. Reaching Chicago very late at night and wearily searching for a bed, he was waylaid by rats who emerged from under the wooden sidewalks and, according to his fantastic account, protested against his intrusion into their realm of darkness and black night. Their leader accosted him sternly, with the inquiry: 'What do you want here, stranger? Why did you not stay with your lovely wife and child? *Why did you come into this distant country, in pursuit of wealth and earthly things? Fool that you are,*' and so forth. To this Schurz made answer, in a manner unconsciously senatorial: 'Mr. Speaker and fellow rats. Though I am not accustomed to speaking to so large and respectable an audience in a language foreign to my native country, yet I feel myself compelled by the reasonable sentiments expressed by your honorable and worthy leader to venture upon a word or two. Mr. Speaker and fellow rats! I am exceedingly sorry to have trespassed upon your nightly rights and privileges by the unfortunate fact of my presence. But, gentlemen, you may be sure I never should have taken such an indecent as well as dangerous course, if not [*sic*] beings of my own race, men with hearts of stone, had kicked me away from their doors and turned me into the deserted streets. I know, gentlemen, that you harbor feelings of kindness in your hearts and that you are not insensible to the sufferings of a distressed stranger, who, *in the vain pursuit of earthly things,* as your worthy speaker expressed himself very appropriately, *has improvidently left his dearest ones and threw* [*sic*] *himself into the wide world.*'[39] Going west to St. Louis, Schurz wrote: 'I am taking a lot of notes and

[39] Letter of September 30, 1854. Italics mine.

having many experiences which will soon come in handy. I am more and more convinced that we should be on easy street here in a couple of years. . . .' So it seems he was positively bent on getting rich quick.

When he reached Chicago on his return trip he found letters from his uncle, Jacob Jüssen, who urgently invited Schurz to visit him and his family at Watertown, Wisconsin, forty miles west of Milwaukee. He must have had such a side excursion in mind, for the uncle's letters were doubtless in response to suggestions of his own, otherwise the time of his arrival in Chicago would not have been known. On that trip he experienced for the first time the natural charms and material enticements of southern Wisconsin. The beautiful moonlight voyage from Chicago to Milwaukee prepared him for a cheerful but not quite open-eyed appraisal of the badger metropolis, and he found the combined rail and stage ride to his destination enjoyable rather than the reverse, a 'splendid plank road' contributing to his satisfaction. Schurz was impressed with all he saw, calling Wisconsin a beautiful land. It compared favorably with flat Illinois 'by reason of its wooded hills and the multitude of lovely lakes.' The development of the southern part of the state surprised him; he had expected to find it less well settled. It was already a fine, prosperous farming region.

There are no more letters, after the one dated Watertown, October 9, 1854, until the following March. But one can easily imagine the eager consultations in the Philadelphia household during the winter about where to go and what to do. Three groups of two each had to be considered—first Schurz and Margarethe, second the parents, third the sisters. The latter had so far been the working members of the family, being employed in a ladies' bazaar. They planned, on settling in the West, to open a millinery business of their own, which they did at Watertown as their advertisement in the local paper proves, but it was only a short time before Tony married Edmund Jüssen and Anna, August Schiffer. The old parents had two interests at heart namely, to continue living with their children in true European patriarchal simplicity, and to be restored to close contact with those among their beloved relatives who were already in America, which meant the Jüssens in Watertown. Carl and Margarethe, while of course duly respecting the desires of the rest, would have as their own special interest to find a location which would be pleasant, favorable to Margarethe from a health standpoint, for she was essentially an invalid, and socially desirable. But, especially, it must afford the coveted opportunity for money making and it must also give Schurz his chance in a political and professional way, for he designed to study and practice law as well as go into politics.

From the result it is clear that sentiments of family attachment played a dominant rôle in the decision. The Schurzs and Jüssens constituted a most affectionate family group. Schurz tells in his *Reminiscences* how all the sons of Heribert Jüssen, together with the two sons-in-law, and their several wives, would sometimes foregather in the Rhenish homeland intent on settling the important business matters which, through the bad management of one of the brothers, had practically ruined them all. But after visiting for a day or two they found their enjoyment of each other's society so charming and so disarming, that no one was willing to say the things involving criticism of one of their number. So, they took affectionate leave of one another without so much as mentioning the matter which was the ostensible reason for their meeting. Carl's letter from Watertown shows how heartily he rejoiced in the affection of his uncle and of his uncle's family. He speaks of the tearful joy with which he had been received, after so long a separation, and lauds the uncle and aunt as people Margarethe would love to know.

Living as a duplex family, a younger pair with an elder, was traditional with the Schurzs as with so many Europeans, whether Germans, Italians, French, or others. Christian Schurz and his wife, as we saw, lived in the *Burg* with the Heribert Jüssens until Carl, the eldest child was four years old. The normal practice is for the son or daughter, on marrying, to be taken into the home of the elders, not the reverse, unless the parents are beyond the working age. But Carl Schurz, as we have seen, was under the deepest obligations to support his parents in view of their sacrifices for him and of their great losses sustained partly on his account. It was a duty he could discharge best by making such a home as would accommodate all the elements of the complex household—his parents and sisters, his wife and himself.

Such a plan could militate disastrously against his purpose to make money fast in order to be free to devote himself to public affairs. It seems strange that the question of investment opportunities should have failed to exercise a more controlling influence over Schurz's movements; or, assuming the motive to have been as prominent as the letters indicate, that it did not issue in a different plan from the one actually adopted. For with the lake port of Milwaukee forging ahead toward the condition of a promising city, the selection by him of the retired village of Watertown requires explanation.

In March, 1855, Schurz accompanied his parents and sisters to Watertown, remaining only a few weeks but securing a location for them by entering into preliminary contracts of purchase for a farm and for a couple of small houses in the village. He then hurried back to attend his wife and child on a voyage to England. Margarethe, just before their departure, had been seriously ill of some lung ailment which created a sort of emergency. But her general health was so unsatisfactory that it was decided to give her the benefit of a summer at the Malvern water-cure where her husband, at the time of his attack of scarlet fever, in 1852, had found such prompt relief. He returned in July to begin business operations in Watertown, the line hit upon being a real-estate speculation. For this purpose he bought a farm at the edge of the village, saved the grain crop growing upon it, and arranged for the building of a good house. He then made a second voyage to England in the fall, joined Margarethe at Christmas, and in 1856 spent with her several months in the mild and beautiful region of Montreux, Switzerland, recommended by her English water-cure physician. In August, 1856, the whole family was reunited at Watertown, in the new house which was to be their home for just ten years.

The selection of Watertown must be considered one of the fatalities which came to Schurz occasionally as an offset to his good luck. On going there he had promised Margarethe that he would be most circumspect about investments, studying all conditions carefully in advance. This he doubtless did, but not without letting family interest and affection impart an uncon-

scious bias to his reasoning on the facts ascertained.
Otherwise he could hardly have fixed upon Watertown
either for business or for politics. Schurz, in his
October letter of 1854, speaks rather slightingly of
Milwaukee, saying the place had not flourished properly for some time, that it could not withstand the
competition of Chicago, that it had too many Germans,
explaining: 'When the Germans in this country have
to live off Germans it goes badly for them.' The impression that he was treating the prospects of Milwaukee too cavalierly, is strengthened by a revised estimate
he gave of that city in August, 1855, just before closing
his contract for the farm at Watertown. He then said:
'No American city, not even Cleveland, has made upon
me such a pleasing impression.'[40] He had gone there
for the express purpose of investigating chances for
investments and, since he had not yet committed himself
irrevocably to Watertown he might still have decided
in Milwaukee's favor. Apparently, however, the family
pull toward the friendly inland town was too strong
and in September, 1855, he signed the papers which
bound him to that place more firmly than he could have
wished.

The arguments in favor of Watertown were super-
ficially convincing. Though small, it was at the moment
the second town in Wisconsin and it bade fair to become
a railway center analogous to Indianapolis. Schurz,
through his recent interest in the Indiana capital, may
well have made that comparison. He had reported to
his wife from Indianapolis the striking fact that, at a
given hour of the day, six trains could be seen moving
out in different directions. Watertown was preparing
for a like distinction, which of course had not been at-

[40] Letter of August 15, 1855.

tained when he settled there. To be quite frank, no railway as yet had reached the place. But the Milwaukee and Watertown was within a few miles of it; the Rock River Railway was pushing south from Fond du Lac in order to connect at Watertown with the Milwaukee and Watertown which would afford access to the lake port; and there was also a railway project from the south having Watertown in view as an objective. After reaching that point, which was accomplished by September, 1856, the Milwaukee and Watertown branched. One division pushed toward Madison where it united with the Milwaukee and Mississippi whose terminus was Prairie du Chien, the other trended northwest toward La Crosse, to proceed thence to St. Paul. The Fond du Lac branch tapped the great pineries near Lake Winnebago, the other roads opened up large farming areas by joining the Mississippi and the Great Lakes. 'All these railroads,' wrote Schurz in August, 1856, 'are called into being by immediate need, and therefore have good prospects.'

The only question of personal significance to him was how the railway development would affect Watertown's prosperity. No doubt these transportation lines were all needed by the state, and would contribute greatly to the building up of the areas through which they passed. But it is not clear why the carrying of freight and passenger traffic through a town should aid materially in building it up. The deceptive element in the Watertown situation was that, when Schurz arrived and for some time thereafter, the place was a railway terminus. This would be abolished by the very process of building the roads farther, when Columbus, Portage, La Crosse, Madison, and Prairie du Chien—perhaps not in that order—would engage the interest of the booster element which for a little while yet were to give Watertown the aspect of a bustling commercial capital. In November, 1855, the editor of the *Daily Wisconsin* (Milwaukee) pointed out that Watertown was likely to remain the terminus for a year. He was literally right in his prediction. If Schurz had investigated properly the evanescent character of western railway termini, he would probably have hesitated long about casting his fortunes with such a town. Western life had many things to teach him, but for its business lessons he was destined to pay dearly.

The farm he purchased contained eighty-nine acres, but the deed from John Jackson to 'Charles' Schurz, dated September twelfth, 1855, does not show the purchase price. Schurz executed a mortgage to Jackson in the sum of of eight thousand five hundred dollars which doubtless represents nearly the whole of it, farm land there rarely bringing one hundred dollars per acre at that time however advantageously it might be located. He probably paid down a few hundred dollars, so small a fraction that he could have regarded the transaction as a kind of option until, by selling a good share of it as city lots, he could pay off the purchase price. That kind of speculation had often succeeded with others, why not with him? His pleasant home, built on the most sightly point of the farm, 'a gentle acclivity' affording charming views of the river, the town, and the neighboring woods, would attract purchasers of home sites. During the progress of the lot sales the farm land could be cultivated.

The sales began in a small way in 1856, but the panic of the following year, combined with the deflation of business due to the passing of the railway boom, stopped the progress of building. The *drang nach*

Westen which Schurz hoped would be illustrated locally by the city spreading into his land at the outskirts of
Watertown leaped over his acres in its precipitate
eagerness to catch the next point of inflation. The Jackson farm of 1855 is still a farm in 1929, save for one
pretty home on the site of the house Schurz built in 1856
and which burned a few years ago.[41] In short, the real
estate business, in so far as it depended on the plan to
convert the Jackson farm into a new addition to Watertown, proved a dismal failure. The town did not require
the additions which sundry realtors were advertising
because, after attaining the proportions of a good sized
village, say nine thousand people, it stubbornly refused
to grow.

Schurz, however, for about two years, was as storm-
ily active in a business way as he later became in public
affairs. He sold some lots, he made investments for
eastern clients, he became president of a local insurance
company, he carried on the official functions of a notary
public. He assumed the duties of commissioner of public improvements and became a member of the city
council. The success of a move fostered by the legislature, to make Watertown the county seat, called for the
construction not only of a court house, but also school
houses, bridges, and so on. 'Although,' Schurz writes at
the close of the eventful year 1856, 'the building and
improving will not actually begin before the spring,
there are many preparations to be made, and one of my
principal duties will be to obtain fifty thousand dollars
on city bonds.'[42] He also served on a committee to raise
a railway bonus.

[41] The owner of the home referred to calls his place *Karl's Huegel*
(Carl's Hill) in memory of the Schurz home on the same site.
[42] Letter to Kinkel, December 17, 1856. *Speeches &c.*, i, 27.

Meantime, he was reading law in the hope of soon beginning practice. The year 1857 was a distressful year for Schurz, what with the panic, his first political reverse, and the financial load he was forced to carry over the period of business stagnation. It might be stated here, once for all, that he did not actually practice law at any time, although he was admitted to the bar and entered into a law partnership with Halbert E. Paine of Milwaukee which was to go into effect January 1, 1859. He also for a short time conducted a Republican German newspaper at Watertown. In a word, he had altogether too many irons in the fire to justify a hope that he would succeed in business.

But fate was against him almost from the start. Instead of real estate rising so much in a few years that 'we need no longer be anxious about our financial situation,' as he anticipated in 1856, he was now really concerned about ways of making a living. The solution of the problem, so far as it was solved otherwise than by adding to his mortgage indebtedness, which he did in 1858, was found in lyceum lecturing, and this too was begun in Watertown. That city, like so many others, had a *Young Men's Association* whose object was to promote the community's intellectual and spiritual welfare, the winter course of lectures being the orthodox means of accomplishing that end. The associations raised funds by charging admission fees, which made it just about as easy to bring celebrities from a distance as to employ local talent, the number of tickets sold often being in some proportion to the number of miles traveled by the lecturer. Many eastern literary men and publicists visited Wisconsin to fill lecturing engagements before such associations, among them be-

ing Ralph Waldo Emerson, Wendell Phillips, and
Horace Greeley.

By a singular coincidence, Horace Greeley gave the
first lecture at Watertown in the year 1858 and Schurz
the second. Greeley spoke, the evening of January
first, on *Europe as I Saw It*. His effort was described
as brilliantly written, but by contrast, the editor of the
Democrat deplored 'the drawling tone, indistinct voice,
and wretched manner in which it was delivered.' He
says, evidently with some partisan animus, 'a donkey
could just about as easily roar like a lion as the renown-
ed philosopher of the press could succeed in appearing
and speaking like an impressive and graceful orator.'
He had hopes, however, for the next time. Mr. Schurz,
scheduled to lecture on January twentieth, had chosen
as his subject *Democracy and Despotism in France*.
The editor says he 'was the ablest and most eloquent
speaker who addressed the people, whether in the German or the English language, during the late state
canvass, and while in a political sense we cannot regret
the result of the election . . . yet so far as he is personally concerned we cheerfully admit that he deserved
success if he did not achieve it'.[43] Among the qualifications for presenting an interesting discourse which the
editor thought deserving of mention was Mr. Schurz's
participation in the German revolution, and his
thorough knowledge of European conditions from
actual observation. The lecture evidently gave much
pleasure to all of Schurz's hearers except those who,
like the Democratic editor, were disgusted by what they
deemed partisan reflections at its close. He had been
defeated for the office of lieutenant governor in the
recent election and the Democratic editor felt that by

[43] Watertown *Democrat*, January 13, 1858.

the remarks objected to he showed himself a very poor loser. But Schurz was now at last launched as a lecturer, a bread-winning business he had contemplated before leaving Europe and which thereafter he pursued interchangeably with politics, diplomacy, soldiering, and editorship for many years.

CHAPTER XI

POLITICAL DISCIPLINE

SCHURZ, as already noted, made his first visit to the national capital in March, 1854. Ostensibly, his object was to use the congressional library in studying American history but in reality he wanted to gain an insight into national politics by meeting leading characters, watching the proceedings of Congress, and interviewing key men to learn the government's attitude toward foreign affairs.[44] He made the acquaintance of Senator James Shields, of Illinois, called on President Pierce, Jefferson Davis, and others. He audited debates in the Senate and House, and conversed with a number of the members of Congress. This visit seems to have intensified and focalized all those ambitions to shine in public life which we have seen developing since his student days at Bonn and which are reflected in the letters announcing his intention to go to America. Gleefully, he reported to his wife a conversation with a group of congressmen wherein he was assured: 'If you settle in one of the new states, we will meet you in a few years in this city, and then we shall listen to you as you now listen to us.'[45] Here was a reason for the removal to Wisconsin even more urgent than the presence there of relatives and friends, for soon we shall see Schurz explaining to Kinkel that in Wisconsin the German element is already powerful, that it is actively striving for political recognition but needs leaders who are free from the necessity of devoting their time to making

[44] See letter to Kinkel, April 12, 1853.
[45] Letter of March 23, 1854, *Speeches &c.*, i, 11-13.

money. He believed that to be the place where he could work, 'without truckling to the nativistic elements,' and there he hoped in time 'to gain influence that may also become useful to our cause.'[46]

Nativism and 'the cause,' together with slavery, were at this time prominent motives of Schurz's political action, while ambition was the dynamic impelling him forward on a political path. The nativistic or 'Know-nothing' movement had been rampant in the United States for about a decade, driving more and more of the foreign born citizens into the Democratic party, because Democrats had always turned a friendly countenance to the newcomers while the Whigs, representing the American aristocracy, treated them with high disdain. The Know-nothings, first cousins to the Whigs, were determined to reduce foreigners, especially if Catholics, to a status of political inferiority. Democrats, in fighting that policy, were contending for the rights of men as men, a principle dear both to the revolutionists and to Jeffersonians, but they were while doing so half consciously violating the same fundamental principle in their attitude toward slavery extension.

Like the Democratic and Whig parties, the Know-nothing party was nation-wide, hatred of foreigners being just as universal and implacable in the South as in the North, although foreign immigration into that region was as yet light. Northern Know-nothings, however, being in the main of New England Puritan stock, were generally opposed to slavery extension while their southern partisans favored it. Carl Schurz quickly saw the weakness in that situation and knew that a change was about due. The southerners, he said, could be consistent in favoring both slavery extension

---

[46] To Kinkel, March 25, 1855, *Speeches &c.*, i, 19.

and the limitation of the rights of foreigners, but not so their brethren above Mason and Dixon's line. These were becoming more and more aroused about admitting slavery into the territories, and in fighting that policy they needed their natural allies from European lands.

An ominous tension existed between the two wings of the Know-nothing party, as Schurz saw when he wrote: 'It will not be long before the slave states become the headquarters of the Nativistic movement, and there it will remain.'[47] The prophecy was fulfilled six months later, the party splitting geographically on the question of slavery extension. The northern wing now promptly drew closer to the foreigners.

Schurz recognized that the new Republican organization, which was forming out of fragments of the Know-nothing, the Whig, the Anti-Masonic, and Free Soil groups, would be sure to contain many of the elements which had always been hostile to foreigners. But he also saw that if, on the issue of free soil, large numbers of foreigners could be won over from the Democrats, old animosities would quickly disappear and the resulting party, made up of native and non-native citizens, would prove a more comfortable political home for anti-slavery Germans than the pro-slavery Democracy had been. This was the reasoning on which, months before the Fremont campaign opened, he had pledged himself to serve the cause of liberty by throwing his influence in favor of the party of free soil.[48]

Schurz's devotion to 'the cause,' by which he meant the revolutionary movement in Europe and especially

[47] Letter to Kinkel, January 23, 1855, *Speeches &c.*, i, 16. The break in the party came in their national convention in Philadelphia the following August.

[48] Frederick Hecker, the erstwhile Baden revolutionist, took a similar attitude, as did Gustav Körner, Francis Hoffman, and other leading Germans.

Germany, conflicted not at all with his determination to
support the free soil movement in America. In fact,
quite the reverse; for a study of political tendencies in
Washington had convinced him that the United States
would never interfere practically in behalf of the liberal
movement abroad so long as slave-holders remained a
power in American politics. 'The slave-holder,' he
wrote, 'fears the propaganda of freedom because he
does not know how far it will go.' But if the slave-
holding, or as he sometimes called it, the country gentry
class, could be overthrown, then the government would
not merely cherish a lively interest in the fortunes of
nations struggling for institutions like their own, as
Webster said in his famous Hülsemann letter of 1850,
but would, he believed, actually use its influence to promote the liberal cause. While this represents an
optimism born of inexperience, it gave Schurz a second
motive for crusading against slavery, and crusade he
did, from 1856 until the question was finally eliminated
from American politics.

He had hoped to make himself economically independent before taking much part in public life, but this
policy his ardent, impatient nature rejected. He was
always unable to restrain his eagerness to participate
in stirring events. 'Why must I sit here—a mere non-
entity occupied with miserable plans for making money,
although my head is full of ideas and the consciousness
of inexhaustible strength—while out there momentous
decisions are being made and scoundrels and medioc-
rities crowd the world's stage?'[49] This outburst was
occasioned by the news of the fall of Sebastopol which
came to Schurz while he was engaged in surveying his

[49] Letter from Watertown, Wisconsin, September 29, 1855, to Mrs.
Schurz. *Speeches &c.,* i, 22.

newly purchased farm into town lots. It is not clear how
he thought he might participate in the affairs that orient
drama symbolized, and the remark is chiefly interesting
as revealing on the one hand the nervous impatience
generated in him by thwarted ambition, on the other the
absence at this time of anything like national boundaries in his thinking. He was as much, perhaps more,
interested in Europe as he was in America, justifying
what he wrote to his friend Althaus before sailing from
London in August, 1852; 'I am saying farewell to
Europe with the certainty of being back at the right
time,' that is, when the next revolution should break
out.

A short time after this the Democrats tried to draw
him into their party. He refused because their political
principles were entirely opposed to his, especially in
regard to national politics.[50] But when, during the following summer, the young Republican party sought his
aid, he gave it in overflowing measure, speaking
throughout the state of Wisconsin wherever audiences
of Germans could be assembled to hear him. That
meant pretty nearly everywhere in the eastern half of
the state, for the immigrations had been increasing for
more than a dozen years and, while the Germans at
first clung timorously to the lake shore, on account of
the assured market at the ports, the progress of road
and railway building was luring them ever farther into
the interior. For reasons already stated, these people
had favored the Democratic party, only a few of them
training with the Whigs and none with the Know-nothings. But their union with the Democratic party was as
illogical as was that of American free-soilers; for the
Germans were naturally opposed to slavery, and partic-

[50] Letter of October 23, 1855, *Speeches &c.*, i, 23.

ularly to its further extension into the territories, where their children would eventually make homes, while the Democratic party, under southern leadership, was becoming ever more pro-slavery in its attitude. Schurz had the arguments calculated to make this situation clear to his fellow countrymen, and these he delivered with tremendous force, earnestness, and eloquence. They were arguments not for a party but for a cause. From the outset he placed principle above all else. But in advocating a non-partisan attitude on the subject of slavery he at the same time was following his convictions and pursuing the most tactful line of approach to his hearers, who were nearly all Democrats and had to be shown why the Republican policies deserved their support.

Schurz, of course, was only one of a group of German speakers who in 1856 worked upon the voters of that connection in Wisconsin, and as yet he was less prominent than some others. Several men of local distinction were kept busy during the campaign, while Judge J. B. Stallo of Cincinnati and Francis Hoffman of Chicago made speeches in the larger cities, with telling effect. Republican newspapers also disseminated, with a keen perception of their influence on German readers, reports of the doings of Frederick Hecker and Gustav Körner of Illinois. The combined results of these diverse appeals, aided by a local and general German Republican press, was to give Fremont, as Schurz estimated, probably with considerable exaggeration, about twenty-five thousand German votes. Even if the actual number were half that large, it would prove that very successful forays had been made into the enemy's country where Germans in masses were wont to vote obediently, not for slavery, but against Know-

nothingism and in favor of the party which could be
trusted to treat foreigners with respect.

The campaign impressed Schurz deeply, as he recalled when writing his *Reminiscences*. Letters dated
soon after its close testify to the same effect. 'A universal struggle of opinion among a free people,' he wrote,
'has about it something unbelievably imposing;' and he
philosophized about the effect such movements produce
upon the popular mind. Possibly because his work had
been mainly among foreigners, he judged them to be,
in comparison with native Americans, 'fast anchored
by futile prejudices' which, however, yielded to the
moving power of oratory, as the returns showed. But
for the conversion of thousands of Germans, Fremont
probably could not have carried the state, an inference
which politicians were quick to make and sure to treas-
ure up against a future time of political need.

Accordingly, it is not surprising that, when the
Republican state convention met the following year, in
order to strengthen the party's chances of success, it
placed Schurz on the ticket for lieutenant governor.
He was charmed with the prospect of advancing 'at a
single leap' from the office of alderman in the little city
of Watertown to that of second officer of the state, and
he plunged into the canvass with zeal, spending four or
five weeks in the field, speaking nearly every day. He
received from Republican leaders the most confident
assurances that he would be triumphantly elected, but
at last suffered the humiliation of being defeated by a
very narrow margin (one hundred and seven votes),
although the rest of the ticket, with Alex W. Randall
at its head, pulled through. It was a bitter experience
for Schurz. He was prone to suspect the loyalty of
some of his associates on the ticket, to believe an elec-

tion fraud had been perpetrated, and what not. There
had been a tremendous falling off in the aggregate vote
as compared with the presidential election of 1856,
which might have been expected, but the Republican
losses were much higher than the Democratic. For this
Schurz blamed the panic, which gave all citizens deep
concern about their economic affairs but kept the American farmers, the backbone of the Republican party, at
home on election day, while the masses of Irish and
German voters constituting the bulk of the Democratic
party, were in the towns where they could be easily
regimented. The reasoning is not particularly convincing, but defeated candidates are proverbially ready,
after an election catastrophy, to explain how it happened, and Schurz was no exception to the rule. The real
reason for his defeat, probably, was the popularity of
his opponent.

Three months after the election Schurz sent to
Kinkel a printed speech which he says was the only one
he made during the campaign that was correctly reported. But since a considerable part of his reputation in
America rested upon it, he would, with becoming mod-
esty, 'lay it at the feet' of his master in the oratorical art.
Portions of it, he says, had made the round of the
American press and were well received. 'I need hardly
say,' he added, 'that I spoke after careful preparation.'
An extemporary speaker he believed himself incapable
of becoming; in debate he got along well enough, but
he would hardly be able to make a great speech by relying on the inspiration of the moment. 'It would be of
the greatest importance to me,' he adds, 'but I believe
I am lacking in the absolute command of form. In this
connection I envy you. Study and experience may

achieve something, but they will not make the master. . . .'[51]

The address referred to was delivered at the court house in Madison, Friday evening, October sixteenth. It was printed—eight solid columns—in the *State Journal* in two installments, October nineteenth and October twentieth, and runs to more than ten thousand words. Editor Horace Rublee called it an 'eloquent, earnest, logical, and finished address.' Mr. Schurz, he said, was 'an easy, fluent speaker, without any of the rant and bluster of the stump orator, but clear, earnest and eloquent with the genuine eloquence of thought expressed in language unusually choice and elegant for the extemporaneous speaker. A slight foreign accent, an occasional idiom or the use of an unusual word, are the only evidence that he is not speaking his mother tongue, such is his perfect mastery of our language, and these only heighten the interest of his remarks as any one who heard or who has read the speeches of Kossuth can readily understand.'[52]

Between the letter quoted above and this editorial comment we can easily conclude something about Schurz's method of public speaking at this our first opportunity to study him. When he writes that he spoke after careful preparation (because he would never be an extemporaneous speaker) he of course meant that the speech had been written out and committed to memory, for he spoke wholly without notes. Mr. Rublee, a competent and interested listener, supposed, or wanted his readers to suppose, that Schurz had been doing his thinking on his feet and expressing himself in language 'unusually choice and elegant for the extem-

[51] Letter of February 23, 1858.
[52] Editorial the *State Journal*, October 17, 1857.

poraneous speaker.' Here we have proof of genuine oratorical art, that rare accomplishment by which a speaker
presents a finished, and perhaps hackneyed address as if
it were the fresh, spontaneous utterance of an admirably
clever talker. This continued to be Schurz's method in
campaigning, for when preparing the great address on
Douglas which he gave in New York City in 1860, his
letters prove that he was engaged in memorizing it. He
was gifted in voice, presence, and dramatic power. He
had the great actor's facility for mastering his 'lines,'
and never required the aid of a prompter.

The Madison speech of 1857 was undoubtedly
printed not from some reporter's notes, but from his
own manuscript, that being Schurz's method of getting
to the public with a message he desired to give them. It
may have been mildly edited, for the printed version
fails to show a single one of the idioms or peculiar words
referred to in the editor's comment. But this editing
would affect at most only a few words or phrases. So
we have here, in our own language, the perfected exposition of Schurz's anti-slavery views, the arguments
he presented to his German compatriots not only in
1857 but also in 1856. Doubtless he gave largely the
same arguments with variations and additions in the
two years which followed.

A reading of the speech leaves one marveling at the
orator's easy command of a classic English style.
Since September, 1854 we have had no means of testing his English, and by comparing this with the
language of the rat story, his progress toward literary
perfection can be easily gauged. It may be said at once
that, aside from Seward, there were few if any public
men in the United States who at that time, in discussing the slavery issue, employed so pure and elegant a

diction, though several—among them Lincoln—were
more successful in producing the effect of simplicity.
Schurz was proving himself a linguistic genius, which
was one basis of his great career.

He begins by arraigning the Democratic party for
its abandonment of the principles of liberty which were
its birthright, and for accepting the increasingly
despotic views of the southern slavocracy. Schurz de-
rides the northern Democracy's professed love of the
constitution and their loudly proclaimed opposition to
slavery. 'If they really are hostile to slavery,' he said,
'then, sir, they love their enemies more than Christians
ought to do.'

He held, with Lincoln and other anti-slavery extension advocates, that the constitution was made to be an
impregnable bulwark of liberty and of the rights of
man. From that standpoint he discussed Taney's Dred
Scott Decision, wherein the jurist argued that the right
of property in a slave is distinctly and expressly affirmed by the constitution, paid his respects to Buchanan's
proclamation of the same views, and dealt with
Douglas's unconventional treatment of the Declaration
of Independence. In the light of Douglas's reasoning,
he points out, the American revolution is no longer the
'great champion of universal principles, but a mean
Yankee trick, a wooden nutmeg, the most impudent
imposition ever practiced upon the whole world.' It
was in this connection that he used against the Little
Giant, whether justly or not, the festering phrase: 'It
requires a prejudiced mind or a disordered brain to mis-
understand the principles contained in that Declaration,
but it requires *the heart of a villain* knowingly to mis-
represent them.'

Toward the close of the address occurs a spirited and effective appeal to Democrats to throw off the trammels of party discipline and vote as they really believe on this great issue. The peroration contains eloquent words on liberty which have often been quoted and which were especially appealing as coming from one who had experienced despotic government. Schurz did not often interlard his speeches with perfervid exhortations, but he had the habit of closing with something in the nature of oratorical pyrotechnics, and this is so good an example that it seems wise to quote the entire passage: 'O, my friends,' he said, 'you cannot imagine what electric thrill the word *Liberty* sends through the heart of a man whose head is borne down by the leaden weight of oppression. You perhaps have never measured the incalculable value of the treasures you possess. Do not, I implore you, do not jeopardize them in a wanton race of ambition and greediness. Do not, like a spendthrift, squander your noble inheritance, vainly imagining that it is inexhaustible. Liberty is valued most when lost, but then it is too late and I tell you your institutions do not stand as firmly as the pillars of heaven. You are wielding yet the formidable mace of self-government. Lift it high and throw it down with a crushing blow upon the head of the serpent!'

This address deserves to be read entire by anyone wishing to gain a true perspective of the career of the brilliant young German scholar who was going up and down the state of Wisconsin giving the people new ideas clothed in language they were but little accustomed to hear. When it is recalled that, in the following year, the people of Illinois heard the speech, or its equivalent, and had the opportunity to compare it with the much heralded speeches of Lincoln and Douglas, and

that in 1859 a large proportion of the Minnesota pioneers
heard something similar, while more and more newspapers were carrying reports of Schurz's doings, we
begin to realize that he was bound to become a force in
American politics whatever treatment the voters of
Wisconsin might accord him. He, in fact, suffered a
reverse in 1859 comparable to his defeat in 1857. For
it was his ambition that year to be chosen governor, the
lieutenant governorship failing longer to interest him.
But this time he was denied the nomination.

In addition to the experience of being twice balked
in his ambition to secure public recognition in Wisconsin, Schurz in these years learned how it felt to endure
every species of criticism and calumny to which in a
democracy an aspirant for high office can be subjected.
In 1857 the democratic papers exploited the charge that
he was violating the law of the land by asking for an
office for which he was not legally qualified, being not
yet a citizen of the United States. His nomination occurred on the third of September. On the seventeenth
of the same month the Watertown *Democrat* criticised
him editorially on the ground that he had not been five
years a resident of the country. The amusing feature
about this particular attack was the fact that on the very
day it was launched Schurz's five years were completed!
Of course, he would not have taken office till the following January. Other and more reckless charges were
later flourished by the thugs of the press as he called
them, for the purpose of putting him out of commission.
Among these was the ridiculous story that he had come
to America, in the interest of the Prussian government,
for the purpose of spying on the political refugees.
'Certain it is,' says Schurz, who was thinner skinned
than most American politicians, 'that if only a tenth

part of the things that were said and written of me had
been true, I should have been rather fit for the peniten-
tiary than for the company of gentlemen.'

Though seeming to pass such attacks by as the idle
wind, Schurz's revulsion to the sordid business is attested by letters to friends and by his later confession of
the pain they caused him. His spirit sang in the sun-
shine of popular favor, but disparagement and unjust
aspersions were as wormwood to his proud and sensitive
soul. He tried to deserve good treatment by according
it to other men in public life. Yet prejudice sometimes
gained dominion over him too, and when engaged in
public debate his opponent could count on taking hard
blows as well as giving them.

The governorship question was a test of Schurz's
willingness to play the game under the rule of give and
take which controls in party politics. The Germans of
Milwaukee had brought success to the Republicans in
that city for the first time, thus intensifying their feeling of political importance which was communicated to
Germans throughout the state. At the same time,
rumors were rife about a resurgence of Know-nothingism, the action of Massachusetts in adopting an anti-
foreigner amendment to the state constitution being
evidence on the point. Certain German editors thought
themselves justified, under these conditions, in demand-
ing that the party nominate and elect Schurz for
governor and they were disposed to make compliance
with this demand the test of the Germans' continued
fealty to the party. Schurz claims the movement took
him by surprise and that he was long in doubt whether
to let it go on or to stop it with an emphatic refusal to be
a candidate. Where he was personally concerned his
judgment was less trustworthy than in other cases, or

he would have been quick to sense, in the attitude of his countrymen, the danger of what Senator Doolittle called a German Know-nothing movement which, confronting an American Know-nothing movement, might bring swift destruction to the Republican party.

Schurz did, in fact, express some hesitation, but it was mainly on personal not party grounds. He dreaded the blow to his own political prestige which a convention defeat following upon his electoral defeat of 1857 would involve. The office of governor he professed to value only as a means of added influence, which would tell in his projected work among the Germans of the entire north in 1860.[53] But ambition overcame prudence, he decided to make the fight and failed, Randall being renominated by a large majority; whereupon some German editors threatened a bolt, intimating that it was Know-nothing sentiment which led the convention to reject their favorite.

Schurz, in some quarters, was criticised for a disposition to rule or ruin the party, but such a charge certainly does not lie against him for anything he did after Randall's selection. He of course declined the proffered consolation nomination for lieutenant governor, which was unanimous, explaining that his reasons were well known to Randall and others. In doing so, however, he formally pledged his aid toward the party's success. The German newspapers which were closest to him also came promptly to the support of the ticket. That Schurz was profoundly disappointed is not in the least doubtful[54] and it was perhaps fortunate that he had campaigning to do in Minnesota which would en-

[53] Letter to Potter, December 24, 1858.
[54] At the state convention the following February he declared that he felt the offer of the lieutenant governorship 'as an insult.'

able him to regain his customary equanimity.[55] When
he returned to Wisconsin in October he plunged into
the canvass with characteristic abandon. He told his
German friends that they were quite wrong in suspect-
ing that a Know-nothing influence caused his defeat at
the convention and urged them to stand loyally by the
ticket, which in the main they did, with the result that
Randall and the entire list of Republican candidates
came through with flying colors, the governor's majority being near four thousand.

If Schurz can be justly criticised for his part in the
governorship incident, it is on his pre-convention attitude, when he believed the party, in a measure, could be
dragooned into taking him for governor; for he would
refuse any other place on the ticket, and a German
would be needed in order to attract German votes. The
convention, unwisely thinking he would accept a unanimous endorsement for lieutenant governor, seems to
have been left somewhat up in the air by his refusal,
and actually made up a ticket which had no German name upon it. Schurz could suggest none
for any of the secondary offices. But it is certain that there were such men, and had he been
ready to propose a name, the convention would
doubtless have accepted it. His failure to do so, unless
we ascribe it to a pure oversight, could be interpreted
either as a slight to the Germans or as a challenge to
the party to get on as best it might without the full
coöperation of the Germans. The convention, it is true,
was quite as helpless as Schurz about discovering an

---

[55] In his speech at Milwaukee a few days after the convention closed,
on being tendered a reception by the Young Men's Association, he voiced
his well known principle that service to a cause does not call for a reward.
At the same time, certain of his remarks indirectly reflected upon Randall,
the party's nominee, whom he had pledged himself to support.

available German. Yet, two years later they took one of his lawyer friends, a man slightly older than himself, similarly trained, and an older resident both in the country and the state. That gentleman, Edward Salomon, not only filled worthily the lieutenant governorship, but when on the death of Louis P. Harvey he became chief magistrate, he proved his adequacy in the midst of all complications of the Civil War period. Good sportsmanship ought to have suggested to Schurz to hold some German in reserve for the second place on the ticket in case he himself failed to secure first place.

Although the Republican party cannot be said consciously to have rejected Schurz because he was a foreigner, it is nevertheless true that the nomination of a foreigner for governor in any party would have been contrary to the established custom of the people at that time;[56] and when a foreigner happened to reach the gubernatorial chair from the office of lieutenant governor, in the case of Salomon, he could not obtain the nomination for a term as governor in his own right. The inertia of habit was too strong for even Schurz to overcome. On the whole, however, he emerged from the Wisconsin political tangle in 1859 more fortunately than might have been anticipated.

[56] The views of one of Schurz's Norwegian correspondents of 1859 cover this very point.

CHAPTER XII

HIS FAME BECOMES NATIONAL

SCHURZ, in March, 1857 made a trip to New York apparently on business connected with his office of commissioner of public improvements in Watertown. Arriving at night, he went to the Prescott House and next morning, before beginning his work of interviewing financiers, even before permitting himself to be seen in the hotel dining room, he visited a clothing store 'as necessity compelled.' He next went in to breakfast where a surprise awaited him, for the landlord, charmed to have the privilege of entertaining so famous a guest, brought out a bottle of champagne in order that he might clink glasses with him. Schurz commented on the incident amusingly, saying: 'My fame is now almost seven years old and in the seventh year it still brings me a bottle of champagne. Is not that a strong testimony against the vanity and transitoriness of human fame?'[57]

The manner in which he dates its origin shows that this fame attached to him more as the rescuer of Kinkel than as the lucky revolutionist who had given the slip to Prussian soldiers at Rastatt. The incident is important as revealing the enormous advantage Schurz enjoyed as an ambitious German seeking preferment in a continent progressively peopling with Germans who still felt their separateness and needed leaders to guide their political future. As he happened upon men in New York who knew the story of his adventurous life, so he found them in Pennsylvania, Ohio, Indiana, Illi-

[57] Letter of March 21, 1857.

nois, Missouri—in fact wherever Germans were making
homes in this country. More than that, the story of the
liberation of Kinkel, and the revolutionary record, commanded the interest of intelligent Americans as well as
Germans, and Schurz was by no means wanting in a
flair for publicity. So, very properly, he made use of
those stories to aid his campaigning, to improve the
chances of his lecturing engagements, to gain the attention of politicians.

Three and a half years later than the incident of the
champagne breakfast in New York, he had a still more
remarkable experience on a Lake Erie steamboat ply-
ing between Cleveland and Detroit. The captain ap-
proached him very respectfully 'hat in hand,' said he
had just learned who his distinguished passenger was,
returned his passage money, remarked that he considered it an honor to have him on board, and would
never accept pay for such an honor, etc. He prepared
his own cabin for Schurz's convenience, commanded all
stewards to be at his beck and call, allowed him to sleep
at Cleveland long after all other passengers were ashore,
then provided a sumptuous breakfast, had the stewards
transfer his baggage to the train, and on parting begged
his guest to honor him by using his boat again. 'Fame
is something,' was Schurz's laconic comment.

This American skipper, we are safe in assuming,
had never heard of Kinkel, and might not have been
able to distinguish the German revolution of 1848 from
the Peloponnesian War. Yet he knew Schurz, and recognized his claim to the respect and honor of all Americans. The explanation is to be found in the story of
Schurz's public activities between March, 1857 and September, 1860.

His speeches of 1856, important though they were as a means of converting Germans to Republicanism, were all made in the German language and failed entirely to attract the attention of the English language press. The Madison speech of 1857 was the first utterance of his which made the round of the Republican English newspapers. But its brilliancy was such that thereafter Schurz had only to speak in English, and hand his notes to some friendly editor, in order to insure more than state-wide publicity for his views. His fixed habit of writing all speeches was a great aid in this respect, enabling him, by means of the newspapers, to multiply his audiences many fold.

While his lecturing and campaigning as a whole need to be considered, one can indicate a series of addresses whose delivery and publication were largely responsible for the reputation Schurz enjoyed at the opening of the Lincoln campaign. In that series the Madison speech of 1857, stands first; the Chicago speech of September twenty-eighth, 1858, second; the Milwaukee speech on *Political Morals*, delivered November eighteenth, 1858, third. Next we have the speech on *True Americanism*, delivered at Faneuil Hall, Boston, April eighteenth, 1859, and lastly the *Douglas and Popular Sovereignty* speech, which he gave at Springfield, Massachusetts, January fourth, 1860. Accessory to these was his speech on state rights in Milwaukee, March twenty-third, 1859.

The first of the series has been sufficiently described. Such quotations from it as were printed outside of Wisconsin quickly impressed the general public with the thought that here was a new champion of liberty who deserved a place alongside of the best known anti-slavery orators; and the fact that this new knight of the

platform was a foreigner proved especially intriguing
to Americans, who are not linguists. The impression of
his masterly powers must have been greatly strengthened
by the publication, in Chicago and eastern papers, of
the speech given in Chicago on the evening of September twenty-eighth.[58] In it he presented a philosophical exposition of the dangers involved in a
conflict between political principles and social institutions, followed by a powerful argument for
putting and keeping slavery in its place as a purely
local labor system supported by state laws. The ideas
were in no sense new, as could be inferred from the public interest in the Lincoln-Douglas debates at that very
time. But the treatment of the subject was much
broader than the Republicans had been wont to hear,
and the oratorical powers displayed by the speaker,
judging from the excited enthusiasm of the great audience, must have been overwhelming. It was after this
speech that a group of Chicago citizens urged Schurz
to settle as a lawyer in their city, offering to guarantee
him a respectable income.'[59]

He began with general considerations, a method of
which he was very fond, and laid down the principle
that a clear knowledge of the logic of things and events
is the only safe foundation of political wisdom. This
knowledge is supplied by history, which teaches that
such antagonisms as that between liberty and slavery,
democracy and privilege in a government like ours are
apt to prove fatal. Slavery and democracy will never
mix, as the condition of southern society amply proves.
For, with all their professions of belief in democracy,
liberty, equality, enlightenment, religion, the controlling

[58] The speech is printed, entire, in the *Press Tribune,* Chicago, September 30, 1858.
[59] Letter of October 18, 1858.

group in the South had actually departed so widely from these fundamentals as to illustrate perfectly the spirit and practise of tyrannical governments. As in the Madison speech, so here, he condemned the northern Democrats for their supine acceptance of slavocracy's political commands, whereby they had been forced from one position to another, from the Missouri Compromise to the Dred Scott Decision, and the end was not yet for the drift still continued. Unless the slavery interest were halted it would continue until all genuine liberty was lost, for the Nebraska Act had now revolutionized the position of slavery. The fathers of the constitution intended to confine it within local areas, and leave it at the mercy of state laws. But now it was declared to be a national interest, claiming a right under the constitution to a preferred status. Slavery now could go anywhere where it was not positively forbidden to go. Free labor could go nowhere in the national domain and be safe against molestation by the favored institution. Schurz, though he had promised to 'indulge in no personal invectives against Buchanan, Douglas, or any other man,' did not quite succeed in treating Douglas as a gentleman; for he spoke of his quibbles between squatter sovereignty and the Dred Scott Decision as one of the 'most contemptible subterfuges by which ever a pettifogger made himself ridiculous.' The remedy for the fatal drift toward slavocratic tyranny over all American life was suggested by the southerners themselves. They contended that, in order to survive, slavery must be permitted to expand. Why not take them at their word, forbid its expansion, and let it gradually disappear?

The process by which slavery (hedged about as a purely local interest with no foot over the nation's door

plate) would in time lose its hypnotic influence upon
southerners themselves and pass away, being abolished
by one state after another, Schurz discussed in considerable detail.   As at other times, even up to the close of
the year 1860, he scoffed at the idea that the South would
dissolve the Union rather than abandon their position on
slavery—which was good tactics if not sound deduction.

This speech seems to have been reported, rather than
printed from copy, which may explain its want of high
finish as compared with the Madison speech of a year
earlier.   It also gives such an impression of complexity,
both in argument and in literary structure, as makes a
strong contrast to the crystal clear speeches Lincoln
was delivering in the debates with Douglas.   However,
Schurz's method of implanting in the minds of his hearers general principles, and making these the basis of his
argument, was tremendously effective as were his surprise illustrations, his flashes of satiric humor, and the
moral force with which he drove home his arguments.
While there was in it less subtlety of thought and a less
insinuating quality of phrase, the Chicago speech is not
unworthy of a place beside those of Lincoln, to whose
leadership Schurz therein referred, as he did to the
forthcoming national campaign of 1860.

The victory already referred to, won by the Republicans of Milwaukee, in November, 1858, was on the
policy of refusing to permit corrupt Democrats to obtain seats in the legislature in order further to debauch
public life through railway and other jobs with which
the people had recently been outraged.   The managers
of the La Crosse Railway had made presents of blocks
of their stock—it was said—to all but one of the members of the legislature, and had not overlooked the governor and other administrative officers. Even one of the

supreme court judges was accused of accepting a gift
of stock.   This had created a great scandal.   In such a
canvass Schurz was in his element.   He called upon Germans of both parties to stand up for public honesty, and
with their aid gained the first success which had come to
the Republicans in that 'citadel of the Democracy', as he
was in the habit of calling Wisconsin's metropolis.   In-
cidentally, it insured the election to Congress of J. F.
(Bowie-knife) Potter,[60] who was one of Schurz's
warmest friends.   So great an event of course had to be
celebrated, and on the evening of November eighteenth,
at the jubilation meeting, Schurz delivered his short
speech on *Political Morals*.[61]

He interpreted the victory as a triumph of moral independence over moral servitude, of manhood over ser-
vile partisanship. He had emphasized the same idea in
the two speeches previously discussed, but now he went
farther and announced the principle that it is the duty
of the citizen to discipline parties by making his support contingent upon their moral rectitude. 'I sincerely
hope,' he said, 'that my countrymen who have emanci-
pated themselves from party despotism will never again
consent to be made use of in corrupt combinations and
political tricks, that they will never again be parties to
dirty political trades and corrupt bargains *on whatever
side they may be attempted*. And I do not hesitate to
prophesy that if the Republican party should be unfortunate enough to entangle itself in the same network
of corruption with which the democracy is choking itself to death, the people will strike it down with the
same crushing verdict under which Hunkerism is sink-
ing now.   And in that case, I confess, my heart would

---

[60] The man who, being challenged to a duel by Roger Pryor of Virginia, chose bowie knives as the weapons and was not obliged to fight.
[61] Carl Schurz, *Twelve Speeches*, Lippincott, 1865.

behold with grief and sorrow its degradation, but would
have no tears for its defeat.' Portions of the speech
were a bit theoretical but it was enlivened by practical
suggestions which rescued it from the suspicion of high-
browism. For example, he supplied a very simple rule
for the treatment of corrupt men within the party, which
was to kick them out and denounce them as traitors; to
inflict the political death penalty 'without regard to person or station, without benefit of clergy.'

The speech, which created some stir at the time, and
doubtless had considerable influence toward inducing
the Wisconsin German press to advocate Schurz's election to the governorship, gives an accurate reflection of
some of his fundamental principles as a politician. Had
the Republicans in 1884 been familiar with it they could
not have indulged such extreme indignation over his
insistence on the defeat of Blaine, the ground for which
was precisely stated in the quotations given above.

The year 1859, which brought Schurz such a humiliating disappointment as a Wisconsin politician, recom-
pensed him through a notable series of contacts with
individuals and communities in the East. Know-
nothingism had raised its head once more, and in the
legislature of Massachusetts had proved strong enough
to pass an anti-foreign suffrage amendment for submission to the voters at the spring election. The act
provided that, before gaining the right to vote in Massachusetts, foreign born persons must not only have
become citizens of the United States, which required
five years residence in the country, but in addition must
have lived in the state two years after becoming citizens. Wise Republican leaders deplored that action
because to again frighten the foreigners of the country
with the bogey of Know-nothingism would mean the

certain defeat of the party in 1860. Some of the young
men of Boston, headed by Edward L. Pierce, a friend
of Charles Sumner, considering ways of overcoming the
anti-foreign influences, decided to invite Carl Schurz
to Boston for an address.

Just at this time Schurz was especially interesting
to eastern radical anti-slavery men on account of his
brilliant exposition of the state rights idea. His speech
on that subject, delivered two weeks earlier in Milwaukee, had been widely read in the East before he reached
there. He accepted the Boston invitation with alacrity,
was present at the Jefferson banquet April twelfth
where he met a number of distinguished public men and
made a brief address. During the week which followed
he was dined and wined and lionized by politicians,
scholars, and literary men to an extent that was wearing
even to him, and on the evening of April eighteenth, before a great assembly in Faneuil Hall, he delivered his
glowing speech on *True Americanism,* probably the
most eloquent and impassioned of all his early utterances. We may have our own opinion of the method
he employed in selecting and diverting from the grand
stream of general history the principles of the American
system, but we must applaud the noble language of his
exordium, the argument for toleration of all races and
creeds, and the proof, throughout the address, of an ex-
quisite sensitiveness to American ideals.

The opening paragraph gives the key to the argument. He said: 'A few days ago I stood on the cupola
of your statehouse, and overlooked [*sic*] for the first
time this venerable city and the country surrounding it.
Then the streets, and hills, and waters around me began
to teem with the life of historical recollections, recollections dear to all mankind, and a feeling of pride arose

in my heart, and I said to myself, I, too, am an American citizen. There was Bunker Hill; there Charlestown, Lexington and Dorchester Heights not far off; there the harbor into which the British tea was sunk; there the place where the old liberty-tree stood; there John Hancock's house; there Benjamin Franklin's birth-place;—and now I stand in this grand old hall which so often resounded with the noblest appeals that ever thrilled American hearts, and where I am almost afraid to hear the echo of my own feeble voice;—oh, sir, no man that loves liberty, wherever he may have first seen the light of day, can fail on this sacred spot to pay his tribute to Americanism. And here, with all these glorious memories crowding upon my heart, I will offer mine.'

The main argument for a generous treatment of foreigners was compressed in a paragraph which begins with a somewhat remarkable concession. Schurz admitted that there were difficulties to be encountered by any society whose basic principle is equality of rights, and he did not deny the social and political deficiencies of many newly arrived immigrants as contrasted with the native born citizens. More surprising still is his obvious allusion to Catholicism as a religion whose principles may not, in all respects, harmonize with the doctrines of true democracy. Know-nothings themselves could have presented no better summary of the social problem foreign voters introduce. He describes them all —the conglomeration of heterogeneous elements, the war of clashing interests and unruly aspirations, the granting of governing power to the ignorant and inexperienced. The counter argument seems weak when stated in language other than his own. The substance of it is that the fathers of the republic, in inviting the

weary and burdened of every nation to the enjoyment
of all the rights of the American born, had exercised
true faith in democracy. He closed with the not
unfamiliar proclamation that 'true democracy bears
[with] in itself the remedy for all the difficulties that
may grow out of it.'

Schurz's Faneuil Hall speech created a genuine sen-
sation in the East. It was widely copied by the newspapers, it affected the campaign against anti-foreign-
ism (though Massachusetts adopted the amendment),
it opened the way for Schurz as a lecturer in Massachusetts, New Hampshire, New York. In a word, it made
him a marked man in Yankeedom. To the reputation
thus acquired, he added again through his searching
analysis of the popular sovereignty doctrine of Douglas
in a speech at Springfield, Massachusetts, January
fourth, 1860. That address contains but little that is new
to the student of Schurz, but his restatement and ampli-
fication of arguments already presented in 1857 and
1858, when printed at large in eastern journals, made a
strong impression on the public mind.

No doubt Schurz's popularity with the more determined anti-slavery people of the North, the group which
was most effective in pushing the cause along, was en-
hanced by his support of the Wisconsin program of nul-
lifying the Fugitive Slave law, and bringing the state
supreme court into direct conflict with the supreme
court of the United States. This came about through
the Glover rescue. Glover was a negro who, in the winter of 1853-54, was employed in a sawmill near Racine.
On the tenth of March he was attacked in his cabin by
B. W. Garland of St. Louis who claimed to be his
owner and who proposed to carry him away into slavery.
Garland and his aides took their victim, bound, to Mil-

waukee, where they threw him into jail and where the severe wounds inflicted upon him in the process of capture were dressed by a physician. During the day a great crowd of anti-slavery men, led by Sherman M. Booth, editor of the anti-slavery *Free Democrat,* gathered at the court house, with battering ram broke down the door of the jail, took Glover and by underground railroad hurried him to Canada. The incident created a furious anti-slavery excitement throughout the state and mass meetings everywhere declared the Fugitive Slave law unconstitutional. Booth was arrested under that law for aiding and abetting the escape of the fugitive but the state supreme court released him on a writ of *habeas corpus.* The reasoning of the court was based on the theory that the Fugitive Slave law was unconstitutional, null and void, though the point was not argued in detail. The United States district court, however, took a different view, reindicted Booth, and sentenced him to pay a heavy fine and spend a brief term in prison. Again the state supreme court of Wisconsin granted a writ of *habeas corpus* and in its decision this time formally declared the Fugitive Slave law unconstitutional and void. The case finally reached the supreme court of the United States which, of course, under the leadership of Justice Taney of Dred Scott fame, promptly reversed the decision of the state court and ordered Booth returned to federal prison. Now the supreme court of the state finally gave way, but by no means gracefully, and Carl Schurz was a vigorous contender for the right of a state to nullify a national law judged by its courts to be unconstitutional. He later deplored his mistake in this matter, as he had occasion to deplore others of his political errors. But he was lucky even in his lapses from sound policy. Everything he did seemed to be water on his wheel.

CHAPTER XIII

THAT TREMENDOUS DUTCHMAN

THE year of years for which Schurz had been impatiently waiting, was now at hand; the time when he was determined to do the impossible as a propagandist in behalf of his sacred cause and allow nothing to stand in the way of the full utilization of its opportunities. In his private affairs that coveted independence was no nearer than it had been in 1856. He was still burdened with debts which, added to the continuing and increasing needs of his family, kept him pretty industriously at work earning money in the lecture field, his one available source of income. Though talking was his forte, he by no means enjoyed repeating the same speech over and over, particularly since it usually had only an incidental relation to the burning issues of the day.

As the year 1860 opened it found him in the East, working off his schedule as patiently as he could. His invasion of New England as a crusader for foreigners' rights in the spring of 1859 had the result expected, giving Schurz a genuine vogue among the lyceum associations of that region. In January he lectured in Boston, Roxbury, Concord, and Springfield, Massachusetts; in Nashua, New Hampshire; and probably at Hartford and New Haven, Albany, and New York City. He made Boston his headquarters for several weeks and, while there, completed a new lecture on the theme: *America in Public Opinion Abroad,* although he was still delivering the old lecture on France because committees continued to call for it.

The most exciting event of his eastern experience was the great speech on *Douglas and Popular Sovereignty,* given at Springfield, Massachusetts, January fourth. It was the address which Lincoln said made him jealous, though inasmuch as the Illinois statesman was to deliver his Cooper Union speech at New York the next month, Schurz had no doubt fulfilled for him the part of one crying in the wilderness. The Springfield speech was not only printed in the newspapers, but in pamphlet editions both English and German which were distributed widely, usually by state Republican committees anxious to be beforehand in beginning the presidential campaign.

Schurz now postponed a series of lecture engagements in Indiana in order to visit Wisconsin. At Madison in February he found 'uncounted copies' of the Douglas speech lying about, which made him an object of much curiosity on the part of the new members of the legislature. It doubtless aided in his political organizing with reference to the state convention, and the national convention to follow.

As already indicated, Schurz had begun his preparations for the Lincoln campaign between the close of the unsuccessful but brilliant effort of 1856 and the opening guns of the decisive battle staged four years later. Oddly enough, the selection of Lincoln as standard bearer was not one of the arrows with which he filled his quiver. He came to Lincoln only after the convention had made good his nomination, but then he accepted him with all heartiness. In the *Reminiscences* Schurz dilates on his pleasant visit in the spring of 1860 with Salmon P. Chase, mistakenly dating it before the state convention in Wisconsin which had made him the first delegate-at-large. Chase tried at that time to pledge him and the Wisconsin delegation for his own candidacy, but Schurz frankly avowed a political preference for Seward. This being so, one comes with a little shock of surprise upon the evidence that, in the summer of 1859, he was not only personally favorable to Chase's nomination but had actually begun to organize for the purpose of insuring the selection of Chase delegates from the state in 1860.[62]

The plan, as it can be inferred from Schurz's correspondent, was to decide on the man early, by conference with a few trusted friends of the anti-slavery cause; then to pledge the German and Norwegian districts to choose for the state Republican convention delegates who would insist on the delegation to the national convention supporting that candidate. Since the state convention would be keenly anxious to guarantee the votes of these elements, it would be strongly disposed to accept their favorite. Before the time for electing the local delegates arrived, however, Schurz had veered away from Chase and with the bulk of the Republican leaders, had fixed upon Seward as first choice. But the tactics suggested the previous year, in the interest of Chase's candidacy, were employed with telling effect for Seward, with the result that the German communities declared for him with practical unanimity.

Schurz had other objects, also, to bring before German voters at the primaries and this he seems to have done largely through the German Republican press. He had formulated the most important planks for a Republican platform designed to attract foreign born voters. It would, as a matter of course, contain pronouncements on the subject of popular sovereignty and freedom in

[62] Letter of William Henry Brisbane, April 4, 1859. (Cong. Lib.; Photostat Lib. St. Hist. Soc. of Wis.)

the territories; perhaps also on a protective tariff as a support to free labor. But he was concerned about a plank pledging the party to enact a free homestead law, and particularly one which would guarantee foreign born citizens against political discrimination such as the Massachusetts constitutional amendment embodied. Such resolutions, accordingly, were adopted by primaries where German voters constituted a dominant or powerful element, and their delegates were pledged to support them in the convention. Also, they were pledged to demand the election of Schurz as delegate-at-large to Chicago.

The state convention met on the twenty-ninth of February. In the list of the two hundred and five delegates, from fifty-four counties, can be found not more than a dozen names of men who were probably Germans by birth. But each one of several important counties—Dodge, Fond du Lac, Manitowoc, Ozaukee, Sauk, and possibly Grant—sent one such delegate, while Jefferson sent two, Schurz and Lindeman. This German block, led as it was by Schurz, enjoying the active alliance of all delegates from the counties harboring large bodies of German voters, and the good will of the whole convention, which was determined to leave no powerful element in the state dissatisfied with its action (particularly not the Germans who were still sensitive over the nominating campaign of the previous fall,) wielded a power altogether disproportionate to its numerical strength.

The result was quickly apparent. When the question of delegates was up, it was resolved that the convention choose one delegate-at-large for the whole state and thereupon unanimously elected Carl Schurz to be that delegate. Schurz was also a leading member of the resolutions committee, which reported precisely the kind of resolutions in which he had been interested, the one on no discrimination against foreigners having been introduced by a Sauk County German delegate, doubtless after consultation with him. As the state's delegate-at-large, Schurz was made chairman of the Wisconsin delegation to Chicago, and there, being once more a member of the resolutions committee, he supported the declaration protesting discrimination against foreign born citizens, which was adopted, and also the free homestead resolution, likewise adopted. On the first of these he was heard in the convention as well as in committee. The platform as a whole being to his mind, and the candidate perfectly satisfactory, he could go forward with spirit and confidence.

From the close of the state convention March first, until after the election November sixth, Schurz was almost constantly busied with work for the national cause. Although up to the middle of May he was nominally engaged in filling his lecture engagements, yet every minute of spare time was employed in surveying conditions and laying plans for the work to be done after the Chicago convention. He spent most of the month of March in Indiana, one of the doubtful states, made many valuable acquaintances, saw to the distribution of his Douglas speech, compiled statistics, and was finally prepared to say that one way only was open to the Republicans for carrying the state, namely, by converting ten thousand Germans who had previously voted Democratic.

Schurz also aided in Chicago to win the brilliant Republican victory in the municipal election in April and, while not fully successful in Milwaukee, had given freely of his time and effort there, with at least encouraging

results. Thus were both Illinois and Wisconsin girded
to resist the prospective Douglas onslaught. After the
national convention he went to Springfield as a member of the committee to notify Lincoln, whom he then
met for the second time, having made his acquaintance
on the train in September, 1858, in the manner so pleas-
antly described in *Reminiscences.*

On the thirtieth of May, at the Milwaukee ratification meeting, Schurz delivered one of the noblest short
speeches published during that historic summer. In it
he pointed out how the convention refused to compromise Republican principles, preserving in their purity
the ideas which underlay the party's foundation. He
stressed the point that, through its platform, Republicanism had become more than an anti-slavery party. It
was now affirmatively pledged to the interests of the
larger freedom, for slavery would be confined to the
limits within which it then existed under the laws of
sovereign states, while free labor would be planted in
the territories by the Homestead Act, and promoted all
over the country by the tariff law for encouraging home
industry. He paid a high tribute to Seward whose long
and conspicuous service to the anti-slavery cause compelled Schurz's personal loyalty. Then he spoke of
Lincoln, using language which must have introduced
him most favorably to the millions, especially in the
East, who had been taught to look upon the Illinois
lawyer as a second or third rate man, like Polk or
Pierce, who had been nominated for expediency's sake.
Schurz called such views infinitely silly. 'Let them,' he
said, 'ask Douglas, from whose hands he [Lincoln]
wrested the popular majority in Illinois; let them ask
those who once felt the magic touch of his lucid mind
and honest heart; let his detractors ask their own secret

misgivings, and in their own fears they will read the cause of the joy and assurance of his friends. They whistle in order to keep up their courage, but methinks it is a doleful sound.'

Before the contest actually began the Democracy found itself fatally crippled by the secession of southern delegates from the convention at Charleston. The Democratic party was thereby split into two sectional factions, hating one another, which imparted to the Republican canvass the spirit of a triumphal march. This made a situation in which Schurz was at his best, for it was always easy for him to work in the confidence of victory. As a member of the national committee he was given charge of the 'foreign department 'and before the nomination was a week old he had developed a complete program for precipitating foreign language speakers upon all communities requiring that type of proselyting. He expected to go to all the principal places and do the heavy work himself. He had stood by Governor Seward for the nomination, he wrote Lincoln, but added that if he were able, he would do the work of a hundred men for Abraham Lincoln's election.

The Republican party being now definitely pledged to maintain the rights of foreigners, thus repudiating such illiberal enactments as the Massachusetts amendment, Schurz had high hopes of the Germans who had been so firmly attached to the Democratic party until, on the issue of free soil in 1856, this unanimity had been seriously disturbed. The Germans, by 1860, aggregated about one and a half millions and were numerous enough in several of the northern states to constitute the political balance of power. In addition to their critical aid in carrying Wisconsin and other northern states for Fremont, they had to their credit signifi-

cant local reforms which raised Republican hopes for
them in 1860. Indiana, though it had gone for Buchanan by a considerable majority, might through them
be carried for Lincoln. Pennsylvania, with its great
mass of Old Pennsylvania Germans, added to the newer
immigrations, might also be won for Republicanism
despite the enormous majority for Buchanan four years
earlier. The Germans would guarantee the majority
in Ohio and might enable Lincoln to carry both New
York and Illinois.

Schurz was animated by the psychology of conquest.
He felt strong enough to agitate, single handed, for the
conversion of the Germans in a dozen northern states
and to make them, if possible, the determining factor in
the election. But for all that he had no intention of
hiding his light under a foreign language bushel as he
had done in the Wisconsin campaign of 1856. He intended, while giving most of his time to his own countrymen, to make some English speeches subsidiary to German meetings, and was resolved also to deliver several
English speeches under circumstances so conspicuous as
to attract the attention of the entire nation. Naturally,
his choicest addresses were printed in both languages
and widely distributed in pamphlet form by the national
and state committees. His ratification speech had been
spread over the whole country as early as July, producing the most wholesome effects everywhere.

At the beginning of July Schurz attended meetings
of the national committee in New York, and also arranged for his canvass in Pennsylvania. On the return
trip west he spoke at Cleveland, and then as his first
major enterprise, toured the state of Illinois, speaking
at places having large numbers of Germans, who came
over in troops to the Republican side. At Springfield

on July twenty-fourth he addressed, in both languages, a great gathering in the state capitol, with Lincoln seated directly in front of him. The presidential candidate had insisted on marching down with Schurz at the head of the wide awakes' procession, because he wanted to hear 'that tremendous speaker.' When the meeting was over he crushed Schurz's hand and said delightedly: 'You are an awful fellow! I understand your power now.' Lincoln's instinctive tact prevented him from using the expression which almost everyone applied to Schurz during this campaign, but had he known that the orator rather gloried in the title 'that tremendous Dutchman' he would not have hesitated to bestow it.[63]

At the Peoria meeting the newspapers reported: 'A complete impetuosity of enthusiasm prevailed among our German friends,' while from Pekin came the news that at least one hundred Germans who were formerly Democrats had been converted by Schurz's speech at that place. And so the merry work went on, the orator gaining power day by day.

His own letters to Mrs. Schurz, frequent, frank, and almost naïvely enthusiastic, constitute both a kind of itinerary for his speaking tours during this campaign and a mirror in which we can view his performance as a stump orator. When he went to Quincy, Illinois, he was met twenty-two miles from the city by an official deputation, and on reaching the station was greeted by the governor in the presence of a vast crowd. There was music, the noise of cannon, etc. He was obliged to respond briefly to an address of welcome. Requests for speeches additional to those regularly scheduled

---

[63] Schurz wrote from Mankato, Minnesota, September 30, 1859, saying: 'The people come from a circuit of 12 to 15 miles, with banners and drums, in order to hear "that tremendous Dutchman."' So the use of the phrase anti-dated the campaign of 1860.

were pouring in, but Schurz wisely fought them off, gauging accurately the amount of work he could do with maximum effectiveness. He also refused to make brief remarks in English after concluding his German addresses, as he was almost daily urged to do, and—after suffering for a few nights—plainly informed the committees that he must not be gotten out of bed to respond to serenades. Appreciating with utmost nicety the orator's duty of conserving his physical powers, and especially his voice, he consistently refused to speak in the open air. Apparently he became hoarse only once during the entire canvass, that being at Easton, Pennsylvania, when addressing an audience of six thousand Pennsylvania Dutch.

The work was severe enough at best. Up to a certain point the crowds which hung about his room at hotels, bombarding him with questions, the torchlight processions, serenades, band music, drums and trumpets were a real delight to Schurz who never outgrew his youthful love of pageantry, but they made large drafts upon his nervous energy. The heat was oppressive, the fare at the hotels often bad, night rides on the railroads sometimes very trying. Still he remained 'cheerful as a fish in water,' and did not feel that he was undertaking too much. At Belleville, Hecker's town, after speaking to a big meeting from the same platform with the old Baden revolutionist, Schurz wrote: 'If it goes everywhere like in Egypt where in 1856 there were hardly any Republican votes, then Lincoln's election is unavoidable. . . . Oh, dear! The cannon are thundering again, the drums rattle, the marshals are galloping past my window. The thirty-four maidens in white are also on hand. Here comes the deputation to fetch me. Adieu.'

He went next to St. Louis where he spoke to the Germans on the evening of July thirty-first, and on the next night gave in English his great speech entitled *The Doom of Slavery,* which was circulated to the extent of hundreds of thousands. It being his purpose in that effort to make a direct appeal to slaveholders one can the better understand the conciliatory tone in which he discussed the great issue. The speaker began by acknowledging the part inertia plays in human affairs and admitted that, having once adopted the institution of slavery, slaveholders were compelled by necessity to protect it. In doing so they would inevitably repress any expression antagonistic to the peculiar institution. But he warned them in language with which we are already familiar, that a system which compels such tactics makes of its votaries the slaves of slavery. He then traced the descending path towards tyranny which such communities are obliged to follow, and showed how natural was the clamor for laws to coerce northern men, by police regulations, to refrain from discussing the vexed question, as Douglas had proposed in the Senate. Equally inescapable was the demand for the acquisition of new slave territory; for the annexation of Cuba, the northern states of Mexico, and in fact any outside regions favorable to the southern system. Slavery must have more power, which is to be gained only by its physical extension.

To this point Schurz had stated the southerners' case. In the second part of the address he set forth the Republican point of view, which it is not necessary to expatiate upon. Slavery, he summarized, required for its security and permanence a type of policy utterly at variance with the principles upon which free labor rests. That, he affirmed, was the essence of the 'irrepressible conflict.' 'Mr. Douglas,' said Schurz, 'boasted that he could repress it with police measures; he might as well try to fetter the winds with a rope; the South means to repress it with decisions of the Supreme Court; they might as well, like Xerxes, try to subdue the waves of the ocean by throwing chains into the water.'

The argument of this address was similar to that of the Chicago, Madison, and Springfield speeches, but it was delicately modulated to the requirements of a slave-holding community and presented in a tone not unappreciative of the problem such a community had to meet. It is an early commentary on the breadth of Schurz's social sympathies. Nevertheless, he powerfully affirmed the necessity of halting the tendencies toward the complete subjugation of free labor with a program which would have exactly the opposite trend, though leaving slavery, where it then existed, to the operation of local laws. The spirit of the age, which was against slavery, would make itself respected; our social institutions must be harmonized with it. The concluding section was devoted to the question of disunion, and in this he gave the South some things to think about, should it be tempted to try that remedy.

Much time in the month of August was devoted to the Germans of Indiana who received him with peculiar friendliness, as the letters and the newspaper reports show. For example, at La Fayette he was handed a bouquet bearing a card inscribed: 'To the patriot Carl Schurz from the German Democrats of La Fayette.' There were welcoming speeches, bouquets from the ladies, a great meeting, a complimentary supper, serenades, etc. He rightly judged that a great many converts were made at that place. Such free time as he had, and the schedule was so arranged as to allow for short breathing spells, was used in preparing his Douglas speech for New York in September. On this effort,

which he seems to have had in mind as the high point
of the season's work, Schurz labored with gusto while
traveling about Indiana, Michigan, and on the steamer
going from Detroit to Cleveland. A special incentive
for making that speech his best was the fact that
Douglas was to speak in New York on the preceding
evening, which would make Schurz in a manner the
official Republican trailer of the *Little Giant*.

The Douglas speech, otherwise known as *The Indictment,* was scheduled for Cooper Union the evening
of September thirteenth. Schurz's feeling about its importance is suggested in the confession that he was
nervous during the whole day and so absorbed in the
thought of the occasion as to be quite unable to write.
The feeling instantly left him on entering the great hall,
which was so packed that no one was able to move.
James O. Putnam was speaking as Schurz stepped upon the stage. The audience greeted him with resounding
applause. 'Then,' he writes, 'was Richard himself again,
and I once more felt the old self-confidence. . . . At
last my part on the program was reached. I was received with endless cheering and during my speech was
interrupted so frequently with applause that the hand-
clapping consumed nearly as much time as the speaking. I have never spoken as brilliantly as last night.
The tremendous audience seemed as if electrified and as
I closed there was a veritable charge toward the platform. It was hard to get done with handshaking. I believe it was the greatest, most scintillating success I
have had yet. I spoke more than two hours and they
told me they had never seen a speaker hold so great an
audience for so long a time.'

The above statement, written next day in a letter to
his wife sounds boastful but is merely frank. Schurz is

telling the sober fact in language, which, though strong, is in no way out of harmony with the reality he is attempting to portray. *The Indictment* was an all but matchless campaign speech, one of the most devastating reviews and criticisms of a conspicuous career that American political history had thus far brought forth. The speeches published during the 1860 canvass, speeches by Seward, Sumner, Wade, Evarts, Grow, Butler, Fernando Wood, Hammond, and Douglas himself contain nothing which even approaches this in the completeness of knowledge displayed, the swordsman-like sureness in attack, the brilliant oratory of triumph, and the excoriating sarcasm with which Douglas's pretensions to superior statesmanship are lampooned.

The speech as a whole was divided into three parts and there was in it a cumulative effectiveness which, toward the end, sent his sympathetic audience into ecstasies. Schurz professed reluctance to attack an individual, but since Douglas's 'supreme statesmanship' and his 'championship of freedom' were being universally urged by the Democratic orators and press as reasons for electing him, the man himself had become the issue and must submit to being treated as such. The order of treatment was, first, Douglas the champion of freedom; second, Douglas the greatest American statesman; third, Douglas the presidential candidate. The reasoning on the first topic has already become familiar through the earlier speeches. But nowhere else did Schurz follow Douglas's sinuous trail so relentlessly, or demonstrate so completely the hollowness of his claims —so far, at least, as the overt record at that time went. He denied to Douglas the credit for saving Kansas from the Lecompton conspirators because it had already become manifest when he began his fight that the forces

of freedom could not be overthrown. The Nebraska
bill had set the edifice of territorial liberty on fire and
Republican fire companies were pumping away with
full force, 'when up rushes the very incendiary, Douglas, with a little teaspoonful of anti-Lecompton water,
throws it into the flames, and then swells himself up and
claims to have extinguished the conflagration. . . If he
was honest, [says Schurz] you will be obliged to confess, it is exceedingly difficult to prove it on him.'

Popular sovereignty, which was the theme of his
January address at Springfield, Massachusetts, he here
treated as an incident, with incisive brevity. At first it
was pretended that the popular sovereignty principle
gave complete power to the people to prevent the
establishment of slavery in a territory. Douglas's Free-
port Doctrine meant that the people, while not empowered to prevent the establishment of slavery in a
territory 'may annoy and embarrass the slaveholder in
the enjoyment of his slave property, so as to *tease*
slavery out of the territory if they can.' Popular rights
were growing thinner and thinner, approximating
Lincoln's 'Homeopathic soup, made by boiling the
shadow of a pigeon that had starved to death.' But
Douglas recently had thinned it still more when he announced that territorial legislatures were just as solemnly obligated to protect slaves as they were to protect
'horses, cattle, dry goods, and liquors.'

At last the degeneracy is complete. Where once the
doctrine of popular sovereignty was represented as a
perfect shield to liberty, it has now become the cloak
of despotism. All that is left to the people of a territory
now is to pass laws *favorable* to slavery.

The discussion of Douglas as a supreme statesman
took the form of an examination of his various propos-

als to empower the president to declare war without the sanction of Congress, and of the recent speech, January twenty-third, 1860, in favor of his plan for a national police. Both cases, Schurz contended, illustrate the statesmanship of tyranny, not of democracy; they reveal Douglas's inability to think from principles or to gauge the force of political tendencies. He dwelt with special vehemence on the second point. The purpose was to break up the Republican party by arming the federal courts with power to imprison its leaders for declaring slavery wrong. It was a proposal to pass a preventive law, a law more drastic than the Federalist Sedition Act, whose passage had been the bugle call for the establishment of the Democratic party. 'And,' cried Schurz, 'there are those who dare to call the man who proposed to inaugurate such a system of policy a great statesman.'

The discussion of Douglas as presidential candidate caps the climax. Schurz gave it as his belief that, for once, Douglas had been honest when, on finding the Democratic forces would be hopelessly split over his nomination, he asked his friends to withdraw his name. But he says: 'Now the moment had arrived when it became manifest that there was justice in history. Douglas's position was disgusting but his punishment was sublime. Then his friends for the first time refused to obey his commands. Those whom he had used so often and so long for his own advancement, saw now there was a last chance of using him for theirs. They said to him: "We have performed our part of the contract; now you have to perform yours. We have nominated you for the presidency; now you have to permit us to be elected congressmen, sheriffs, county clerks or constables, on the strength of your name. There is no backing out. Dost thou think because thou hast suddenly become virtuous there shall be no more cakes and ale? Yes, by St. Ann! and ginger hot in the mouth, too!" And so the saddle of the rump nomination is put upon his back, and the whole ghastly pack of office hunters jump upon it. The spurs are put to the flanks, the whip applied to the panting, bleeding jade, and so the spectral ride goes, east and west, night and day—and may the steed go to perdition, if only the riders reach their goal.'

This Cooper Union speech made no break in Schurz's program. Elated beyond measure by its success he moved forward, making conversions literally by the thousand in Pennsylvania, Ohio, and Indiana, states whose local elections came early and heralded the Lincoln triumph in November. His reception at Milwaukee befitted one who could say of the campaign as a whole: 'It seems as if victory could not fail us and, by Jove, I have done my share towards it.' It was known that Lincoln, watching the progress of events from the calm of his Springfield home, had singled out Schurz for special mention as one of the greatest orators of America.[64] He was hailed, on his return to Wisconsin, as the peerless hero of the hustings.

Assurance of a favorable outcome, so far from inducing him to lower the intensity of his efforts, rather spurred him to still greater ones, in order not be chargeable with neglect if the campaign should ultimately fail. His most strenuous labor was performed in his own state during the last two weeks of the campaign. In that interval, he made numerous speeches in the city and county of Milwaukee and covered, by team, a large share of the

[64] New York *Tribune* (daily), September 29, 1860. A correspondent of the Missouri *Democrat* had been with Lincoln on September 21, just one week after the Douglas speech of Schurz had appeared in print in the *Tribune*. The correspondent wrote: 'In speaking of the leading speakers of the nation Mr. L [incoln] regards Carl Schurz as one of the foremost.'

great German community near Lake Michigan. The vote when it came showed the effect of his propaganda, for the Fremont majority of thirteen thousand in the state had been changed to a Lincoln majority of twenty-one thousand over Douglas, and it can be shown that one-half of the increase was supplied by four of the strongly German counties. The results in Indiana, Ohio, St. Louis, and especially Pennsylvania spoke similarly in praise of his almost superhuman effort to swing the German vote for Lincoln. 'I have been told,' he wrote to a friend a few years later, 'that I made Lincoln president. That is of course not true; but that people say so indicates that I contributed something toward raising the breeze which carried Lincoln into the presidential chair and thereby shook slavery to its foundations. I devoted my entire strength to it and became exceedingly weary with the Herculean labor.'[65]

One thing was left to do, before Schurz dismissed the campaign from his mind and started out once more, with a portfolio of lectures, to tour the East. He was never slow to assert the representative character of his leadership. In February he had warned the state convention that, if the Republicans wanted the Germans who were under his influence, certain policies would have to be followed. Now, after Lincoln's election, he not improperly looked upon himself as representing, better than any other one man, the Germans of the entire North. Therefore, when the southern states threatened to secede in consequence of the election of an anti-slavery president, Schurz at the Milwaukee jubilation meeting on November eighteenth in directing his remarks to the South really spoke to the Germans of the nation. The victory, he maintained, though marking one of the great

[65] Letter to Petrasch, September 24, 1863.

turning points in human history, boded no attack upon the slave states, no violation of the fundamental law. It simply meant that the constitutional right to prevent the farther spread of slavery would be upheld; that freedom must henceforth be national, slavery sectional. He warned the South against the fatuous hope that by threatening secession they could prevent either Lincoln's inauguration or the faithful performance of Republican pledges. By this pronouncement Schurz was preparing the German supporters of Lincoln for the policy the Republican president was bound to proclaim, and was teaching them the logic on which the Union must be sustained, should it be threatened by the action of the discontented southern slave states.

CHAPTER XIV

THE CRISIS

THE election of 1860, as if to convict Schurz of being a bad prophet, incited the southern states to rush madly over the precipice of disunion, South Carolina appropriately taking the first plunge. Then came the inevitable effort at conciliation and compromise with— as Schurz felt and Lincoln feared—a fair chance that the gains of the election would be bartered away, leaving the main problem to be solved at a later and perhaps less auspicious time. Schurz was extremely anxious that no step of an irrevocable nature should be taken before Lincoln's inauguration; after that, the cause would be safe.

He was so worried about his own finances in 1860 that, aside from staying at the farm several days to obtain a prolonged sleep and get his lectures in order, he was able to take no vacation whatever after the nerve shattering labors of the campaign. But he capitalized his great reputation as a stump orator in making a lecture schedule which was much more comprehensive than those of previous years. It took him first to Auburn, New York, where he delivered a new lecture on *American Civilization;* then to Tremont Temple, Boston for another new lecture, completed five minutes before time to go on the platform. It was on *Freedom of Speech,* a theme he selected because a band of Bell-Everetts, the self-styled 'Union and Constitutionalists,' had recently broken up an abolitionists' meeting in that city. Schurz could not let pass so good an approach to the public. Success was insured by the timeliness of the lecture, which was printed in the Boston papers and aroused general interest through the East.

Engagements now came so thick and fast that they robbed him of the Christmas holiday with his wife and children, who were then visiting in Philadelphia. He made Boston his headquarters until the end of December, and gave twenty lectures in various New England towns during that month, being obliged to decline a number of proffered engagements for which no free evenings could be found. There followed a series of seven or eight, perhaps more, in the state of New York. Then he entered Ohio, where he completed the month of January. One week of February he spent in Michigan, lecturing at Hillsdale, Detroit, Ann Arbor, and other places. On the ninth he spoke in Springfield, Illinois, and afterwards in other Illinois towns and also at Burlington, Iowa. Obviously, he was in a good way to make the lecturing business relatively profitable for his engagements netted him not less than twenty-five dollars per night.

Schurz prized the opportunity which his Springfield visit would afford for a talk with Lincoln. While traveling about from place to place he had been in constant touch with members of Congress, and the reports received by letter and from the newspapers were beginning to disquiet him greatly. In December things looked favorable enough, for Ben Wade's doughty speech defining the position of the Republican party had been generally applauded by party leaders, to Schurz's infinite relief. No humiliating compromise seemed to threaten at that time. Still, he 'fired his charges' into the Washington situation almost daily, telling his political friends what ought to be done, and how. At one time he wrote out a speech which was to be delivered by a member of the

House. By Christmas eve he had come to the conclusion that a struggle between North and South was inevitable and he semed almost to welcome it as a means of settling the great problem for all time. Apparently, too, the idea of participating in a prominent way affected him for he writes: 'It is a time for men of decision and resource, and I would not be surprised if your husband would be called into the service again.' He did not expect to carry a sword, but to contribute in an administrative capacity. Already he had sketched out a plan of organization which he was sending in advance to Lincoln and which, at the right moment, would be precipitated upon the various northern governors.

One thing, at this Christmas season, gave Schurz real concern. The secessionists were using every effort to draw Virginia and Maryland into their movement. Should the plan succeed, an attempt would surely be made to seize Washington and thereby prevent Lincoln's inauguration. The South he thought was relying upon the fallacy that the North would not fight. That delusion they would give up, together with the designs against Washington, only in case the northern states should arm as quickly as possible and make clear their determination to sustain the government. His distaste for lecturing increased with the excitement about public questions. But money had to be earned and he stuck doggedly to his program, speaking evenings and spending free hours during the day in keeping up a vigorous correspondence with public men at the national capital and elsewhere.

Whether or not he wrote to Lincoln during these anxious weeks we do not know. It would be strange if he failed to do so and almost equally strange if the non-letter writing president-elect had replied. But at the end of January Schurz was reassured by a newspaper report quoting Lincoln as preferring to die rather than surrender a single one of the Republican principles. He would not be guilty of the cowardice of leading a retreat of the conquerors before the conquered. 'Glory to him!' he writes, 'We live in a wonderful time. It is not merely an age of the adventurer and upstart whom cleverness and favoring circumstances have raised up [a charge sometimes launched against himself]; it is likewise the age of conscience-ruled men, who dominate affairs by the force of honesty and shatter all opposing obstacles. . . . Is it not a proper ambition to want to be worthy of such a time?' As usual, when a great decision was about to be made, Schurz found himself striving to prepare his sick and suffering wife for further sacrifices.

Now came disappointing news. Cassius M. Clay, who had asked Schurz to write Lincoln in behalf of his (Clay's) cabinet aspirations, on the ground forsooth, that the Republican administration would require a man of his firmness to save it from the danger of compromise —that very man had made a speech in Washington advocating concessions to the South! 'It won't be long,' Schurz remarks, let us hope with a chuckle, 'till I shall be able to believe in no one but myself.'[66] But worse things yet were in store, for five days later he wrote bemoaning the defection of Seward himself, a stroke which would have broken Schurz's heart had not Lincoln stood firm as a stone wall, and Chase likewise. He speculated on the problem whether Lincoln might not withdraw his invitation to Seward to head the cabinet, which, though a dangerous move, would be justified in view of the latter's rashness in compromising the new administration's policy.

[66] Letter of January 31, 1861.

Schurz hoped, at that juncture, to participate in the
conference which had been called by the state of Virginia, to meet at Washington. He believed it would be
wise for the northern states to send delegates, in order
to show their disposition toward a pacific policy, tell the
southerners some things they sadly needed to hear, and
above all gain time, so that Lincoln's inauguration might
take place before overt hostilities occurred, threatening
the national capital. He accordingly urged Governor
Randall of Wisconsin to recommend to the legislature
the plan of sending delegates and asked that he be named
as one of them. He followed the matter up telegraphic-
ally with zest, but nothing came of it because the conference met and adjourned before affirmative action was
had at Madison. He not unnaturally suspected Randall
of a desire to frustrate his plan. Schurz had no illusions
about the chances of a favorable outcome, for in case an
adjustment were reached on the slavery issue another
and insoluble question would at once take its place,
namely, should the laws be enforced in the seceded states
and the Union preserved at any cost?

The high point in Schurz's winter program was, of
course, the visit to Springfield, February ninth and
tenth. Lincoln had a moment with the lecturer before he
went upon the platform, and promised to visit him at his
hotel next day for the purpose of talking over the whole
situation. He assured Schurz that Seward's views were
made public without his (Lincoln's) knowledge or consent. For himself, there would be no compromise, a
statement he was making freely to everyone. On the
tenth they had their long talk, agreeing marvelously on
all points and becoming profoundly confidential. This
argues an extraordinary degree of harmony in the views
of these two men, for the visiting lecturer had a reputa-

tion for being an exacting if not querulous conferee.
His experience at this time with Lincoln must have been
most happy for he writes: 'Suddenly bringing our conversation to a halt, he [Lincoln] said: "I will give you a
mark of confidence which I have given no other man."
Then he locked the door and read to me the draft of his
inaugural address. After we had discussed it point by
point, he said, "Now you know better than any man in
this country how I stand, and you may be sure that I
shall never betray my principles and my friends." ' He
told Lincoln at this time that he would ask for a few
offices for his friends and was not only encouraged to do
so, but assured that the new president would 'never forget' his own case.[67]

When Schurz arrived in Washington for the inauguration he was bombarded with congratulations on the
report, prematurely published, that he would receive the
Sardinian mission. But, though Lincoln wanted to give
him that post, the political situation was too knotty to
permit him to bestow favors at his own sweet will. Complications arose when influential eastern politicians
urged another candidate for Sardinia. Then, too, something had to be done for Cassius M. Clay and others.
The result was a game of political battledore which at
one point threatened to deflect Schurz to Rio de Janeiro,
an eventuality he was prepared to resist if necessary,
because he considered himself peculiarly fitted for the
European diplomatic field. Finally the skies cleared.
Clay announced himself ready to accept the mission to
Russia. His dispatch to that effect reached the president at eleven on the night of March twenty-eighth.
Next morning Schurz called at the White House early,

[67] Letter of February 10, *Speeches &c.*, i, 179-180.

when the president handed him a paper upon which was
written: 'I nominate Carl Schurz of Wisconsin to be
minister plenipotentiary and envoy extraordinary to
Spain. Abraham Lincoln.' 'Warm handclasps, &c.'
writes Schurz, who begins that letter with the phrase:
'This is the day of victory,' and closes it with the declaration: 'This outcome is better than the Turin [Sar-
dinian] mission would have been. Next to Mexico,
Spain is the most important diplomatic post—and it is
mine.'

He now hurried to New York to make the necessary
financial arrangements for a speedy departure, Seward
insisting on the necessity of his reaching his post promptly. But the attack on Fort Sumter altered his plans.
Schurz was convinced that to a country as poorly organized as the North was, he could perform a very great
service by recruiting a powerful force of cavalry made
up of the thousands of able bodied foreigners who had
received thorough training before coming to America.
His political leadership of the Germans would thus
bear fruit of a very special excellence. The thought
obsessed him to such an extent that he finally decided
to lay his plan before Lincoln, resign the ministry if
necessary, and at least gain a period of leave from it for
the purpose of raising his cavalry division. Lincoln,
always glad to meet Schurz's views and being impressed with the practicality of the idea, secured Seward's
consent to give him three months leave of absence from
his post. He went to New York to begin the work of recruiting but had not advanced it far when the European
situation made his presence in Madrid imperative, and
early in June he sailed on the *Persia* with his family for
Liverpool.

It was distressing to Schurz to leave the country just at that moment—'in a disturbed time to enter upon a quiet life.' But he felt that service could be rendered abroad too. As a matter of fact his chief concern during his short stay in Spain was to convince European diplomats that the anti-slavery professions of the Republican party were honest and would finally result in general emancipation. Therein he was very prone to outrun the administration, which seemed to him excessively slow in coming to the great decision to free the slaves as a war measure. While his public correspondence was always decorous, some of his private letters fairly blaze with angry impatience. Schurz's mind, brilliant, and in some respects philosophical, was affected by a temperamental impulsiveness difficult to subdue. It rejected that long view which led Lincoln to harmonize all the discordant northern interests through a policy requiring time but operating inexorably to the desired end; an end sought by him no less earnestly than by his restless friend near the Spanish court. After the defeat of Bull Run, Schurz felt he could bear the suspense no longer and he then insisted on being permitted either to come back on leave or to resign. The leave was granted and in January, 1862, the minister and his family sailed for home from Hamburg, he having at last, after twelve years banishment, obtained permission to travel in Prussia.

From what Lincoln said to him on his arrival at Washington, he inferred that the president desired his presence in the country because of the political aid he could render in the approaching congressional election. The idea appearing to please him, Lincoln promised to find him a situation corresponding in importance to his diplomatic post. 'That,' wrote Schurz, 'could only be a position in the army, for there are no more civil offices open.'[68] He was obliged to undergo a tedious wait, till the tangled strands of administrative red tape could be unravelled, but finally in May, the commission as brigadier general came and he was attached to Fremont's division in the valley of Virginia.

It is interesting to read Schurz's frank statement, written to his mother, of the reasons for going into the army.[69] By that time he had seen enough to get him over the opinion formerly held that it would be a short war. He believed, nevertheless, that the North had the resources to overthrow the South, and that two principal battles might end the military operations, provided there were no great reverses. But then would begin the more serious problem of reconstructing the nation in a manner to guarantee a great, free, and peaceful future. He thought his own exertions might be needed toward its solution, but in order to have his chance, since the spirit of the army would be a controlling influence after the peace, it would be necessary for him to gain a good footing in the army. Military service to him, from this point of view, was a mere incident in his political career, and had as one leading object to improve his political prospects.

This does not mean that Schurz would be satisfied to be a political general. On the contrary, in order to further his cherished ambitions it would be necessary to make a name for himself in the army, and this he was just as determined to do as he had been to make himself felt in the politics of 1860. His military record, when

[68] Letter of March 13, 1862.
[69] Letter of May 5, 1862.

finally completed, was highly creditable. But he was not as fortunate on the field of war as in the political arena. He was not as well fitted to work in a closely knit organization like an army with its rigid hierarchy of officers, as he was to bring about results through efforts largely personal and individual. In 1849 he wrote from Rastatt that subordination under superiority had never come hard for him, and that he had never denied recognition to superior power wherever it had been encountered. But he also said: 'I did not want to be second where I could be first; I did not want to serve where I understood how to command.' In the Civil War he tried to play the military game according to the accepted rules. But Schurz was so frank in his suggestions, so impatient of stupidity wherever exhibited, so hopelessly unable to disguise his contempt for blunderers, that his superior officers must have found him a somewhat trying subordinate to get on with. To this should be added the circumstance that some prejudice existed against European trained officers, partly because they were apt to vaunt their own military attainments as superior to the American. On the other hand, some American generals were quick to blame their own mistakes upon the foreign officers or troops, a fact deeply resented by them in turn.

But Lincoln himself, endlessly patient as he is supposed to have been, found the hotspur German brigadier trying, and once—only once, for his friendship never wavered—he gave his difficult friend what can only be described as a good 'dressing down.' Then he sent for him, and explaining all his own perplexities, attached Schurz to him by stronger ties than ever; for these extraordinary men had too much respect and affection for each other to permit them to differ fatally.[70]

A present day military historian, General John M. Palmer, has found circumstantial evidence that Schurz communicated to Lincoln the military philosophy of Clausewitz, which only came to its own in Europe after the Franco-Prussian War. If this surmise is correct, Schurz can be said to have influenced the course of the great struggle far beyond what the overt records show. These reveal both successes and failures. Schurz won commendation for his conduct at Second Bull Run, where his brigade covered the retreat of the army. But at the battle of Chancellorsville he suffered a heart-breaking reverse, due to no fault of his.

He had been promoted to a major-generalship in March, 1863, and for a time hoped he might be given Sigel's command, that general being employed elsewhere. But he had the misfortune to gain the displeasure of General Hooker, with whom, after the battle of Wauhatchie, he had a serious falling out over a statement in Hooker's report which reflected upon Schurz's conduct in that engagement. Schurz demanded a court of inquiry, established his point against Hooker, and then, because of the bad relations between them, left his old command in the Eleventh Army Corps to take up whatever service might be found for him. The consequence was that most of the year 1864 had to be spent by him either in the quiet of a training camp at Nashville or in

[70] Compare Schurz's letters of November 8, 1862, and November 20, 1862, with Lincoln's replies of November 10 and November 24, 1862. In the last mentioned letter Lincoln says: 'If I must discard my own judgment and take yours, I must also take that of others, and by the time I should reject all I should be advised to reject I should have none left, Republicans or others—not even yourself. For, be assured my dear Sir, there are men who have "heart in it" that think you are performing your part as poorly as you think I am performing mine.' *Speeches &c.*, i, 220. Schurz also printed the letter in *Reminiscences*, ii, 394-395, with comments of his own upon it.

the political campaign at the North, while 1865 also afforded him comparatively few opportunities for service in the field, though he was much engaged in organization work.

Early in April, 1865, immediately after the surrender of Richmond, Schurz was sent to North Carolina to give such aid as he could in the concluding phases of the war. He was at Raleigh on the fateful fourteenth of April, but the news of the murder of Lincoln appears not to have reached him until the seventeenth. His letter dated on the eighteenth reflects not only his own profound grief, but the vengeful attitude of the soldiery at what they considered the final enormity committed by the expiring confederacy. Schurz felt thankful that the war was over, for were it to continue 'it would resemble the campaigns of Attila.' May first he was back in Washington, resigned his commission, and with unfeigned joy wrote: 'the uniform has been laid aside; the sword hangs on the wall; the children play with the riding whip and spurs.'

CHAPTER XV

RECONSTRUCTION

WHEN Schurz, on entering the military service, suggested that it would be likely to give him a chance to be useful in helping to solve the problems which would confront the nation after the war, he of course had no inkling of the intimate relation he was destined to sustain to the overshadowing question of reconstruction. Yet, in the sequel, through a strange concatenation of events, he influenced reconstruction history more perhaps than the 1860 election and also more than the course of the war itself.

The manner in which he was brought into this third phase of the great social revolution of the sixties is suggestive of the Schurz luck. He had met Andrew Johnson, then governor of Tennessee, at Nashville in 1864, and gained a pleasant acquaintanceship with him. Schurz's vigorous canvass for Lincoln and Johnson in the fall election could hardly fail to develop in the latter a sense of friendly obligation to the brilliant foreigner, and the reflection that he might prove as useful in the future as he had been in the past would not be without its appropriate effect. Accordingly, when Schurz returned from the war and called on the president to talk things over, they got on so famously together that he was encouraged to think his relations with the new administration might prove as satisfactory as they had been with Lincoln. He at this time was well impressed with Johnson, believed him to have overcome his former bad habits (which related to strong drink), considered him able if not broad-minded, and hoped he would carry out the Lincoln policies successfully.

Johnson was just then giving much attention to the question of rehabilitating the states lately in rebellion and was disposed to follow the Lincoln policy in that respect consciously and almost literally. That policy, designed of course for conditions as they were in war time, was to empower a group of technically loyal white citizens (those who would take the oath prescribed by the president and who did not belong to specified excepted classes) to re-erect the civil government in their state, under a proper constitution, and prepare to re-enter the union by electing congressmen and senators. The entire process of reconstruction was to be supervised by the president, but the houses of Congress would of course retain the constitutional right to determine whether the members from states seeking their former place in the national councils had been properly elected.[71] On this general plan Lincoln had encouraged the restoration of state governments in Tennessee, Arkansas, and Louisiana. Johnson now called on the people of North Carolina to proceed with a similar though not identical program, and soon thereafter undertook to reëstablish all of the rest of the lately rebellious states.

The mere question of the restoration of civil government in the southern states need not have produced serious friction between president and Congress. If the president could in anywise conjure a passably loyal constituency which would set up a government able to manage local affairs, the nation's work of pacification would be completed, the military forces could be withdrawn in whole or in part, and the federal courts reopen,

[71] McCarthy, Charles H., *Lincoln's Plan of Reconstruction* (New York, 1901), 461.

thus bringing back the healing influence of customary procedures and habits. This would be so great a boon to all parties concerned that any president might have counted on the northern people supporting a policy having only this object in view.

Unfortunately, the presidential program far outran the above minimum and looked to the full participation of the former rebel communities as states in the Union, with representatives and senators in Congress, the right to choose electors of president and vice-president, and all other powers and privileges which fully equipped states enjoy. The unwillingness to contemplate a distinction between 'states' reorganized for purposes of local government and states in full panoply hinges back upon theories maintained by the North during the war. Secession, so the argument ran, meant revolution, because the American system was an 'indissoluble union of indestructible states.' Lincoln's doctrine of rebellion was that groups of persons in the South, by raising an insurrection, had conspired together to overthrow the laws of the national government. The states of the southern confederacy, notwithstanding their own solemn declarations and the fact that they had participated as states in the rebel government, had never been out of the Union. To employ the political scientist's phrase, the states 'perdured,' or 'lasted through' all the troubles of the war years. When the rebellion was finally crushed, and the victorious power's heel withdrawn, they must be permitted to spring right back into the Union they had flouted and fought until overpowered.

Nothing is clearer than that the doctrine of 'perdurance' is a refinement of political philosophy out of harmony with the facts. Lincoln himself, unfortunately in this case, refused to define the relations of the conquered 'states' to the Union, saying those relations were not what they should be and the sooner they were improved the better. If he had employed his really great powers of analysis on this problem as he did, while writing the first inaugural, on the problem of secession, there can be little doubt his solution would have been equally sound. For he would have seen that, however the war began, the states during the course of it had ceased to be states in the Union and had become by conquest practically communities under the jurisdiction of the Union, which could therefore be reorganized at the will of the national governing power. The relation was, with a difference, like that of territories, but as a concession to habit—and a balm to violated consistency—the expression 'late seceded states' would have served just as well. Civil organization, modeled as far as practicable on the territorial structures, utilizing the self-government principle to the fullest extent consistent with safety, might then have been set up, to last until such time as the 'late seceded states' were by Congress judged fit to be reintroduced into the Union.

Instead of such a simple, logical policy, based on a common sense principle, the actual history of reconstruction illustrates the attempted application of two contradictory philosophies with a variety of deformations of each. The presidential policy was based on the 'perdurance' theory, though this was not adhered to consistently, the congressional at first on the territorial theory and later on the conquered provinces theory, but neither one was applied with clear logic. In consequence of the confusion of views, the president and Congress maneuvered themselves into hopeless controversy, the late seceded states became recalcitrant, the drastic policy of 'through' was finally applied to them with results incalculably disastrous not only to those communities but to the entire country. Black supremacy, force bills, the Ku Klux Klan, the Solid South, are only a few of the evils for which the régime must be held responsible.

Now, at the outset of his proposed activity toward reconstructing the states, perhaps at a time when his policy was still plastic, President Johnson asked Schurz to make a tour through the South, study conditions in the several states visited, and report to him his findings. Whatever may have been the condition of the president's mind at that juncture, we are left in no doubt as to Schurz's general views. For he described them briefly in a letter to a friend just before he started on his southern journey.[72] It would be, he thought, a trifling matter to restore the Union in its political outlines, but that was by no means what was wanted: the problem was to reconstruct it so as to guarantee the results of the great social revolution effected in the South by the war. 'A free labor society must be established and built up on the ruins of the slave labor society.'

This involved the stupendous difficulty that the southern whites had accepted abolition through necessity solely, without actually changing their views on the slavery question, and therefore as soon as the states became autonomous again they would bring back a system as nearly like slavery as possible, and the national government would then be powerless to interfere. So long, he said, as the rebel states are not fully restored to their former places in the Union, the federal power can 'find means by which the results of the revolution can be so fixed that thereafter the southern population can no longer alter them.'

[72] Frederick Althaus, June 25, 1865.

When we compare the above with the summary at the close of his famous report, it is seen that practically his tour through the South, assembling of testimony, and so forth, had but the effect of confirming views with which he entered on this important public errand. But, if for that reason we incline to criticise Schurz as an investigator, in the way some have done,[73] certain facts need to be considered. In the first place, the opinions expressed in June had experience and observation behind them quite as truly as did those expressed in December. For Schurz had but recently returned from service in the far South, he had been in Virginia during one period of the war and in Tennessee during most of 1864. Wherever he was stationed he observed, inquired, and reasoned about conditions as bearing on reconstruction after the war should be over. So, when he writes, after starting South, that the opinions with which he went were quickly and easily confirmed, this may quite as logically be taken to imply that his previous observations and his inferences from them had been correct, as that he refused to see new facts which would disturb complacent predilections. It is probable, indeed, that Schurz's opinions on the whole were based more on insight than on investigation, but even that would not of itself invalidate them. Schurz, with his unusual intellectual equipment and his experience in judging the effects of social revolutions, might very well arrive at his conclusions in a manner different from that of the imperfectly trained observer without necessarily being open to the charge of bias.

At all events, his trip through the states of North and South Carolina, Georgia, Alabama, Mississippi, and

[73] Cf. Dunning, W. A., *Reconstruction, Political and Economic* (New York, 1907), 50.

Louisiana provided a good fund of confirmatory evidence, derived partly from personal observation, partly from military officers, agents of the Freedman's Bureau, provisional governors, and a wide variety of southern witnesses. All his inquiries had as their main objective to determine the attitude of southern people on the question of substituting a free labor system for the recently abolished slave labor system, which was surely logical if the war meant anything at all for the blacks.

Stating the results more at large than in the letter mentioned above, he explains why the southern whites are not in a frame of mind to legislate calmly with reference to a system of free labor. They are universally so near financial ruin as to feel under a strong compulsion to try for quick gains by means of a labor supply managed as far as possible on old habitual lines. Nineteen out of twenty southerners, he estimated, were convinced that negroes would not work without compulsion. Some were willing to lease their plantations to Yankees who held the opposite views on that subject, and let them try their moral suasion on the blacks, but they fully expected to see the experiment fail. They had indeed given up the idea of personal property in negroes, but the whites as a whole looked upon the entire mass of black folk as existing for the benefit of white society. The proof on this point was cumulative and it began to come in strongly when the reconstructed states adopted their black codes, their apprenticeship laws, and laws governing vagrancy. In all of these there was a marked tendency in the direction of making peons of the blacks. Schurz looked upon this as a natural reaction to the fact of the forcible freeing of the slaves, but was not prepared to condone it on that account; and he posed his practical question, whether the immediate restoration of the late rebel states to absolute self-control was so necessary that it must be done even at the risk of endangering one of the great results of the war and of bringing on in those states insurrection or anarchy, or whether it would not be better to postpone that restoration until such dangers were passed? So far the change from slavery to free labor had been known to the southern people only by its destructive results. It was therefore not strange that they sought to throw obstacles in its way. But this made it all the more necessary that the movement of social reconstruction 'be kept in the right channel by the hand of the power which originated the change, until the change can have disclosed some of its beneficial effects.' Every case of successful planting on the free labor, contract and wages plan, would make new friends for the system and he felt sure that 'one good harvest, made by unadulterated free labor in the south, would have a far better effect than all the oaths that have been taken and all the ordinances that have as yet been passed by southern conventions.'

If the southern people knew that the nation would accept nothing short of a genuine free labor system, as a basis for the rehabilitation of the late rebel states, they would incline to adapt themselves to the change. But, since they were hoping within a few months to have the unrestricted control of their internal affairs, as fully restored states, they simply refused to make the effort toward adjustment. Their hope was, through the influence of the president, supported by northern Democrats, to be able soon to bid practical defiance to the power that brought about the freeing of the slaves.

An important influence toward the creation of a free labor system in the South would be immigration

from the northern states. Opportunities for northern-
ers with means and enterprise were good. But they
would not come unless the safety of person and property
were guaranteed, which could not be done as yet by
governments wholly controlled by the southern whites.
Nor would the much needed northern capital migrate to
the South without guarantees of protection.

The most radical suggestion contained in Schurz's
report has reference to negro suffrage. But, while in
this matter one cannot acquit him of a certain trend toward a speculative idealism, the reading of his statement will show that he looked upon the proposed voting
right mainly as the negro's means of protection to his
other civil rights. 'Practical liberty,' he says, 'is a good
school, and besides if any qualification can be found, ap-
plicable to both races, which does not interfere with the
attainment of the main object, such qualification would
in that respect, be unobjectionable. But it is idle to say
that it will be time to speak of negro suffrage when the
whole colored race will be educated, for the ballot may
be necessary to secure his education.' Schurz found a
universal prejudice against negro education as well as
negro voting and believed it would be necessary for the
national government to hold the position of umpire over
southern affairs until these prejudices had been softened
by experience under new conditions. The fact that, in
the very period of his observations in the South, the
convention in Mississippi called under the president's
own initiative, flouted Johnson's suggestion to enfran-
chise such of the negroes as could read the constitution
and write their names, is all the comment needed on the
correctness of Schurz's diagnosis.

In concluding the report he says there are many
well meaning individuals among the southern people,

but they are not numerous or strong enough to stem the popular tide. 'There are good reasons to hope that a determined policy on the part of the national government will produce innumerable and valuable conversions. This consideration counsels lenity as to persons, such as is demanded by the humane and enlightened spirit of our times, and vigor and firmness in the carrying out of principles, such as is demanded by the national sense of justice and the exigencies of our situation.'

It needs hardly to be pointed out that Schurz entertained the best of good will toward the southern people, whose renewed prosperity was desired by him quite as earnestly as by President Johnson or anyone else. He simply was unconvinced of the correctness of the president's policy of getting the southern states back into the Union at once, with all that this implied in the way of power to thwart the will of the North and to undo the work achieved at so great a sacrifice. In these views he was on the whole correct, though he probably underestimated rather than overestimated the intensity of southern prejudices against negro education, negro suffrage, negro equality before the law, and the reforms which he hoped might be secured with comparative ease were bound to come very hard. Moreover, they would have to be worked out through the agency of the better class of the southern people themselves, which does not mean that the states must perforce be rendered immediately autonomous, but that a general amnesty should have been passed promptly in order to permit the real custodians of southern opinion to assume the leadership in their respective communities.

It is hard to see how views very different from Schurz's could have been made to prevail in the North.

His report became the factual basis of the congressional system of reconstruction. He cannot, however, be held responsible for the aberrations and the needless rigors of that unfortunate system, the resultant of the contentious wrongheadedness of a narrow-minded and tactless president and the wrongheadedness of equally tactless war embittered leaders in Congress. There is, in Schurz's report, no evidence of that war psychosis which influenced some northern radicals. But neither was his investigation influenced by the desire to make propaganda for a prematurely hasty restoration of the late rebel states, as was obviously the case with the cursory investigation of General Grant, reported to Congress by the president simultaneously with the Schurz report for the sake of discounting the latter. So far from having a motive to cross the president's plans, Schurz realized that the character of his findings would probably end the good relations he had earlier established with Johnson and that his hopes of a career in the public service would go glimmering. He must therefore be credited with exercising all of his stubborn public honesty in dealing with this great question in strict accordance with his best judgment.

CHAPTER XVI

INDEPENDENCE AND POWER

IN SEPTEMBER, 1863, Schurz wrote from his camp at Catlett Station, Virginia, one of the most important letters relative to his American career. In it he gave his boyhood friend Petrasch, who had just broken a fourteen year silence, such an account of himself as might bridge the gap between the revolution in Germany and the events of the day in this country. At the conclusion of the narrative he says: 'I have labored much, struggled much, endured much, and also suffered much—so much that I needed strong convictions to keep me upright. How often, in moments of discouragement, have I wished I could be of those who, assured of some definite occupation, can eat their bread in peace with their loved ones. The petty jealousy of Germans who would rather subordinate themselves to natives than to a fellow countryman who overtops them; the ambitions of natives who begrudge to the foreigner his influence and his distinction; the poisonous slanders of political opponents to whom not even personal honor is sacred—all of this has given me many bitter hours. I might have worked myself up to that sovereign contempt of men which is said to make a man great, but that is against my nature. I would rather remain insignificant. I love the people in spite of themselves and possess that invincible confidence which, deceived a thousand times, is also a thousand times revived. This is perhaps artless but I cannot do otherwise and that keeps me young, and cheerful, and hopeful. The main thing is this; that in a calling such as mine a man should

THEODORE PETRASCH ABOUT 1863

not permit himself to be ruled by a false ambition. The
ambition to *do* something can be boundless, but it must
free itself from the ambition to *be* something. I am
glad to have gained official positions which, according
to the usual interpretations, are brilliant; I have learned
to recognize their worthlessness for they have never contributed to my inner satisfaction. I believe that I could
now, without regrets, cast from me a crown if I had it.
Such things are only means to an end and as such are
sometimes of consequence. I have happily come to the
point where externalities no longer have any tempta-
tions for me. I believe I am able to say that in practise
I have become even a better Republican than in theory.'

Public office as a means of service was to him a price-
less boon; dependence upon public office for one's livelihood was the most wretched slavery, because it puts
fetters on the mind. If Lincoln, 'the good, good Lincoln,' as he wrote of him after his death, had survived,
Schurz could have had his choice of available civil or
diplomatic offices but he might have declined them all,
for he was always intent on an opportunity to do work
which carried a reward in itself quite apart from any
emoluments attached thereto. Work which did not
bring him such a natural gratification, however well paid
pecuniarily, was distasteful.

To be sure, a man of his economic limitations and
business inaptitude was sometimes obliged to perform
sheer task work for the sake of a livelihood. It was so
now, on his return from the South. He was through
with government employment, there was little or no income from private sources, and an accumulation of
debts was pressing heavily down upon him. When,
therefore, Horace Greeley offered to put him in charge
of the *Tribune's* Washington office, although its duties

were arduous and of a routine uninspiring character, he took the position and spent in it some four months, giving it up to assume the editorship of the new Detroit *Post,* a radical Republican organ which was soundly financed and offered a reasonably good salary. He remained at Detroit about one year, when another and as it proved, very fortunate newspaper opening enticed him to St. Louis.

Schurz's financial situation in the years 1866 and 1867 was pitiable, to say the least, and, if we consider the almost superhuman labors for the public which had engrossed so much of his time and energy during the space of ten years, we might call it tragic. The family's resources had consisted in the main of that portion of Margarethe's patrimony which was available at or near the date of her marriage. After supporting them for several years, providing for the Watertown investments, including the building of the excellent country house, that source of support was apparently exhausted. Schurz, in April, 1858, laid a second mortgage[74] for $3,500 on the Watertown farm which, as we have seen, had been mortgaged at the date of purchase for $8,500. This would seem to indicate that his money worries became acute about that time. Also, he now began to give lectures in order to eke out his income, and he took stump speaking engagements which contributed something.

Unfortunately, Schurz was never quite free from the temptation to try out projects which promised larger returns, and at some time prior to 1866 he had ventured heavily in a railroad land speculation. This failed, leaving him short approximately $5,000. On

[74]In favor of Francis A. Hoffman. Court House Records, Dodge County, Wisconsin.

the heels of that reverse came the judgment in a suit
for foreclosure of mortgage by the administrator of the
estate of John Jackson, deceased, the man from whom
Schurz in 1855 had bought the Watertown farm.[75]
This completed his financial ruin and Carl Schurz, re-
nowned for his patriotic services to two nations, admired and revered by millions, stood before the world
stripped of everything save honor, loved ones, friends,
and an inveterate habit of work.

His wife and children had removed from the farm to
Detroit in August, 1866. His parents had been a part
of the Watertown ménage from the beginning, the
mother acting as housekeeper, the father as gardener
and general supervisor of the work of the farmer. After
the loss of the property they took up their residence with
the eldest of the married daughters, Anna (Mrs.
August Schiffer) at Monee, Illinois, not far south of
Chicago. This was the family situation in the early
spring of 1867.

Schurz had received overtures about newspaper
work from certain persons in St. Louis as early as January, 1866 and weighed the advantages of that prospect
against the offer from Detroit. Evidently, however,
this was not the project which he finally accepted,
though even at the earlier date he would have preferred
St. Louis to Detroit as a permanent location.[76] The
Detroit position was laborious and confining, though he
did find time to write some speeches, to attend at Philadelphia in September, 1866, the big political meeting
which assembled at the invitation of the Southern
Unionist Convention, and, in the winter, to deliver a
number of lectures in Illinois and Missouri. He also

[75] The judgment was dated January 22, 1867. Court House Records,
Dodge County, Wisconsin.
[76] Letter of January 23, 1866.

wrote an article for the *Atlantic* on 'The True Problem' which restated some of his well known views on the reconstruction question,[77] and prepared at this time (December, 1866) his lecture on Germany. He regretted that the days were so short and that the brain will not always remain fresh and clear, words which proved that he was overworked.

From Princeton, Illinois, March fourth, 1867—the date is interesting in view of what transpired between that day and the same date two years later—Schurz wrote to his wife a significant letter. He had vainly expected to receive one from her in St. Louis, and to punish her for the disappointment, playfully threatened to withhold some very important news. He says: 'It relates to nothing less than the purchase for me of a half interest in a St. Louis newspaper business and the advance of the purchase price in such a way that I can repay it out of the business itself in three years. So now I have spoken in dark mysteriousness and you shall receive not another word until I am with you again. Still I will say this much more that the outlook concerning the prospect of the plan is good if we upon mature family discussion decide to take it up.' The contract, by which Schurz, with no capital of his own, became half owner of the *Westliche Post,* a leading western German daily of wide circulation, and with a very profitable printing business, was closed in April, and he became the partner of Dr. Emil Preetorius, the famous editor.

It appears that the family lived together in St. Louis for only about a month or six weeks, when the death of the youngest daughter completely shattered the delicate health of Mrs. Schurz who, in the middle of June, sailed for Germany with the two remaining children, Agathe

---

[77] *Atlantic Monthly,* xix, March, 1867.

and Marianne ('Hans' and 'Pussy'), in quest of health
for herself and the best school opportunities for them.
They remained abroad more than two years, being ab-
sent at the time Carl's most signal honor came to him
in America. He, however, joined them at Wiesbaden,
remaining from Christmas, 1867 to the following
March. That was the occasion of a visit to Berlin during which he was invited to call on Prince Bismarck
with whom he had several illuminating conversations.[78]

Schurz's absence on the visit to Germany, which began at the end of November 1867 and ended with his return to St. Louis April third, 1868, divides the period
we are now considering into two unequal parts—March
fourth, 1867 to December first, 1867; April third, 1868
to March fourth, 1869. The first part, because of the
distressful condition of his wife, who required the encouragement which his long and cheerful letters might
afford, yielded a relatively larger body of correspondence than the second and longer period. And, for once
in a way, the letters were not wholly devoted to politics.
Schurz chats with her about the health conditions in the
city, about the German outdoor theatre where he diverts
himself for an hour in the evening, about the reputation
he has gained of being a hard man because he dresses
down the office hands occasionally when they neglect
their duties. He also says a few words now and then
about the staff, mentioning Udo Brachvogel with special commendation and referring to his distinguished
partner, Dr. Preetorius, in whose home he lived, with
genuine affection. One letter contains an amusing pas-

---

[78] Schurz inferred, from some questions the Iron Chancellor put to him,
that his idea had been to draw Schurz into the Prussian state service. One
can only speculate about how he might have responded to such a suggestion had it come a year earlier, in the midst of his financial worries and
before a prospect of relief had presented itself.

sage about a young man from Texas who is a worshipper of his and whom he had to get rid of by the use of guile. Aside from incidental items like the above, his space was divided more or less equally between politics and descriptions of brief jaunts into the Missouri country.

Of such journeys, made partly to stimulate business and partly for recreation, there were four. The first was a steamboat voyage up the Missouri to Augusta, a settlement of educated Germans about fifty miles from St. Louis which was begun in the eighteen thirties. There the partners (for Preetorius accompanied Schurz) were entertained by a Dr. Münch, brother of Frederick Münch, who wrote over the pen name of *Far West*. Münch, though once a university professor, was now a Latin farmer, living on one of the Augusta hills, which overlooked not only the Missouri River but also miles of vineyards developed in that limestone shale region by these transplanted vintners of the Rhine valley. Life among those country people was simple, plain, but clean and wholesome. The little community, of about three hundred, all spoke German save the shoemaker's apprentice, a newcomer, and he was learning it. Even the children of the few negro families could speak German. The coming of the St. Louis dignitaries was the excuse for a Sunday's festivities held in a near-by grove, where Schurz and Preetorius both had to speak, where Augusta wine flowed freely, and good feeling and jollity prevailed. The German spirit and training had been preserved, he says, through the influence of the old families. The next generation would be purely American, a fact which Schurz, unlike many Germans, did not deplore. The mission of Germanism (*Deutschthum*) as he saw it, was to meliorate Americanism, not to become a substitute for it. As he states the matter, there should be produced: 'A modification of the American spirit through the German, while the nationalities melt into one. In a few years the old patriarchs in pleasant little Augusta will be dead and their successors will be carried away by the universal movement.'[79]

In August a visit was paid to St. Charles, near which place, at Cottleville, the Germans took up the defense of northern Missouri, August sixth, 1861. That anniversary was now celebrated as a kind of secondary Fourth of July, and Schurz was invited to deliver an address which he did. The Missouri Germans were more attractive to him than those in Wisconsin had been, probably because they were more largely of the forty-eighter class, and especially because Republicanism was almost universal among them, whereas the majority of the Wisconsin Germans, in Schurz's day, still persisted in their Democracy. Probably the difference between the Germans of the two states was more apparent than real. He found cultured German families in Missouri because he was Carl Schurz, editor of their *Westliche Post,* whom these Germans delighted to receive in their rural homes.

A week-end spent with Udo Brachvogel's elder brother, at Vineland, was a pleasant occasion. This gentleman, a middle aged person of considerable property, had arrived from the old country in the previous year. He bought six hundred acres of good farm land, planted vineyards, erected mills, and was doing a thriving business. But, enthusiastic as he himself was in the American prospect, his wife, a highly cultivated woman, yearned for the comforts of her German home, her dis-

[79] Letter of July 8, 1867. Cf. *Reminiscences,* iii, 259-262.

cussions with her lord and master over the relative
merits of America and Germany reminding Schurz of
his own domestic arguments with Margarethe.

The most amusing outing story of the series is in the
letter of September twenty-third about his visit to the
fair in Booneville. The good friends of that town had
invited Schurz, out of pure good will, in order to give
him a jolly time. They did not wish him to feel responsible for a speech, or anything of the sort. But they were
bound to make him forget his labors for a day, to show
him their countryside, in which they seem to have made
a hit, for he pronounced their Booneville hostelry the
nicest country hotel he had seen in America.[80] He visited the fair also, admired some of the exhibits, witnessed
a peculiar tournament (*Ringelstechen*) such as was
customary in Europe at the end of the middle ages, and
lunched with his friends at the Booneville battle ground
where a home guard of one hundred and fifty citizens
withstood an attack by fifteen hundred rebels. There,
as elsewhere in Missouri, he says, it was the Germans
who held aloft the banner of the Union.

Then came the account of what happened on his
second night in Booneville, a bit of fun which doubtless
reminded his wife of the famous rat letter of thirteen
years earlier. The pleasantry lay in his description of a
serenade given him at the Booneville hotel by the American glee club consisting of 'several singers, two violins,
one bass viol, and one bass horn. The singing,' he says,
'was introduced by a kind of prelude in which every instrument semed to amble quite at will through all possible keys. Then a tenor voice struck in and sang a song
whose refrain was: "Mother, kiss me in my dreams."
The climax of the song was the following voice and in-

---

[80] 'And how I slept in the soft wide bed!' he says.

strumental effect: tenor voice in highest pitch, and
piano, "Mother, Mother," violins (very softly), "Diddle
dee;" tenor voices *pianissimo,* "Mother," violins, (still
softer), "Diddle dee!" Chorus in thunder tones and
crashing bass horn: "Kiss me in my dreams." '

The year 1867 was not so very exciting politically,
and yet there were the 'antics' of President Johnson to
amuse Republicans. One thing he did was to remove
General Sheridan from his post in Louisiana, on account of the complications resulting from the New
Orleans riot of July thirtieth, 1866, and have him ordered West to the Indian country. Since the general had to
pass through St. Louis on his way west it was decided
to give him a great demonstration by way of showing
the president how the country felt about his action.
Schurz was at the head of the committee of arrangements and prepared for a tremendous torchlight procession as the spectacular feature. On behalf of the city
and the state, he gave a speech of welcome which, as
usual with his pronouncements on politics, coursed
through the Republican press. Besides all this, he was
personal escort for the little general, took him to the
German theatre where he nearly lost him in the crush,
and finally got him off on the train, he himself being at
the point of collapse. But it was the first conspicuous
stroke of the year against the Johnson policy and that
was quite compensation enough for Schurz.

The fall elections of 1867, while not critically important, yielded clues for the presidential contest in 1868.
A number of states called for Schurz's aid, but he was
chary about responding. Many features of party management displeased him, particularly the trend toward
control by 'wire-pullers and speculators' which was producing restiveness among the voters. He did not pro-

pose to make good the foolishness of other people, and wherever the party was in bad straits through the fault of its own leaders he pointedly let things take their own course. There was, however, particularly in Illinois, Wisconsin, and some of the eastern states, a renewed drift toward temperance agitation, which troubled him because of the way it affected German voters. Believing that the American element of the party was unwise in paying so much heed to temperance propagandists, he wrote an article expressly for their consumption which, like his Sheridan speech, was welcomed by the Republican press and had its influence upon policies in 1868.

Wisconsin Republicans gained his aid because they had behaved well and because he could not disappoint old friends like Governor Fairchild. Half a dozen speeches in important centers were his contribution to the campaign in that state, the concluding one being made in Milwaukee before a great gathering on election eve. He found the Germans a bit skittish on account of the 'temperance humbug,' but they were nevertheless held in line sufficiently to enable the party to win the state contest. At the Milwaukee meeting Schurz at last had the opportunity, deferred for nearly a decade, to pay off a score against Alexander W. Randall, who having 'Johnsonized' was of course outside the pale and became fair game. He received little mercy at Schurz's hands.[81]

The elections of 1867 netted a Republican reverse. The defeat in New York was decisive and was due, Schurz held, to the Sunday law and corruption in the party, while in Massachusetts the temperance people suffered a severe defeat. The Ohio legislature went

[81] His speech is printed in the Milwaukee *Sentinel* (daily), November 3, 1867.

Democratic, so did the city of Philadelphia and—in a
word—the Republicans had need for a careful stock-
taking in preparation for the great campaign to follow.
Schurz was rather pleased than otherwise at the result.
It would force the party to clear out the wire-pullers
and speculators from among its managers, and to relieve
its platform of disturbing non-political questions like
temperance and Sunday laws. This would impart spirit
and unity to the presidential canvass, and hold the Germans in the fight to chastise 'traitors' like Andrew
Johnson.

From Washington, March twenty-ninth, after his
return from abroad, Schurz wrote: 'Greatly as many
things in Germany pleased me, I am bound to say that
this country seems home to me. How fresh and hearty
life is here and how one feels at every step that he can
accomplish something! This is a very great matter.'
Then he plunged into an account of the hopeful political situation and ended with comments on the trial of
the president, by impeachment, which would begin next
day. He was perfectly certain that Johnson would be
convicted, but after hearing the opening statement of
the prosecution by General Butler, discouragement
took the place of confidence. 'What an opportunity
that would have been for a great orator,' he says, apparently wishing he could have made the speech. 'Butler made a commonplace lawyer's argument of it. . . .
I sat there filled with impatience. . . .'

A good test of the accuracy of even the best of memories is Schurz's remark, written a generation later:
'When I arrived in the United States again the impeachment trial was over and President Johnson had
been acquitted.'[82] The final vote on the impeachment

[82] *Reminiscences*, iii, 382.

charges did not in fact occur before May twenty-sixth, more than two months after he arrived at New York. Such discrepancies are not surprising to those who understand the difference between memoirs and contemporaneous records, but too many intelligent persons still are satisfied to accept reminiscences in lieu of history. The trial, indeed, was not concluded at the time of the adjournment of the Republican national convention in Chicago over which Schurz presided as temporary chairman and to which he delivered the key-note speech containing the finely ironical sentence: 'Abraham Lincoln was struck down in the fulness of his glory and we are now left to measure our loss by what he left behind him in his place.'

In that convention, where he really starred, Schurz moved to amend the platform resolutions as reported by adding one which declared: 'We favor the removal of the disqualifications and restrictions imposed upon the late rebels in the same measure as the spirit of disloyalty will die out, and as may be consistent with the safety of loyal people,' which was adopted with substantial unanimity, and raised to the dignity of a national political issue conclusions of his which were as old as his report on conditions in the South. That sentiment not only represented his just and magnanimous views, but it served as a significant rallying cry during the Liberal Republican agitation inaugurated by him later, and which swept into the reform movement a large proportion of intelligent southern opinion.

Schurz's campaigning in 1868 was very strenuous, though not equal to that of 1860. He was not one of the original Grant men, although he had long been convinced that Grant would be the nominee. Once more he was employed in such doubtful states as Indiana, Ohio,

Illinois, and Pennsylvania where German voters abounded, and he was proud to convince communities which had heard him in 1860 that he still retained his old fire. The journey through Pennsylvania he described as a genuine march of triumph. In 1867, after ten years of strenuous experimenting, he had found the right tone for extemporaneous speaking, and it seems clear that his appeals had gradually become less formal than they had been in the earlier period. Also, some of his extemporary speeches justify the judgment he expressed in 1858 that he was deficient in the control of form. But he never lost his habit of careful preparation, of thoroughness in argument and dignity of style. At Cooper Institute, New York, on the evening of September fifth, he apparently again reached the climax of his speaking in an address to an immense gathering of Germans. For once the friendly enthusiasm of his reception momentarily overcame him and he was obliged to struggle for self-mastery. Several hundred of his old soldiers occupied reserved seats directly opposite the stage. They leaped to their feet at his entrance, stretched out their hands, and repeated their ringing *'Lebe Hoch'* until it fired the vast assemblage. 'Finally,' he says, 'I took myself firmly in hand, and made a speech which even the critical New York Germans appraised as the most classical and striking I had ever delivered. . . .' Two weeks later he gave his big speech in Chicago. It was easy for him to fight in the feeling of victory, and having already devoted twelve years to the cause, which he believed would be rendered permanently safe through Grant's election, he was not disposed to spare himself in a last gruelling effort.

On the ninth of August, Schurz wrote his wife saying he would devote the last five or six weeks of the campaign to Missouri. One reason for doing so, he added, was because a new senator would be chosen by the next legislature and since Henderson's reëlection had been made impossible on account of his vote to acquit Johnson, there was a chance that he (Schurz) might be chosen, particularly if he should make a good impression on the people during the electoral canvass. As the writer of *Reminiscences,* Schurz failed to remember the true history of that capitally important episode in his own life, to which we must now give some attention.

Republican dominance in Missouri came as a result of the war, although the city of St. Louis, where Germans were exceedingly numerous and virtually unanimous for Lincoln, went Republican in 1860, as did some other localities under similar conditions. After the close of the war the control by that party was maintained through the disfranchising of rebels, and later, by means of an unfair registration act; Missouri, therefore, continued to be ruled by radicals. Schurz nominally belonged to that faction, although his natural impulses, as we have seen, were more generous than those of his faction. As leader of the Germans, who under the restricted suffrage which prevailed in the state constituted about thirty-five per cent of the radical strength, he was in an excellent position to appeal for political support, and it is all but certain that the idea of seeking the senatorship came to him as soon as the Johnson impeachment vote eliminated Henderson. He had already considered running for Congress in the St. Louis district, and the chances for a senatorship, which it was his most cherished ambition to attain, would not be permitted to escape him. A difficulty was that Charles D. Drake, the other United States senator, elected in 1867, was also, like

Schurz, a resident of St. Louis. He would naturally try to keep the way open for his own reëlection in 1873, which might be problematical if another St. Louisan were chosen in the meantime, it being a tacit but fixed rule that there should not be two senators from the same locality. For this reason Drake supported General Benjamin Loan, of St. Joseph. Schurz counted on a number of rural aspirants cancelling one another, which might permit him to win the prize despite the handicap of locality, and he deliberately planned to have the demand for his own candidacy come from the rural section rather than from St. Louis.

His campaign tour in behalf of Grant covered large portions of the state and he made friends everywhere. The demand for him to become senator, beginning doubtfully and far away in a small town newspaper at the end of July,[83] had swollen by election day to a considerable chorus, though there were not wanting some familiar discordant notes. By some too it was regarded as probable that Grant would offer him a place in the cabinet, but he discounted the idea as highly speculative. Besides, he would prefer a senatorship to any cabinet post except the highest, and he knew Grant would not make him secretary of state. He could achieve more as senator, would be able to retain his business connection with the newspaper, and besides, a senatorial post would be the best stepping stone to the headship of a later cabinet.

The Saturday Dinner, which Schurz's memory later pictured as the scene in which the suggestion of his becoming a candidate for the Senate was first made to him, was an institution founded by himself for the os-

[83] It is said by Barclay, Thomas S., *The Liberal Republican Movement in Missouri*, 152, note 5, that the LaGrange *American* first proposed Schurz's name July 30, 1868.

tensible purpose of bringing about better relations
between Americans and Germans in the city. He says
he started it shortly after the election, and in fact the
first meeting was held at the Planter's Hotel on
November fourteenth. Eighteen or twenty persons,
'Journalists, advocates, and a couple of merchants—all
men of consequence,' were in the group, which sat from
three to seven o'clock. 'I am convinced,' he writes on
November twenty-eighth, 'that in a short time the Saturday dinner will exert a decisive influence upon the
politics of the state. Has not your husband here again
had a happy inspiration? He has to amuse himself now
as best he can and in this business he is trying to com-
bine the useful with the pleasant. . . .' If the dinner
promoted his candidacy, as it almost certainly did, the
above statement justifies the inference that it had
been planned with that very object in view; yet some
still insist that Schurz 'was no politician!'

However, he still had a hard fight on his hands.
Senator Drake came home to lead the opposition to him
and Henderson supporters also joined in the attack. He
had the vigorous aid of the Missouri *Democrat,* which
was the most important Republican paper in Missouri,
of a large and growing number of rural papers, and the
good wishes of the Republican press of the nation generally. But his problem was to secure the votes of
radical members of the legislature and of these the
majority were long in doubt. The opposition tried to
array the national administration against him, but he
received word from Grant's intimate friend, Elihu B.
Washburne, that the newly elected president was much
interested in his success. They circulated the report
that Schurz's family were already in Europe and that
he intended to return there permanently. They charged

that he was an infidel, which was for the consumption of
the fundamentalists, a wine-bibber, a foreign upstart
whose God was ambition, a mere 'talker' without ability
to achieve anything useful.

Under the able leadership of Colonel W. M. Grosvenor, editor of the *Democrat,* Schurz's forces were successfully held together when the legislature met in January. The super-heated attacks upon him were arousing his friends with the result that mass-meetings were
called in various parts of the state to bring pressure upon the legislature in his interest. Finally, Schurz enticed
Drake and Loan into a debate, which was the best possible strategy; for in such an encounter he was a
dangerous opponent and since the discussion was held
in the presence of the legislature and a great concourse
of visitors his triumph was spectacular.[84]

Schurz was often guilty of writing over-enthusiastic
letters, but none of the others quite equalled in that respect the series penned immediately after the senatorship was assured to him. He was positively jubilant.
'The battle has been fought. It is the greatest triumph
of my life.' So he wrote when the nomination had just
been made, and added: 'My rooms at the hotel were
crowded until three o'clock in the morning. They sang
the John Brown song and shook hands as if the yoke of
a tyrant had been loosed from the people.' This referred
to the feeling, which became an element in the campaign, that Schurz would liberalize the laws affecting
political rights of ex-rebels, and bring about an era of
good feeling. He had promised to do so and, as we shall
see, kept his word. His election initiated a new régime

[84] It was called the 'Battle of the Giants,' not in allusion to Loan, who
was ineffective, but to Schurz and Drake the real contenders. Schurz believed he had never spoken better than in the final reply to Drake, which
was crushing.

for Missouri and also, as the sequel shows, for the South as a whole. 'You see,' he concludes, 'I am swimming on the crest of the wave. Only one thing was lacking; that you were not there to see my victorious fight and that you cannot be in the capitol when I take my seat in the Senate. Your brilliant eyes would have made my triumph doubly sweet. I shall see them in my dreams.'

When the formal election was over he wrote[85] describing the unanimity with which the Republican press of the country applauded his success, saying the German Republican press as well as the American was unanimous in their recognition of him. The Democratic papers, also, treated him respectfully. 'Only Heinzen,' he says, 'scolds away lustily in the old manner.'[86] His election was by many considered the beginning of a new era for Germanism in America. Carl's aged parents were overcome with joy and pride.

Schurz wrote from Washington February sixteenth, acknowledging receipt of letters from his wife and children congratulating him on his triumph. He could see Margarethe's joy 'peeping out from every line.' The thought of how it would cheer her, he says, had been with him all the time as a source of his inspiration. Then he adds this revealing touch about her former pessimism, a burden under which he probably had to struggle continuously: 'Do you remember how occasionally, in moments of depression, you gave me to understand that you felt as if I was losing my grip? When I tried to cheer you up you would shake your head and believe me to be mistaken in saying that my best days were not yet past. I was right, was I not?'

[85] Letter of January 24, 1869.
[86] Karl Heinzen, of Cincinnati, editor *Der Deutsche Pionier*.

They had agreed upon a senatorship as the highest post
to which he could aspire, the presidency being reserved
for the native born. Now he had it. It would enable
him to employ his powers to useful ends, give him
honorable distinction and, in contributing to the success
of his business, enable him to lay by a neat sum annual-
ly. Already the newspaper had brought in profits
enough to pay for itself, with an excess from which he
was able to wipe out old debts. So the senatorial election, which made him politically triumphant, found
him for the first time in his life enjoying financial
independence.

CHAPTER XVII

THE SENATORIAL PERIOD

SCHURZ took his seat in the United States Senate March fourth, 1869, the day of Grant's inauguration as president. Two days earlier, March second, he had celebrated his fortieth anniversary. From this time he operated on a widely different plane and under stimuli which varied in essentials from those which had been effective earlier. His newly achieved economic freedom was the main feature in the relief he enjoyed. Bread-worrying, the ancient enemy of his spirit, was finally laid. While he never acquired what could be called great wealth and sometimes, as during the years of his cabinet service, found it necessary to conserve his resources thriftily, he did not in the later period feel the pinch of want, or the burden of debts he was unable to meet. Thenceforward he could labor with a new satisfaction.

It was not in his nature to give himself ease. On returning from Jefferson City with the certificate of election in his pocket he wrote: 'But now comes the work. I have decided to be a distinguished senator and that involves a great deal.' The very first week in office convinced him that no legislative body in the world had to work harder than the American Congress. What with attending the sessions, receiving twenty-five or thirty callers every morning, most of them office hunters, running around among the departments in the interest of constituents, and attending to his correspondence, he consumed not only the daylight hours but also the night till one or two o'clock. He often dropped asleep at his writing desk with a mountain of letters unanswered. But, fortunately, a portion of his duties afforded compulsory exercise, which he needed, so that he could awaken in the morning as fresh as ever.

At the moment he became senator the problem of civil service reform was one of Schurz's major interests. His experience, dating from the election of Lincoln, had made office seekers intensely distasteful to him, and gradually produced the conviction that the method of distributing government patronage was the fountain head of the evils threatening American institutions. By good fortune, he had an opportunity within a few days to make his maiden speech on that general theme. The tenure-of-office act, passed for the purpose of tying the hands of Andrew Johnson, was regarded with black disfavor by Grant, who promptly asked Congress to repeal it. This the House was prepared to do, but the Senate showed reluctance, its judiciary committee recommending a suspension of the act until the next session of Congress. Schurz was disposed on general principles to favor a repeal, but he saw that if the question were definitely scheduled to come up again in the fall there would be a chance to introduce a full fledged civil service reform bill, and for that tactical reason he spoke and voted in favor of suspension. Being immediately made a member of the committee on retrenchment which would have the civil service problem in charge, he decided to make that subject his specialty. During the summer spent in St. Louis, he prepared his bill and the speech he designed to make in its support. The project was presented on the twentieth of December. Schurz's measure was modeled upon the Jenckes' bill introduced in the House four years earlier, but it contained many modifications, was more thoroughgoing, providing for applying the examination test to more classes, and proposed a longer initial term of service. He spoke upon the subject several times during his term, and a half measure of reform was actually secured through the impulsive urgency of President Grant, but on the whole the state of the congressional mind proved discouraging to civil service reformers.[87]

Schurz, fortunately, was not a one speech or one idea senator. If Dolliver's definition of a Progressive, as one who insisted on reading bills before voting on them, is correct, then he was an arch-Progressive; for he not only read bills before voting, but on all major issues he usually amassed information enough to enable him to clarify the subject in debate. Only the most unrelenting industry, coupled with foresight, and an immense capacity for study made this possible. Schurz's method was to forecast the leading topics of each successive session and make systematic preparation upon those topics. Examples are found in his study of international law during the first summer, because he anticipated a discussion in the winter of American-British relations; of his assembling, during the same summer, a library of books on India, Japan, and China, because the development of the Pacific Coast made it certain that the diplomatic and commercial relations between this country and Asiatic countries would assume importance in the near future.

Like other senators, he was often taken by surprise and in such cases he knew how to burn the midnight oil in efforts to perfect emergency preparations. A case in point was President Grant's treaty for the annexa-

---

[87] Perhaps the most complete statement of Schurz's reasons for the reform bill is found in his speech of January 27, 1871. For an outline of the legislation secured, see Fish, Carl Russell, *The Civil Service and Patronage*, 212-213.

tion of San Domingo. Schurz, through the resignation of one of the former members, had gained a coveted place on the foreign relations committee. This was precisely the appointment he wanted. On that and the committee on retrenchment he achieved his most important results. When Grant requested the Senate to confirm the San Domingo treaty most of the Republican senators, though looking upon the scheme itself with coldness, were complacently disposed to let the president have his way. Not so Schurz and Charles Sumner. These two men worked out fully the argument against annexation and succeeded in preventing it to Grant's extreme annoyance. Schurz's opposition, as his great speech on the subject shows, was based on the dangers for Anglo-Saxon civilization which would be involved in controlling portions of the tropics. He presented as proofs historical testimony of the most diverse kind, and with the fiery earnestness of an ancient prophet uttered his dramatic warning: 'Beware of the tropics!'

The discussion of the San Domingo question, thanks to the president's ill-advised pertinacity, was continued during several sessions. It widened more and more the breach between Schurz and Grant, finally giving rise to a definitive critique by him on the president's unconstitutional assumption of the war powers. In that speech, delivered on the twenty-eighth and twenty-ninth of March, 1871, Schurz reached the high water mark of his senatorial debating, and it is doubtful if anywhere in the record of Congress the question of executive usurpation is treated with such ample knowledge and inexorable logic. The president's apologists, Morton, Frelinghuysen, Stewart, and Howe interjected questions and interrupted continually for the pur-

pose of stating their own interpretations of facts; but
Schurz was more than equal to the occasion, and when he
concluded there was left no sun spot of doubt upon the
great principle involved. The case is summed up best
in this extract: 'Sir, that simple provision of the constitution that Congress *shall have power to declare war*
cannot by any rule of construction be interpreted to
mean anything else than that Congress, and not the
president alone, shall define the contingencies in which
the belligerent power of the United States is to be used.'
Another sharp difference with the administration came
over the force bill which, with some show of justice because of the Ku Klux outrages, brought the South back
under rigorous military rule, a policy Schurz condemned.

The temper of his speeches was usually admirable,
so far as references to Grant were concerned, and he
took special pains to disavow any wish to injure the
president's standing with the party or the country.
Schurz was endowed with a good measure of magnani-
mity and was regardful of the amenities. Grant, however, showed himself quite unable to look upon the
matter impersonally, and made it plain that he considered Schurz an enemy of the administration and a
renegade from the Republican party. Schurz had for-
feited the president's favor as early as the 1870 election,
when he led a revolt in Missouri against the radical
wing of the Republicans which, for the sake of party
success, was bent on barring ex-Confederates from the
ballot indefinitely. He united the liberal Republican
elements, including the Germans, with the Democrats
and by that means won a complete victory in the state.
The restrictive laws were at once repealed and Missouri
became fully reconstructed. But, from a party point of

view, the result redounded to the advantage of the
Democrats, a circumstance Schurz regretted and which
brought down upon his head the severest condemnation
of those who believed, like Savonarola, that the interests
of their party were the interests of the 'kingdom of
God.'

By 1871 Schurz was prepared to cut loose from the
administration entirely. He had become completely
disgusted with the government of President Grant,
which he regarded as personal, autocratic, and through
the machinations of bad men to whom the president
confidingly entrusted power, corrupt to an unprece-
dented degree. He accordingly announced that, under
no circumstances, would he support Grant for reëlection in 1872. This was burning his political bridges but
he knew where the materials were out of which new ones
could be built. Missouri supplied an example. The
moderate Republicans and the moderate Democrats in
that state found it possible to agree on a platform. The
Germans were a coherent body of voters who, though
stanch unionists during the war, were not extreme
partisans, because they were too new to American political practice to have developed the dyed-in-the-wool
attitude represented by the radicals. To match the
Germans, with which group went a body of the more
intellectual, moderate, mostly young Republican voters
of American nativity, there was a large group of Democrats who also looked forward rather than back. These,
too, were mainly young men, concerned about the prosperity of the state, who wanted to put an end to the war
feeling, to secure a revision of the tariff, and an improved civil service. Many of them, from ancient prejudice,
disliked the negro suffrage amendment, but they were
at least nominally willing to support it in consideration

of the benefits to be derived from union with liberal Republicans.

Missouri conditions were duplicated in some of the other states, save that the German element was smaller, and all over the South were to be found hundreds of thousands of order loving, intelligent citizens who realized the folly of continuing to struggle against fate and who were now willing to join with moderate men throughout the country in a bona fide policy of peaceful reconstruction. They wanted to put an end to terrorism of all sorts, to get rid of military surveillance, and to give free labor and the negro franchise a decent trial. Tariff revision downward was a fixed demand of these people, also universal amnesty and a restoration of local self-government. They were responsive to the propaganda, so dear to Schurz's heart, in favor of civil service reform.

Having gained an insight into the political possibilities in Missouri, Schurz in 1871 penetrated other border states and at Nashville, Tennessee, in September of that year, launched the movement for a Liberal Republican party. This he did not do without the active sympathy of many prominent Republicans who, like himself, despaired of good government through the *waribund* Republican organization. But the actual work of setting the new forces in motion was his own, and he continued to be the head and heart of the movement.

The plan was to establish political clubs through the South—the so-called Reunion and Reform associations—and over parts of the North as well, to systematize the discussion of reform principles during the winter, and then to crystallize the results in a great convention which some hoped might influence the

Republican party to adopt a liberal platform and particularly to eliminate Grant as a candidate. The local troubles of the Republicans in New York, Pennsylvania, Illinois, Ohio, Massachusetts, Iowa, and elsewhere, troubles which grew mainly out of the impolitic course of the national administration in reference to the patronage, threatened widespread revolt and opened much soil for the seed of reform. At the same time, it insured the movement against becoming too ethereal, for the practical politician, the place-hunter, and the sorehead would be on hand as well as the aspiring patriot and the intellectual, seeking perfection in government.

The Missouri State Liberal Convention, January twenty-fourth, 1872, adopted a platform under Schurz's guidance. It included general amnesty, a readjustment of tariffs, civil service reform, and the non-interference of the national government with local affairs. It called upon all Republicans of the nation, who believed in these principles and desired to see them adopted, to meet in mass convention at Cincinnati, May first, 1872.

This Cincinnati Convention is a political phenomenon which evoked much satirical comment at the time, and has continued to be a source of amusement to historians and others. Much of the derision leveled against it was deserved. And yet the movement which it focalizes was of profound significance in our political history. It was the first general reintegrating of the elements which revolt against a political system resting on war psychology had rendered fluid. Grant, the victorious soldier, who deserved the reverence of the people for his military services, had been elected to an office for which he was ill-equipped, though it must be remembered that the moral backwash of the war was bound to multiply the difficulties of any president in that period. The spirit of his administration was the spirit of the army, and the official leaders of his party were almost feudally bound to him, and to the policies so recklessly foisted upon him by designing sycophants. The masses of Republicans continued to give him their confidence, but defections were multiplying, especially among the educated classes, and the arguments based on misgovernment and corruption lay almost sun-clear before the public. The immediate prospects of a new party movement were less hopeful because the southern states were pocket boroughs of the party in power, the leading southern whites being excluded from the ballot which at the moment was wielded by nationally enfranchised negroes supported by federal bayonets and regimented by northern carpet-baggers.

The old, war-time coalition of Union Democrats with Republicans in the North could not be expected to last forever, and in fact many of the former Union Democrats had already dropped back into the Democratic party, albeit reluctantly, on account of that party's evil reputation for unpatriotic conduct during the crisis. A new party, calling itself Republican and standing for some of the liberal policies like a lower tariff, and reduced taxes, general amnesty to the ex-Confederates, and the restoration of local self-government in the South, would appeal strongly to such men. Then, there were the Germans, who might prove amenable to the propaganda of men like Schurz, provided nothing about the platform or the candidates repelled them. The factionalizing of the Republican party within so many of the states made the shift from a *regular* to a *liberal* Republicanism easier than it would have been earlier. All in all, while the outcome must have been doubtful from the first, the time seemed propitious for the attempt to launch the new party, whatever the immediate result might be.

But what of the candidates and what of the platform? Schurz, who was rightly regarded as the leader of the movement, was chosen permanent chairman of the convention. His acceptance of the post was a cardinal mistake, as he ought to have known in view of the heterogeneous assemblage of politicians, good and bad, who had been attracted to Cincinnati. He was needed here, there, and everywhere but was chained to the rostrum. Good advice, lofty ideals, the proclamation of the convention's mission to purify the body politic through the outlawing of all that is degrading in party government and convention practice: with such ideas he edified the rank and file, but evidently produced a very slight impression upon the managing class of hardened politicians, of whom a sufficient number were present to make sorry work of the idealist's program.

When the convention opened, three men were most talked of for the presidential nomination: Charles Francis Adams of Massachusetts, Horace Greeley of New York, and Judge David Davis of Illinois. There were various favorite sons also, one of them being B. Gratz Brown, the man whom Schurz had used two years earlier to help make the Liberal movement in Missouri a success, and who was chosen at that time for governor of the state. The Davis boom was handicapped by being too heavily financed, all Davis shouters having received free passes on the railways, and expense money, making the manner of his candidacy quite alien to the pristine spirit of the convention.[88]   Mr. Adams

[88] See *That Convention* by F. G. W. Ebals, illustrated by Frank Beard (New York & Chicago, 1872). Also Ross, Earle Dudley, *The Liberal Republican Movement* (New York, 1919). Bancroft and Dunning, *Carl Schurz, Reminiscences,* iii.

fulfilled best the ideals of the movement as conceived by Schurz. He would have been glad to see Adams nominated, though he unaccountably kept strictly clear of the question of who should be selected. This was Schurz's second error of management. Samuel Bowles at the time and Joseph Pulitzer later, expressed the opinion that a word from Schurz would have gone far to determine the outcome. That word he did not utter, though his intimates knew that his hopes were fixed on Adams. But Adams aroused no spontaneous enthusiasm, and his record made him positively unacceptable to the Irish voters. Besides, he virtually gave the convention to understand that he cared not a fig for their nomination, though he did not actually threaten to decline it.

Greeley was the best known of all the leading candidates on account of his long connection with the Republican New York *Tribune,* which under his editorship had practically fathered the party. He was an extraordinarily able man, a brilliant writer, a lover of mankind, and an enthusiast in promoting human welfare. But a dominant intellectualism, which gave an aspect of liquid instability to his policies, the plentiful crochets and cranky notions he displayed—his Fourierism, land reformism, woman suffragism, prohibitionism—made him seem to many the very last person who ought to be risked as a presidential candidate.

Strange as it may seem, Greeley had a strong following in the South by reason of his vigorous advocacy of amnesty and local self-government, and his resounding opposition to the radical policy of coercion. He had lectured in the region during the year 1871, gaining a wide popularity, for it was seen that his sympathies were genuine. He also had a great following in the

West, as well as in New England and the Middle States. So far it would appear that his candidacy would justify itself despite his personal idiosyncrasies, 'white hat,' and ridiculous appearance. But, it was understood from the beginning of the movement that, as in Missouri, success depended upon either the tacit or official acceptance of the Liberal Republican candidate by the Democrats and Greeley had some glaring defects as a lamp expected to attract that variety of moth. Liberal Republicans and Democrats were agreed on the need of tariff reform, but Greeley was the high-priest of protectionism. Besides, he had fought the Democrats so long, had so scourged them with his rhetorical cat-o-nine-tails, that they 'would have to love their enemies more than Christians ought to do' (as Schurz once said in another connection) in order to accept him.

Greeley had still another weakness. In 1867 when Schurz put forth his views on the undesirability of the Republican party taking up the temperance issue, he called special attention to the harm Greeley was doing by keeping that issue to the fore. German voters, he well knew, would become unmanageable as soon as the party should declare itself for prohibition in any of its forms. It was therefore certain that if Greeley were nominated all hope must be abandoned of attracting the Germans en masse, and the danger of their general defection would be very critical. Against this should be placed his splendid record of helpfulness to labor, his liberalism as respects the treatment of the South, his sound social democracy, and militant hatred of corruption.

As all the world knows, Greeley became the standard bearer. Perhaps his nomination was inevitable, but a combination effected between his managers and B.

Gratz Brown, who withdrew in Greeley's favor, no doubt helped to bring it about. If any man could have prevented that outcome and insured a more desirable ticket than Greeley and Brown (for the latter was rewarded with the vice-presidential nomination), it was Schurz, and he abdicated the function of president-maker. He may have had private reasons which justified the act, but we do not know what they were. He said after the convention that perhaps he might have directed the result but he scorned to become a president-maker, and besides, as a foreign born citizen, he thought it would have been unseemly in him to be too active in selecting the candidate. These reasons have all the earmarks of the 'poor' excuse which is supposed to be 'better than none.' Schurz was not too modest in 1860 to try to nominate Seward; and at that time he had been a citizen less than three years. It is more likely that his hands were tied through his relations with Brown, or with Trumbull of Illinois—another favorite son upon whom he looked with considerable favor. The nominations once made, the reprehensible trading between Brown and Greeley forces having been conducted without Greeley's knowledge, he ought under the circumstances to have made the best of it. But, as in 1859, it proved impossible for Schurz to control his disappointment promptly enough to gain credit for playing the game in the way which, under our system, good sportsmanship requires. His correspondence with Greeley revealed a querulousness which would hardly be relieved by Greeley's salty and, it must be said, just reply. Schurz based his complaint partly on the ground that the nomination left the revenue reformers in a ridiculous position and particularly that the 'trickery' employed by Greeley's aides made the convention and its

work unpalatable to reformers. Notwithstanding the
professed frankness of his statement, he said nothing
about temperance. But Greeley bluntly told him: 'Of
course most of the Germans dislike me, not so much that
I am a protectionist as that I am a Total Abstinence
man.'[89]

But once more, Schurz's sober second thought
brought him round to the view that it was better to support Greeley than Grant—and there was no alternative,
because the Democratic convention had adopted the
Liberals' ticket, incongruous as it was. So he stumped
the country again, not with the enthusiasm he threw
into the Lincoln canvass, not 'in the feeling of victory'
he had experienced in 1868, but with a grim sense of
duty and in the expectation of defeat. The task of holding the Germans in line turned out to be impossible, and
the rank and file of the Democrats showed so little enthusiasm for Greeley that the vote almost everywhere
fell far below the figures for 1868. The Republican
totals were also affected by the stay-at-home vote, but
not to the same extent. The election was a half-hearted
affair despite the work of the campaign speakers, newspapers, cartoonists, and rhymesters.

Notwithstanding the failure of the Liberal Republicans in the election of 1872, the organization did not go
for nought. Among other things, it rendered easier co-
operation between reforming elements from both great
parties in local and state elections. This facilitated a
movement throughout the Middle West and the West
looking to agrarian reform, the control of railroad rates
and the curbing of monopolies, principles already recognized by the Liberal Republicans in 1872. The Granger

[89] The correspondence is in Schurz, *Speeches &c.*, ii, 370-377, and *Reminiscences*, iii, 350-351.

legislation, so important in the domain of monopoly regulation, was one outcome of that movement which culminated in 1874 and 1875. So strong did the reforming group of intellectuals become in their appeal to the more independent voters, that the triumphant Republican party itself was now compelled to heed the warnings trumpeted in local defeats and in congressional losses. The radicals accordingly dealt more kindly with the reformers, tacitly readmitting them to the inner councils of the party. So far as Schurz was concerned, Grant's veto of an inflation bill in 1874 gave him a much friendlier feeling toward the president.

Schurz's experience of public life in the Senate was to him infinitely agreeable. A phrase he often used in correspondence was 'cheerful as a fish in water,' which would accurately describe his enjoyment of the legislative medium in which he swam so valiantly. As this story of his life reveals, he was specially equipped to deal with important, urgent public affairs, and he always worked best at close grips with his subject and with those who were directly coöperating or contending in connection therewith. The forum, in a word, was his natural instrument of achievement. We have seen how his method of public speaking, beginning with completely formal preparation, was gradually modified to the extemporary basis, and two years before he entered the Senate he had discovered a tremendously effective campaigning tone to use in platform speaking. In debating he had never been limited to the formal word, emotional turbulence incident to verbal encounters opening to him the treasures of the subconscious so that if he 'needed a thunderbolt he had but to reach out and take it as it went smoking by.'⁹⁰ That he was as effective if

---

⁹⁰ Said by Webster in commenting on his speech in reply to Hayne.

not as deft in word fencing as in the gentlemanly art
practised with swords, is attested by numerous senatorial situations in which he starred. For example, when
twitted by Matt Carpenter with disregarding the good
old West Point doctrine: 'My country right or wrong,'
he countered instantly with an amendment, adding to
the phrase: 'When right to be kept right, if wrong to
be set right.' Perhaps the best example, however, is his
reply to Conkling who accused him of strutting and
boasting. 'If I did anything yesterday which looked
like strutting,' Schurz retorted, 'then I must humbly
ask the senate's pardon; for certainly I did not want to
encroach upon the exclusive privilege of my honorable
and distinguished associate from New York. If I did
and said anything that looked like boasting, let me as-
sure you, Sir, it was not the remark [quoting Conk-
ling] "If I met a thousand of his kind I would not
quail," for I would not consider that a striking demonstration of courage.' The difficulty was Schurz enjoyed this intellectual swordsmanship for its own sake
and sometimes, playfully, he inflicted wounds which refused to heal, creating enemies where such a course
would not have been necessary. It is certain that Conkling never spoke to him after the sally just described.
On the whole, however, his parliamentary manner was as
admirable as his enjoyment of the practise was keen.

The question of sound money or greenbackism was
tending to divide Democrats from Republicans, and
Schurz found it easy to swing Germans into the movement for sound money. On that issue, in large part,
Rutherford B. Hayes was elected governor of Ohio in
1875, with the aid of the Germans proselyted by Schurz
and others. Meantime, Schurz's term as senator ex-
pired March fourth, 1875, and Missouri having become

safely Democratic, he did not become a candidate for reëlection. Compared with many senatorial careers he had been granted only a brief lease of power, yet measured by achievement, and the quality of the work performed, it stands out conspicuously among the great parliamentary careers of the age. Rhodes speaks justly when he says of Senator Schurz: 'He gave his country six years of almost ideal service.'

CHAPTER XVIII

CABINET MINISTER

CARL SCHURZ seemed fated to be the originator of new and important political changes. Though the post-senatorial period in his career represents, on the whole, a gradual ebbing of the spring tide of his influence, yet there appear in that period at least two resurgent movements which are significant enough to command special attention. These are his positive effort for the election of Hayes, followed by his service in the cabinet, and his negative effort for the defeat of Blaine. With the first of these we shall be concerned in the present chapter.

During the summer of 1875, the senatorial term having closed, Schurz spent several months with his family in Europe receiving many honors especially in Germany. He was recalled by some of his reforming friends, who on the sound money issue were exceedingly anxious to throw the German vote in Ohio to Hayes for governor. Schurz cut short his vacation, greatly to Margarethe's distress[91] and, delivering his thorough-going financial speech in Cincinnati, Cleveland, and elsewhere turned the tide in Hayes's favor so far as the Germans were concerned.

He now showed an intense eagerness to rescue the country from the sordidness into which the two Grant administrations had plunged it, and looked to the centennial of independence as an auspicious time for arousing reforming zeal. So he planned with his friends for

[91] This proved to be her last visit to beloved Hamburg, for Mrs. Schurz died March 15, 1876.

a great conference whose object was to regiment the independent political elements.

The result of the preliminary planning, in which he was aided by men like Charles Francis Adams, Samuel Bowles, William M. Grosvenor, Francis A. Walker, William Cullen Bryant, Theodore D. Woolsey, Horace White, Alexander H. Bullock, and Henry Cabot Lodge was a call, dated April sixth, 1876, for a conference to be held at New York on the fifteenth of May. This call was sent out to men in all parts of the country who were undoubted patriots, whether avowed reformers or not; personal correspondence was opened with a goodly number in addition, and well known reformers were urged to bring in men of weight whom they could influence; but it was understood that managing politicians should be ignored in the invitations.

When the meeting convened at the Fifth Avenue Hotel, Tuesday, May fifteenth, it was found that one hundred and seventy names were on the list of delegates to this purified 'Cincinnati Convention,' which some of the newspapers called *The Schurz Council* and others *The Reform Conference* and *The National Reform League*. Nearly all of these were present on the first day. The roll, read by Henry Cabot Lodge as secretary, included many of the most prominent publicists, professors, clergymen, lawyers, retired public officers, and aspiring young men who became famous later. Theodore Roosevelt and Lodge represent the last named class. William Cullen Bryant, Thomas Wentworth Higginson, Parke Godwin, Horace White, the Adamses, and Grosvenor, the first; Woolsey, Mark Hopkins, William G. Sumner, Julius H. Seelye, David A. Wells, W. H. Tyler, Professor Perry, John W. Hoyt, the second; Dr. Samuel Osgood, James Freeman

NEW YORK—THE GERMAN BANQUET AT DELMONICO'S IN HONOR
OF CARL SCHURZ, EVENING OF APRIL 28, 1875

Clarke, Leonard Bacon, J. Cummings, H. Blanchard, W. Adams, and R. Heber Newton, the third; Franklin MacVeagh, Edward Salomon, Edward L. Pierce, and John Jay, the fourth; ex-Governor Alexander Bullock, and ex-Lieutenant-Governor Müller and, in a sense, Schurz himself, the fifth. One is struck with the paucity of German names; still some important ones are on this list. In addition to ex-Governor Salomon of Wisconsin, who was now settled in New York as a lawyer, there were Schurz's old friends Dr. Tiedemann of Philadelphia and Dr. Jacobi of New York, his cousin Edmund Jüssen of Chicago, and August Thierne of Cleveland. In addition to these one can identify as Germans, Althof, Bissenger, Ellinger, Glaubensklee, Wallach, Schaack, Ottendorfer, Kaufmann, Klamroth, Kramer, Wendt, and Schlegel of New York, Baumann and Schmidt of Illinois, Brinkerhoff of Ohio, Esslinger of Indiana, Fred Horn of Wisconsin. There appear to be no Scandinavian names, but one Staistney suggests a Czechish origin.

The vast majority of the conference consisted of American intellectuals whose confidence Schurz had enjoyed from the days when, as a crusader for foreigners' rights, in 1859, he first invaded the East and spoke in Faneuil Hall, Boston. It is doubtful if any other man could have assembled such a gathering and directed it to the important end he set out to achieve. This was to declare the purpose of independant citizens to 'support no candidate who, however favorably judged by his nearest friends, is not publicly known to possess those qualities of mind and character which the stern task of genuine reform requires. . . .'

The account of the meeting as given in the newspapers reveals Schurz in control of the deliberations at all points. Some delegates were eager to name a candidate they would be glad to support. It was Schurz's judgment that no name should be brought out, thus leaving both the Republican and the Democratic conventions free to make their nomination in the assurance that the independents would have to be reckoned with and with the peril of their displeasure should the candidate named fail to come up to the requirements they had fixed for him. Schurz was chairman of the committee to prepare the address to the American people, which he wrote. On the sixteenth he read it before the assembly 'in a clear, well modulated voice, and was repeatedly interrupted during the reading by applause.'[92] It described the kind of candidate who would not be acceptable as well as the type who would meet with favor. Having received the conference's unanimous endorsement of the address[93] Schurz next procured the appointment of a permanent committee of which also he was made chairman. This move was designed to convince the political conventions that the independents would remain on guard during the canvass, and that if the party nominations should both prove unacceptable, a nomination by the National Reform League might be anticipated.

Schurz was disinclined to foster an independent nomination except in case of extreme necessity. In opening the business of the conference, he remarked that the independents 'didn't want to camp out all their lives, but they were not suffering from stress of weather enough to run to any party roof, however dilapidated.' He also admitted there was some truth in the charge that they were 'on the fence,' but justified this attitude

[92] Report in the New York *World* (daily), May 17, 1876.
[93] Printed in the *World* as above, also in the *Tribune*, May 17, and conveniently in Schurz, *Speeches &c.*, iii, 240-248.

as being prudent 'since there is too much mud on both sides to jump into.' He was determined to fight to the death against a nomination like that of James G. Blaine, but if the Republicans would put up a true blue reformer like R. B. Hayes he was decidedly prone to support him.

This the Cincinnati Convention did and, while Schurz made no premature proffer of aid, but first elicited from Hayes definite promises of definite reforms, especially in the civil service, he finally announced his adherence to Hayes and took a very active part in the campaign for his election. This time, however, the reform elements were split. The Democrats, by nominating Samuel J. Tilden who had cleared out the Tweed Ring in New York, could claim with some show of justice that they had fulfilled the independents' requirements specifically by giving the country a candidate with a reform record. Among Schurz's conference friends Charles Francis Adams, Parke Godwin, and many lesser lights came out for Tilden. His German friends likewise were divided, Körner of Illinois, his cousin Colonel Jüssen, Oswald Ottendorfer, editor of the New York *Staats-Zeitung* and many others among the leaders going in vigorously for the election of Tilden. Still, while it cannot be denied that Schurz was an independent with Republican leanings, he marshalled very strong reasons for his faith that Hayes was a better hope for reformers than Tilden and he fought for his views with much of the old fire and persistence.

When, after the agony of suspense due to the contested votes, Hayes was declared elected, it was understood that Schurz was certain to take an important place in the national councils. He had not met Mr. Hayes in 1875, despite the fact that it was probably his canvass among the Germans in Ohio that made Hayes governor and put him in line for the presidential nomination. After the Cincinnati Convention the two men corresponded in a way to become very well acquainted. Hayes asked Schurz to suggest paragraphs on civil service for the letter of acceptance, which he did, to the candidate's satisfaction. He added a paragraph on the currency question which also was accepted and, in substance, used in the letter, making it a personal platform for Hayes. This, Schurz believed, was the only thing that prevented the campaign from ending in a complete rout for the Republicans. By his pertinacity, which was not altogether relished by the candidate, he induced Hayes to oppose the campaign managers in their plan to assess the civil servants of the government for the benefit of the campaign treasury. This Schurz believed had a decisive influence on the German vote.

The debate over the ethics of the 1876 election has not yet closed, but just prior to March fourth, 1877, Hayes received notice that he had been officially declared to be president.[94] His inaugural address had been prepared so as to be ready in precisely such an emergency, and to it Schurz had contributed trenchant ideas especially with reference to pronouncements on civil service and resumption of specie payments. Hayes also consulted him on cabinet appointments, and he centered his reply on the problem of helping to find men who would be stanch supporters of the civil service reform principle. The result pleased him only in part, for he was not convinced that a man of John Sherman's political antecedents would prove a simon pure reformer when he became the head of the Treasury Department.

[94] 'Nicht erwählt nur eingezählt,' said the Illinois *Staats-Zeitung*. (Not elected, merely counted in.)

When his own case was brought up by Murat Halstead, who had discussed him with Hayes, Schurz gave out that he would be glad to enter the cabinet if the new president needed him to carry out his policies. His personal choice of departments would be either the State or the Treasury, though he felt good work might be done in the Interior Department also. The Post-Office Department was too purely a business concern to suit him. He had recommended Evarts for secretary of state and Bristow—who as Grant's reforming treasury head had been his choice for the Republican presidential nomination—for secretary of the treasury. Hayes ruled Bristow out because he proposed to include in his cabinet none of the presidential aspirants. That disposed, at a single stroke, of Morton, Conkling, and Blaine, as well as Bristow. Schurz contented himself with the Interior Department and took office under President Hayes.

One point in connection with this cabinet appointment must not be passed over. When Halstead wrote Schurz about his long talk with Hayes, he asked pointedly: 'Is there some danger that if you went into the cabinet you would be a disturbing element? How would you get along with Sherman if Evarts, Hawley, and Harlan were in?' Schurz had a reputation as a 'difficult' councillor; he had wearied Hayes with long insistent letters during the campaign and Halstead had 'misgivings' about the appointment being made at all. But doubts on that question were satisfied, and the friendly relations of the two men throughout the balance of their joint lives is the best proof that the president was not disappointed in Schurz.

But the Republican politicians were profoundly disturbed, greeting his selection with unmeasured scorn, for in their eyes Schurz bore the brand of Cain upon his brow. They could never forgive his heavy blow to Republican success involved in the organization of the Liberal movement of 1872, and they felt outraged by his Catonian insistence on civil service reform. Hayes's cabinet was the target of violent criticism on account of its inclusion of such a man and Schurz was destined to find rough going for his departmental measures in Congress, and particularly in the Senate, where Blaine was on the watch for chances to hamper and discredit him.

So far as the politicians' opposition to Schurz was based on the fear that he would actually carry out in the Interior Department, the 'crazy' notions about civil service reform which he had so long championed, it was not misplaced. For the new secretary's very first step looked to the preparation of examinations both for new appointees and for those who were candidates for promotion. He then advertised the plan and adhered to it unflinchingly. All applicants, no matter how politically strong their support might be, found themselves obliged to go through this testing process and to abide its results. Wherever graft was suspected to exist, as in the Indian Bureau, he changed important officials; in cases where too many clerks had formerly been employed, he discharged the least efficient, by these means toning up the department from every point of view.

Administration was not Schurz's strongest counter, but he enjoyed outlining policies calculated to improve it, and took pride in executing such policies. This being his first opportunity to practically influence the great cause of reform in civil service, he was bound to make his department the best concrete argument in favor of the ideas he had been advocating for so many years. Besides, if the value of these doctrines could be demonstrated in one department of the government, they would have all the more chance of being adopted, or at least respected, in other departments. Admittedly, Schurz made himself a model head and every branch of his widely ramifying department felt the revivifying effect of his earnest, wise and inspirational supervision. He shirked no labor required to keep the diverse bureaus functioning at a high level of efficiency.

His chief delight, however, was in developing and carrying out policies. The secretary had under his supervision the Indian Bureau, the General Land Office, the Bureau of Patents, the Bureau of Pensions, the Geological Survey, the Entomological Survey, the National Parks, the Public Buildings and Grounds in Washington, the Bureau of Education, the Census Bureau, the Territories, and Railroad Accounts. Not one of these was neglected or dealt with in a perfunctory manner. Students of American history have long been conscious that the census of 1880, taken under the acts of March third, 1879, and April twentieth, 1880, urged by Schurz though the actual superintendence of the work was in the competent hands of Dr. Francis A. Walker, marks a revolution in the statistical basis for the study of American life. The secretary took a very keen personal interest in putting through the great scheme of national stock taking, but he generously credited Walker with achieving the result.[95] He was equally interested in the improvements designed for the national capitol, the plans for the congressional library, the rebuilding of the Interior Department structure which had been partly destroyed by fire; the Hot Springs and Yellowstone Parks; the improvement of railroad accounting; the just and generous treatment of

[95] New York *Evening Post*, October 28, 1881.

ex-soldiers under the several pension acts; the progress
of scientific research; the control of the grasshopper
pest; surveys and triangulations in the Rocky Mountains; schemes for utilizing under regulated individual
development, the non-irrigable grass lands of the semi-
arid region.

But, notwithstanding the remarkable proof we
have of his earnest attention to all these interests, his
heart was clearly in the two subjects of forestry and
Indian affairs. The American people, in this period,
were only just beginning to slough off that feature of
pioneer psychology which looks upon forests as an obstacle to civilization, fit only to be slaughtered and burned. They as yet had no general appreciation of the in-
direct utilities of forests for conserving soils, especially
in hilly or mountainous lands, and in governing stream
flowage. Besides, in popular opinion our timber resources were still, as they always had been, 'inexhaustible.' Even Senator Blaine declared in debate, discussing
the timber supply of Montana Territory, that the child
was not born whose great-great-grandchild would see
firewood in that region worth twenty-five cents a cord
stumpage.[96] Schurz, by reason of his knowledge of world
conditions, realized the tragic shortsightedness of such
views and made it one of his special duties, as the officer
charged with the oversight of the forests on public
lands, to educate Congress and the people upon that
subject.

The devastation of the forests, through the most
wasteful method of lumbering, through fires, and
through the deliberate taking by private operators of
government timber, was progressing in his day at an

[96] *Congressional Record,* 45th Congress, 2nd Sess. vii, pt. ii, 1721 ff.

unheard of rate. This timber stealing he attacked at once under an old law and, while it could not be wholly stopped, he succeeded both in limiting the evil and in covering into the treasury some half million dollars obtained through judgments against timber thieves. He pressed in every one of his reports for more adequate laws on all phases of the forestry business, for the reservation of timber lands from homestead or preëmption entry, for the sale of timber from United States land under such restrictions that settlers and miners could obtain wood honestly, that the lumbering operations should be so regulated as to leave a young crop for a future harvest for the protection of the soil and of streams, and for severe laws against the setting of fires on public lands. He recommended, in his first report, and repeated the recommendation each year thereafter, that the president be empowered to appoint a commission to study the 'laws and practices adopted in other countries for the preservation and cultivation of forests,' and to report suitable plans to Congress. 'I am so deeply impressed with the importance of this subject,' he said, 'that I venture to predict, the Congress making efficient laws for the preservation of our forests will be ranked by future generations in this country among its greatest benefactors!' Unfortunately, these remarks, which bore good fruit educationally, were directed to Congresses in which the timber barons and 'practical' lumbermen or their apologists were too strongly entrenched. Schurz was derided as an impractical idealist; as a Prussian who did not realize the vastness of this great country; as an oppressor of the poor pioneer or miner. Instead of passing laws to correct the inadequacy of existing laws, Congress under Blaine's leadership, passed an amendment which practically legalized the taking of timber from unsurveyed government lands in certain states and territories except for export. Schurz described this legislation as more in the interest of timber thieves than of the public welfare. Another quarter century of fearful destruction would be permitted to pass before Schurz's wise plans for forest conservation could be enacted into law.

With respect to Indian affairs, reforms could be initiated more easily. The Indian service when he came into office was in a critical state due to the Sioux and Nez Percé wars and other disturbances which had given rise to a demand for placing the Indian Bureau under the War Department. Being convinced that the problems to be solved were mainly those of peace, not of war, Schurz opposed this move effectively. The study of the Indian question brought him to the view that there were too many semi-independent agencies and too many reservations; that the Indians ought to be more compactly settled, say within the Indian Territory; supervised more responsibly; industrialized as fast as possible through the encouragement of farming and cattle raising; the young educated at least in an elementary way, and taught the English language; civilized occupations like teaming, police service, and mechanical employments introduced among them; and boarding schools established for industrial training of both boys and girls. Above all, and as a fundamental condition of success, absolute faith should be kept with the tribes, their common lands defended against white incursions, and given to the families in severalty, with restriction of alienation for a certain period. Lastly would come, as the final step, the breaking up of the tribal relationship and adoption of American citizenship.

Schurz soon gave up the idea of concentrating the Indians, for he had bitter proof in the removal of the Poncas from the Missouri to the Arkansas that Indians are attached to their home land and can be transplanted only at a frightful social and moral cost. The other features of his general policy were carried out as rapidly as possible. The time was auspicious for developing agriculture and grazing among the tribes, since the great herds of buffalo were being decimated so that they could no longer rely on hunting for their livelihood. They therefore welcomed the government's offer of cattle and farming tools, as well as instructors to show them how to use them. The secretary authorized the employment of Indian wagoners to draw government supplies to the reservations. This was liked by the young men, it proved advantageous to the government, and was extended very rapidly with the best results. The same is true of the native police, to keep order on the reservations; of Indian blacksmiths to shoe horses, sharpen plows, and iron wagons; carpenters to build the houses for which the government contracted; harness makers to supply gear for the dray teams; tailors and shoemakers to provide white man's garb for increasing numbers who wanted to live like civilized beings.

This naturalizing among the Indians of the common trades and occupations of civilization had a very important relation to the educational policy for which Schurz is responsible, and which more than any other one thing yields the hope that we shall ultimately solve the Indian problem on the Christian principle of regeneration instead of the frontiersman's principle of extermination. He saw that Indian day schools were relatively ineffective because they left the Indian children without the necessary contact with civilized life. He made the ex-

periment of placing a group of Indian children in
Hampton Institute under the direction of General
Armstrong. This succeeded marvelously. He then
acquired, by transfer from the War Department, the
barracks at Carlisle, Pennsylvania, installed Captain
Pratt as head, with Miss F. A. Mather to assist, and
opened the Indian industrial school at that place.
About the same time a similar but smaller school was
opened at Forest Grove, Oregon, later removed to
Chemawa, near Salem. The graduates of these schools,
when they returned to their tribes, would find openings
for practising the arts of civilized life and need not re-
vert in their habits to the life of barbarism from which
they had been rescued. The plan was soon so popular
among the Indians, committees of whom came east to
visit Hampton and Carlisle, that other schools were demanded and Schurz was convinced of the economy to
the government of spending money freely on these
institutions. He believed that at least ten more industrial boarding schools ought to be established without
delay and facetiously declared that, as against the old
method of dealing with Indians, the government could
afford to bring all the tribesmen to New York and
'board' them at the Fifth Avenue Hotel.[97]

Schurz did not undertake to solve the Indian problem from his study and his office. In August, 1879,
accompanied by a group of seven or eight gentlemen,
including the president's son, Webb C. Hayes, a member of the German legation, the Washington representative of the New York *Times,* and his own private
secretary he made a tour of inspection among the
western Indian agencies which kept him out about six
weeks and covered a vast area of country. They went

[97] New York *Evening Post,* Editorial, June 21, 1881.

first to Yankton, Dakota Territory, thence to the Santee and Rosebud agencies, to Red Cloud, Camp Robinson, Laramie, Rock Creek, Denver, then to Wichita, Kansas. From Wichita they took private conveyances through Indian Territory. After visiting an Indian agricultural fair on September thirtieth, they returned to Washington.[98]

On this tour the secretary not only learned much about Indian affairs and Indian customs from direct observation, but he made such an impression of honest sympathy and concern for the redmen's welfare that he gained their unlimited confidence. He might be criticised by reformers among his own people, as he was—very severely—for his refusal to let the Poncas return to their original reservation, and for other features of Indian policy before these were fully understood.[99] But the Indians generally believed in his determination to see that justice was done them by the government. A striking illustration, both of this point and of the increasing willingness of the Indians to submit to the white man's plan of life, is the following: Some of the Brulé Sioux murdered a white man in Nebraska and also stole some horses. Their Indian police arrested six of their young men and handed them over to be tried in the white man's court. No effort whatever was made to shield the accused, but Schurz received from Chief Spotted Tail a letter, enclosing a check for $332.80, with the request that he employ a lawyer to insure that

[98] *Daily Press* and *Dakotian* (Yankton), August 25, 1879.
[99] A defense of his policy is in the letter to John D. Long, December 9, 1880, *Speeches &c.*, iv, 50-78, and his open letter to Senator Henry L. Dawes dated September 7, 1881. The latter is a crushing answer to his critics, *Speeches*, iv., 91-113. The problem of the Poncas, however, refused to settle itself. Many friends of the administration opposed Schurz on that question and in his last annual message the president assumed personal responsibility for the policy involved as the best way to quiet criticism.

none of the men be punished unjustly. Spotted Tail
wanted them to have the chance of a white man, if
innocent. It had been possible for the chief to collect
the money from the members of his tribe, such was their
faith in the secretary's desire to be helpful to the
Indians.

The best general comment on the trials Schurz had
as head of the Interior Department is in his letter to
Garfield of January second, 1881, in which he urged the
appointment of Francis A. Walker as secretary to succeed himself and continue his policy. He would never
forget the difficulties encountered, or the mistakes
made, before getting things under control. 'It is a constant fight,' he said, 'with the sharks that surround the
Indian Bureau, the General Land Office, the Pension
Office and the Patent Office. . . .' There was a maze
of perplexing problems, 'especially in the Indian Service.' After the Massachusetts philanthropists had got
through passing resolutions of censure, and their
spokesman in the Senate had been silenced by the secretary's letter laying bare the essential falsity of his
charges, James Freeman Clarke wrote: 'I believe you
to have been the best friend the Indians have had.' This
forecasts the sober judgment of history. It has been apt-
ly said of Schurz that he 'brought justice and the Indian
together,' though he himself admitted that the removal of the Poncas was a mistake.

Of course, the more exciting feature of his activities
as secretary was his participation at the president's
council table. Here he had the happiness to see many of
his cherished ideas about the treatment of the South decided according to his views. He had the ear of the
president at all times and was influential in promoting
important minor reforms, such as the abolishing of

party assessments upon civil servants, and the requirement that these servants abstain from unseemly partisan activity. He got on so well with Hayes that the two men remained ever after warm personal friends, the best proof that Schurz could, if he would, moderate the zeal of his reforming disposition to the requirements of coöperative statesmanship. Schurz conceived a strong attachment for President Hayes whose steady, loyal support and wise counsel were no insignificant factors in his success as secretary.

CHAPTER XIX

POLITICAL FREE LANCE

SCHURZ, as ex-secretary of the interior would have been in a favorable situation from which to influence Republican policies. He might, indeed, have hoped to play an important rôle as cabinet minister again, although, unless fate should bring to his hand the coveted department of State, of which there was small chance, he would hardly have been tempted by the offer of a secretaryship even had he felt financially able to hold it. This he did not nor would he permit his friends to endow him, as they at one time wished to do.[100] He had but just passed his fifty-second birthday, was in perfect health, and equipped for rendering more distinguished service than at any earlier period in his life. His acquaintance with public men and with conditions throughout the country was all but unique. It is true, the Hayes-Tilden contest had seriously disrupted all reform aggregations, the German among the rest, so that Schurz would not in future be looked up to by his fellow countrymen as their political high priest. Nevertheless, his influence among them, revivified by their prideful recognition of his great service as the first German born secretary, was sure to be potent in any case and might, in certain contingencies, become determinative once more.

Schurz, in 1880, accepted Garfield with a good measure of satisfaction. The two men were personally congenial, always addressing one another in a familiar

[100] See letter to Gustav Schwab, March 21, 1884. *Speeches &c.*, iv, 197-198.

way, and writing confidentially. The Ohio statesman's
record as a liberal and reformer in Congress had been
thoroughly respectable. Garfield as president would only need to let himself be guided by 'Garfield the member
of Congress,' Schurz told him, with characteristic
frankness, in order to make his administration an assured success. This language, to be sure, implies the suspicion that he might not permit himself to be thus
guided. Schurz aided in the canvass, and at the successful candidate's request, wrote him his views about cabinet appointments. He protested against Garfield's over
emphasis on geography, insisting that he would be held
responsible for the men he named wherever they hailed
from, and unless all possessed distinction, character and
ability the president would be sure to invite trouble for
himself. He said nothing about Blaine, perhaps deem-
ing it useless to do so; but insisted on the extreme
necessity of having trustworthy men in the Interior,
Post-Office, Treasury, and Justice departments; and
reiterated his views on the significance to the Republican
party of making a good record in civil service reform.
It was his belief that Sherman should continue at the
head of the Treasury, his opinion of that gentleman having risen decidedly in the course of four years' close
association with him. He warned against taking a Wall
Street banker for secretary of the treasury and, as we
have seen, hoped Garfield might make Francis A.
Walker chief of the Interior Department in order to insure the continuity of his own line of policy therein.

As editor of the New York *Evening Post,* a position he assumed very soon after leaving the cabinet,
Schurz dealt kindly with Garfield, and also had many
good words to say for the specific acts of his advisers,
not excepting Blaine. But he lamented the president's

evident disposition to seek party harmony at the expense of the civil service reform policy. When the bullet of Guiteau prostrated the chieftain and evoked that outpouring of popular affection which constitutes one of the striking social phenomena of the past generation, Schurz felt that Garfield, after his hoped for recovery, would be sure to experience a renewed consecration to his work and continue it on a plane representing his true ideals. Realizing then as never before his popular strength, he would go his own way in entire disregard of the factions which had fettered him, and to gain whose support he had allowed himself to be deflected somewhat from his natural course. After the president's death, Chester A. Arthur, till then regarded as an orthodox New York spoilsman, solemnly promised to administer the affairs of the government in the spirit of his predecessor. Schurz was glad to infer that Arthur had been so chastened by the nation's grief for the lost leader that he might be inspired to carry on in the way Garfield would have done had he survived. He approved the cabinet appointments (though the idea of mild, credulous Timothy O. Howe for post-master general, did not promise much in the way of Star Route prosecutions), commended Arthur's messages with reservations, and in general treated the administration with a dignified, discriminative sympathy. But he never missed an opportunity to drive home the point that further improvements in the civil service were needed and to show in a helpful spirit how these could be brought about.

Civil service reform sentiment was growing apace, all over the country. In eastern cities and also in several eastern states associations were being formed to bring about administrative improvement from that specific point of view, the movement everywhere emphasizing the superiority of principles to partisanship, thereby segregating the independents in ever growing numbers. The shot, fired by a disappointed office seeker, which killed Garfield, woke the great heart of the people to the reality of the evil about which Schurz and others had been preaching. Now, at last, civil service reform came to be demanded in deadly earnest, so that Congress and the executive could not avoid it if they would. Thousands upon thousands of the more intelligent citizens quietly resolved to set the issue of good government where it obviously belongs, above partisanship. And now, as a reaction to the new popular determination, politicians suddenly abandoned their sneering attitude toward reform and reformers. Brilliant aphorisms, like Conkling's subtitution of the word *reform* for Johnson's *patriotism* as the 'last refuge of the scoundrel,' suddenly faded out from the literature of political humor.

Schurz watched the growth of independence, fruit of the popular conviction that good government was more to be desired than party government, with the keenest interest and from his editorial vantage point promoted the progress of organization in the several states. In New York, Pennsylvania, Massachusetts, and other commonwealths the leaven was working in a manner to promise practical results. He finally announced that, on the national plane also, a 'genuine and thorough reform of the civil service will be attainable only by an organization created for that purpose.' The further remark: 'It will come in time,' was hardly prophecy, for largely through his urgency a National Civil Service Reform League had already come into being which was destined under the leadership of men like George William Curtis and himself to leave its impress upon national affairs.[101]

Only one matter, related to the purity of government, was by Schurz considered more significant than a sound policy covering administrative appointments, namely, to prevent the election to high office of any man known or widely believed to be corrupt. The tendencies of the period being toward a morality which, to say the least, was shorn of all excess austerity, the placing of a doubtful character in conspicuous public office would invite to rapid and dangerous moral decay. Schurz had in mind one such man whom he regarded as more dangerous than any other because he was possessed of rare personal gifts, brilliant talents, a genius for popularity, and an ambition which compassed the highest office in the gift of the people. He had been watching James Gillespie Blaine for a long time, and while acknowledging his unusual abilities, thoroughly distrusted him.

When Blaine made his famous tenth of January onslaught on the ex-Confederates in 1876, as a bid for northern support for the presidential nomination, he had shown a willingness deliberately to slap the independents in the face; for one of their basic principles was to heal the differences between South and North instead of opening up old wounds by irritating talk. Schurz believed the speech would kill Blaine off as a candidate. In this he was mistaken, for northern Republicans of the 'thick and thin' stripe were elated by it as Blaine, a very clever psychologist, expected they would be. But Schurz was right in his prediction that the gentleman from Maine would 'die of too much

[101] The reports of the League begin in 1883, the same year in which the general civil service law was secured.

smartness at last,'[102] for it was the Mulligan letters' investigation, probably, that prevented his success. But it was well understood that the independents' Fifth Avenue pronouncement against unworthy candidates tacitly placed Blaine in the forefront of those who were wholly unacceptable, which also influenced the convention. We are told, on good authority,[103] that Blaine paid ardent court to Schurz in order at least to gain his promise not to oppose him. But he found in that unbending idealist one public man who was proof against his much belauded personal magnetism. No doubt Schurz sometimes misread men, despite his phenomenal power of character analysis, but he did not fail to oppose those he regarded as unfit, whatever their party status might be.

The convention of 1876 was weathered safely. The election of Hayes made way for administrative reform. Now, as secretary of the interior, Schurz was made to feel the sting of Blaine's 'smartness' on more than one occasion. But the brilliant Maineite was both too wary a politician and too magnanimous a man to adopt the feudists' attitude toward his opponent. He was careful to make no move until he could present at least a plausible case, as in the matter of the secretary's levying a tax of one dollar per cord on firewood taken from government lands by certain persons at Helena, Montana. His opposition in this instance can be shown to have been purely demagogic, for the imposition was not upon the individual settler to prevent him from obtaining needed fuel from reserved lands, but only affected speculators who were trying to make fortunes out of the public's timber. And the tax actually 'broke the com-

---

[102] Letter to Samuel Bowles, January 16, 1867. *Speeches &c.*, iii, 219.
[103] Bancroft and Dunning, *Reminiscences*, iii, 366.

bination,' permitting small dealers to enter the wood
business, with the result that the consumer obtained
cheaper fuel, instead of dearer.[104]   But it gave the
'plumed knight' his chance to pose as protector of the
oppressed frontier settler, 'in latitude 47°, 5000 feet
above sea level,' who at the opening of the terrible winter season was told by this heartless government official,
who had come from the small European state of Prussia, not to burn a stick of wood till the government had
received its tribute.[105]

Two years later, when in working out a delicate
piece of diplomacy in the hope of averting a war between the people of Colorado and the Ute Indians,
Schurz caused a treaty to be brought before the Senate
in the form of a bill, Blaine supported the measure. In
doing so he made a most conciliatory speech, saying:
'It has not been my fortune in Congress during the past
three years, always to agree with the Secretary of the
Interior. Sometimes I have taken occasion on this floor
to disagree with him, and I have risen the more readily
to do an act of justice to that officer by saying that in
this case I shall vote for the measure which is the recommendation of his department.' He also said the treaty
was calculated to avert a war and that the most expen-
sive way to settle Indian difficulties was by the use of the
military power.

Schurz doubtless gave due weight to the fact that
this olive branch was extended just prior to the Chicago
Convention,[106] but neither that circumstance, nor Gail

---

[104] Commissioner of General Land Office. Report for 1878, 124.

[105] Blaine was supported in his attack by senators from California,
Mississippi, and Florida, states where timber stealing had become notori-
ous. The most comprehensive speech in defense of the department was by
Stanley Matthews of Ohio. He was supported by Hoar and Dawes of
Massachusetts. *Congressional Record*, March 19, 20, 21, 1878.

[106] April 9, 1880.

Hamilton's fusillades against him in the New York *Tribune,* which he believed to have been inspired by Blaine, could swerve him from his policy in regard to men such as he firmly believed the nimble-witted senator from the Pine Tree state to be. He did not hesitate, on favorable occasions, to announce his settled determination to keep Blaine out of the presidency if he could. A broad hint was conveyed in a very short editorial written in a strain of seeming jocularity which masked a purpose grim as death.[107] 'Mr. Blaine,' he said, 'was never more mistaken in his life than when he stated "personal discussion of candidates, in the presence of really important issues, sinks below the notice of intelligent voters." We have no doubt,' he continued, 'that Mr. Blaine, as a matter of personal convenience, would like the intelligent voter to abstain from examining the character and record and general fitness of candidates. But never within the memory of this generation has the intelligent voter seen more reason and been more inclined to scrutinize the personality of the candidate closely. And the more intelligent the voter is the more keenly and searchingly will he look at his man. If Mr. Blaine wants to satisfy himself of this, let him, for instance, run for the presidency himself.'[108]

When Blaine, a little later, in his public speeches, professed a belated sympathy with civil service reform, the *Evening Post,* in Schurz's absence, and without his knowledge, published an editorial probably written by Godkin (to judge from its tone) in which Blaine was charged with having, as secretary of state, 'wallowed' in spoils like a 'rhinoceros in an African pool.' The article deserved notice, particularly if its professed facts

---

[107] For Blaine's comment on this see the Chicago *Tribune,* interview, September 19, 1882.

[108] New York *Evening Post,* August 8, 1882.

were wrong, and Blaine in his Chicago *Tribune* interview already alluded to certainly let himself go in denouncing Schurz as a pretender, who in four years as secretary of the interior had done far less for civil service reform than he, Blaine, had done for that cause in ten months as secretary of state. In fact, he charged that Schurz, after a great 'flourish of trumpets' abandoned the reform principle and made his appointments on the old spoils basis.

While one cannot but sympathize with a public man who is unjustly attacked by a prominent newspaper, the ascription of the article to Schurz disregarded a very well-known characteristic of his editorials, which were never of the 'swashbuckling' variety and adhered with unusual scrupulosity to the facts of the case. But as Schurz pointed out in a letter to the *Tribune* which reached the readers of that paper one week later,[109] there was another difference between Blaine and himself that went beyond the question of civil service reform. 'To make a clean breast of it' he says, 'it consists of my entertaining, as Mr. Blaine knows, quite seriously the opinion that the author of the Mulligan letters will, in spite of "booms" and "plumes" and reform professions, never get votes enough to be elected president of the United States. And, as I not only entertain this opinion, but have sometimes expressed it, Mr. Blaine cannot be expected altogether to restrain his feelings.'

The incidents just narrated will make it clear that, between the man who was the popular idol among the rank and file of regular Republicans, and Carl Schurz the most militant among the leaders of the great and growing body of independents, there would have to be

[109] Chicago *Tribune*, September 26, 1882. Also in *Speeches &c.*, iv, 155-156.

war to the knife before Blaine's ambition to be president of the United States could be realized. When the
proper time came, the independents proclaimed their
opposition formally, but the Republican convention this
time, influenced by an exceedingly doubtful view of the
availability argument, gave the nomination to Blaine.
So the battle was on.

Schurz's first move was to try and secure an understanding between the Cleveland and Bayard forces in
the Democratic party which might insure the nomination of one or the other of these men. With either one
of the two as leader of the hosts opposing Republicanism he could fight with cheerful ardor for the defeat of
Blaine, but he had made up his mind to do that whoever
might be the Democratic nominee; for he was sure no
one would be named whose election could possibly be as
undesirable as that of the Republican candidate. The
reason for that seemingly extreme view Schurz explained with apparent calmness to several correspondents, although there is evidence that the Blaine nomination really excited him to an unusual pitch. He said that
the Republican party had been known as the party of
'moral ideas' and rightly so. As all the world knew, the
national honor and good faith had always been safe in
its hands. But the party's involvement in the ethical
question presented by the nomination was clear. For,
so far from discountenancing the demoralization and
rottenness which since the war had become so ubiquitous,
not only in public and private life but also in politics
and business, this 'party of moral ideas' was the first
to succumb. How? By declaring worthy of the highest
honors in the people's gift 'a man who by his public
record, by his own published correspondence, stands
convicted of trading upon his high official position and

power for his own pecuniary advantages. It says to the youth of the country that such things may be done with public approval, and that the men who do it may become presidents of the United States if they are only "smart" enough to strike the popular fancy.' This action, if successful, would, he believed, result in an orgy of corruption among all classes of the people. The party responsible for it was a different aggregation from the Republican party he had been proud to aid for so many years, and in his best judgment he could now serve both the party and the country best by helping to make it plain to everybody that 'a man with such a record can be nominated but cannot be elected.'[110]

On the fifth of August, 1884, at Brooklyn, Schurz made one of the greatest speeches of his political career. It reminds one in some respects of the Douglas speech of twenty-four years earlier, but there are some striking differences in style between the two utterances. To begin with, the analysis of Douglas was political for the most part, that of Blaine personal. The speaker's attitude in the one case suggested the victorious champion rejoicing in his superior strength and almost disposed to gloat over his worsted antagonist. In the last case the tone is that of a man deeply moved by moral considerations to take an attitude which yields him not pleasure but pain. He has a duty to perform, however, and this he will not shirk. The reasoning is that of a skillful lawyer presenting evidence to a jury. Mr. Blaine, when after he had wrested the letters from Mulligan, read them to the House of Representatives, had exhibited not only 'brilliant audacity in handling the truth,' as Hoar said, but according to Schurz, had so intermixed

---

[110] I have summarized the statement Schurz gave in a letter to W. M. Pittman. He said essentially the same things to Henry Cabot Lodge, J. W. Hoag, and John B. Henderson.

and confused the statements from various letters of different dates as to confound the House in its not very incisive effort to get at the truth.

It is not necessary to repeat the substance of the argument. By bringing the letters into their natural relationship several points at once stood self-revealed. One is that Blaine, as speaker of the House of Representatives, was in close business relations with builders of a railway the material basis of which was a land grant from the state of Arkansas to the railway company, which grant originally was made by Congress to the state of Arkansas for that purpose; that is, Congress was the actual grantor, the state only an intermediary. Second, the speaker received shares of stock in this company from one of the partners, and asked for a share from the other partner. Third, he expressed the opinion that he could be 'useful' in the business, and explained how, on one occasion, he had actually, by a fortunate bit of advice to a member of the House, saved the government's grant from lapsing, thus saving the road itself.

Schurz contented himself, in the Brooklyn speech, with discussing the ethics of the case on the basis of the correspondence as Mr. Blaine himself had given it to the public. But when Republican speakers, like Senator Hoar, challenged some of his interpretations, he went further and produced a contract signed by Warren Fisher and showing that Mr. Blaine was to receive, as commission for handling one lot of bonds of the face value of $130,000, another $130,000 in seven per cent land bonds and $32,500 of first mortgage bonds, all without expense to himself. Hoar argued that Blaine's act had not been 'condoned,' but that, through his later election to the Senate from the state of Maine, through his appointment as secretary of state, and his nomination as president, he had been 'triumphantly acquitted.'

That was a slip which gave Schurz the tactical opportunity he prized. Did those things, he asked, in any way alter the facts of the case? Did Mr. Blaine not 'write the Mulligan letters?' Did he not make false statements before the House? Did he not protest against any meddling with his 'private affairs?' Nominations and elections showed only that 'some people' were disposed for party reasons to overlook his record. They did not absolve other people from taking that record into account when engaged in the high duty of choosing a president. How about other cases of similar character? Schurz is informed that Hoar has long held a quite unfavorable opinion of General Butler. That gentleman, in 1882, had been nominated and later elected governor of Massachusetts, and at this very moment he is a candidate for the presidency on the greenback ticket. 'Did that change in any way the facts constituting his record? Did it change your opinion of those facts? Were that election and these nominations in your opinion a "triumphant acquittal?" '

The Brooklyn speech and the reply to Hoar were sent out by the independent organization as campaign documents in both English and German to an extent that insured their reaching voters everywhere. But Schurz campaigned that year, not only in New York, but in most of the states of the East and Middle West. He is said to have made twenty-two speeches in Ohio. He delivered four or five in Wisconsin and did not overlook the states of Indiana and Illinois. But he was especially concerned about New York, believing that success there meant success in the nation. From the first week in August till election day he was very actively engaged in the canvass and all of his work was done without compensation, he paying his own expenses. It was the offering Schurz laid upon the altar of good citizenship.

The excitement at Milwaukee, when he spoke there on the evening of September sixth, was intense. Report says that six thousand German auditors sat before him in Schlitz's Park. The night was intensely hot; everybody suffered, but though cooling drinks could have been had a few yards away, no one left the audience room in the course of his two hours' address. When heckling by German 'regulars' began, the audience cried them down. Witnesses of that evening's work by Schurz describe it as one of the great events of Wisconsin political history.

The result of the election in Wisconsin was to reduce the Republican majority from nearly thirty thousand for Garfield in 1880 to less than fifteen thousand for Blaine. Of this reduction, Milwaukee County, strongly German, accounted for three thousand (notwithstanding Blaine's appearance there after Schurz's), Manitowoc, one thousand, and other German districts something like the same proportion. On the other hand, the 'rock ribbed' Yankee counties gave Blaine slight increases over the Garfield figures. It appears, therefore, that the Germans were not yet so stanchly partisan as to be proof against the kind of propaganda with which Schurz belabored them. And if that were true in Wisconsin, it was equally true in Indiana, which was lost to the Republicans, and in New York whose controllingly numerous electoral vote also went to Cleveland by a very narrow margin.

The outcome, of course, was conditioned by a number of influences. *Harper's Weekly,* with George William Curtis as editor and Thomas Nast as cartoonist, performed yeoman's service for the independent Democratic cause. Its editorials were widely copied and its cartoons, 'Fort Boodle,' 'The Plumed Knight in a Clean Shirt,' and so forth, became familiar everywhere. Religious periodicals like the *Independent* and the Boston *Christian Register* came over to the anti-Blaine side, many clergymen, as may be supposed doing the same. The intellectuals were divided, but a considerable number of those who were nominally Republicans were found opposing Blaine. Others supported him, but without genuine enthusiasm. This was true of Roosevelt, one of the Fifth Avenue conferees of 1876 and an outspoken opponent of Blaine's nomination. He went to his Dakota ranch immediately after the Chicago Convention where, as a member of the New York delegation he voted under Curtis's chairmanship for Edmunds. At Mandan he was quoted as advising young men of the country to 'assume a spirit of independence in politics. He would rather be forced to the shades of private life with a short but honorable career than be given a life tenure of political prominence as the slave of a party or its masters.' Two weeks later he wrote, over his own signature: 'It is impossible for me to say that I consider Blaine and Logan fit nominees, or proper persons to fill the office of president and vice-president—and unless the democratic nominees are hopelessly bad I should not think it probable that I would take any part whatever in the campaign—indeed, I may be in Dakota on election day.' Nevertheless, he came back, stumped actively for Blaine, and denounced the 'Mugwumps' almost as picturesquely as did Whitelaw Reid in the New York *Tribune*.[111] Much was made of

[111] See Malin, James C., *Roosevelt and the Elections of 1884 and 1888*, Miss. Valley Hist. Review, xiv, 25-38.

Burchard's 'rum, romanism, and rebellion' speech as an explanation of Blaine's defeat through the loss of New York, but its effect was uncertain.

Whatever the causes, the margin was exceedingly narrow and this emphasizes all the more the significance of Schurz's complete dedication of his powers to the defeat of the Republican candidate. For without him it could not have been brought about, and James G. Blaine would have been the twenty-second president of the United States. Some contemplate this circumstance with intense chagrin, and with indignation against the wrecker of Republican hopes in 1884; others with deep thankfulness that the country was spared, through his exertions, a trial such as it had never yet undergone, and which might possibly have resulted in some such moral debauch as Schurz feared.

CHAPTER XX

AUTHOR AND PUBLICIST

CARL SCHURZ'S youthful ambition to become known as a writer of books had a tardy but substantial fulfillment following a train of disheartening episodes. Among the latter it is not necessary to consider his novel, discarded because ripening taste was revolted by its immaturities; or the half-finished play, abandoned with such cheerful alacrity in February, 1848, at the first blast of the revolutionary trumpet.

The book on French history from 1789 to 1851, written during the first American period, experimentally devoted to literature, failed to find a publisher and it would be interesting to know the reason. On this point the author gives us no hint. In the absence of the manuscript itself we lack the basis for inference, so we are reduced to the necessity of guessing. The narrative may have been too much submerged under generalizations to suit a reading public educated to appreciate Ranke and Niebuhr, Arndt, and Dahlmann; or possibly the book was discredited in advance by its attempt to cover events down to the minute. Its design suggests a thesis in political science rather than history.

After Schurz had spent some years in the field of political propaganda, speeches accumulated on his hands and some of these he believed might appeal to the reading public as political-historical literature even after the particular occasion for them had passed away. Correspondence on the subject with publishers at first brought discouragement, some of them judging that the people, during the progress of the Civil War, would

be in no mood to read such books. Finally, the Lippin-
cotts agreed to bring out his volume, containing twelve
speeches, which accordingly was issued early in 1865.
But the book failed to gain the attention of the public
in a way to make it a success.

A point of some interest is Schurz's mode of editing these manuscripts for the printer. Instead of leaving them in their original form, as he had prepared
them for delivery, he dramatized the delivery itself by
naming place and date and by inserting all interrup-
tions, after the manner of congressional reporting.
Whether or not he succeeded in exhibiting these accurately cannot now be known. The reader is apt to suspect
that his narrative is punctuated with 'cheers,' 'applause,'
'great applause,' 'loud and prolonged applause,' 'dis-
turbance,' and 'tumultuous applause' pretty much according to the taste and fancy of the author though in
some cases he doubtless followed newspaper reports.
This plan of editing seems a bit grotesque in the case of
speeches which were not reported but printed from the
author's finished texts. It is a testimony to Shurz's
occasional over emphasis on the dramatic, his actor's
craving to occupy the center of the stage and to decorate
himself with the floral tributes thrown at him from bal-
cony and pit. But, in extenuation, it must be remembered that the author was then but thirty-five, and that
his forensic triumphs had really been great enough to
affect an older, less enthusiastic head than his. It is
probable that the speeches would have been more popular had they been printed as essays, their high literary
quality thereby gaining more appreciative attention.

The correspondence of 1853 reveals that Schurz had
a plan for a book on America. This project was never
carried out, although his later lectures on *American*

Civilization and on *America in Public Opinion Abroad*
may have embodied material originally designed for
that book as his lecture on *Democracy and Despotism
in France* made use of data assembled for the book on
recent French history. His reading on the political
history of this country was wide and, for a busy legisla-
tor, administrator, and journalist, exceedingly thorough.
One of Schurz's outstanding characteristics as senator was the intensity with which he prepared for
the treatment of any important question. He, in fact,
brought to his legislative task the ideals of the research
scholar. For example, when the subject of the sale of
arms by government officials to France during the Franco-Prussian War arose, he and Sumner both took
ground opposing the practice. Sumner was technically
in charge of the debate on that side. But his mind 'would
never master the details of a matter of this kind if they
were in any degree complicated.'[112] Sumner recognized
this weakness and, his own speech failing to do the subject justice, the breach was held by Schurz who, in three
notable addresses, treated the complex topic with a
thoroughness that left nothing to be desired.[113]

That Schurz in his day was almost uniquely equipped for writing a political history of America, particularly as covering the more recent period, became
abundantly clear to his associates in the Senate, to President Hayes, and others; so that aside from his own
inclination to take the matter up he had the urgent advice of friends to stimulate him. The idea intrigued him
powerfully, but he never gained what he regarded as
the requisite leisure for the task. It was definitely
among his plans when he left the cabinet in 1881. Why

[112] Schurz to Edward L. Pierce, Sumner's biographer. November 3,
1889. *Speeches &c.*, v, 33-37.
[113] Speeches of February 15 and 20, and of May 31, 1870.

he abandoned it for editorship, unless to recoup his depressed finances, we do not fully know; but it is doubtful if this fiery devotee of politics as a going concern could ever have cloistered himself long enough to execute a task which occupied James Ford Rhodes the better part of a generation.

Had he entered the field of history writing in early manhood, and adhered to it, Carl Schurz might have gained a place among the great names of the guild. He was endowed with the insight, impartiality, and industry to achieve success in research, while his literary gifts would have guaranteed the readability of his books. Unfortunately or fortunately, in the period when he might have habituated himself to the service of the austere muse his scant supply of worldly goods prohibited the adoption of a program such as brought renown to his wealthy friend Henry Adams. Circumstances forced Schurz to be a maker, rather than a writer, of history.

In 1887, however, he published a book, the *Life of Henry Clay*,[114] which ranks among the very best in its series and reveals him as a happy and efficient laborer in the historical field. His picture of Henry Clay is at once convincing, charmingly sketched from within outward, and free from superficial or merely decorative lines and flourishes. The character fits into its setting, for the author made an uncommonly careful study of Clay's historical background in Virginia, Kentucky, and the country at large. In tracing his career he had the opportunity to utilize much of that detailed knowledge of American statecraft which marked him as the historian condemned to practise politics and political propagandism.

[114] Houghton, Mifflin and Company, Boston.

The biography of Clay was written, in the course of about four years, as a favorite task superadded to a heavy program of regular and special duties. For Schurz, aside from editorial work which engaged most of his time, was in constant demand for addresses on all kinds of problems of immediate public concern. He spoke before the Forestry Association, the Reform Club, the Commonwealth Club, various state civil service associations; wrote essays on the Indian problem, the New South, and a score of controversial questions treated in the form of elaborate letters. Still, though convinced that the story of Gallatin's life, which he would have preferred to treat, might be written with far less difficulty, he gradually worked his way into the scattered materials bearing upon his subject in a way to develop a genuine enthusiasm for it. Notwithstanding the long delay he imposed upon the editor,[115] who seems at one time to have raised the question of Schurz dropping the study, he would not permit himself to be hurried, but kept quietly at work until the book was finished to his own satisfaction.

The life of Clay proved an instant success. One of the earliest congratulatory letters received by the author was from ex-President Hayes. He had been sure of Schurz as an author who would treat Clay justly but knowing his aversion to hero worship, had questioned a little if he would see, as others did, 'the wonderful combination of attractive qualities' possessed by Clay— his sound human nature, magnetism, grace, eloquence— which, taken together gave him a unique character. 'You have satisfied the demand of his admirers,' said Hayes, 'and still kept faith with historical accuracy and justice. It is well done, exceedingly.' Similar com-

[115] John T. Morse. See *Speeches &c.*, iv. *Passim*.

ments were made by other correspondents, including
Moses Coit Tyler, and the *Atlantic* reviewer pronounced the book not merely the best so far published in
the American Statesman series but perhaps the best
biography ever produced in America.[116]

The quality which most distinguishes the book, apart
from the charm of its narrative style, is discriminating
judgment, the most fundamental prerequisite of success in historical writing. Schurz's insight, aided by a
penetrating study of his sources, yielded a true interpretation of the man in both his strength and his weaknesses. This is recognized by readers of the biography
who may or may not know that the analysis of character
was with this author a gift raised by long practise to the
plane of a fine art. He mentions the interest in his
youthful letters, the intensive experience as liberal
leader in the university, and as revolutionist, fixed it as
a habit of mind. His later letters give us delightful
cameos of public men including Lincoln, Grant, Sheridan, and Bismarck. In his editorials we find pen pictures of several Indians he had known, especially Ouray,
Ute chief, 'probably the wisest Indian of this generation,' and the 'pretentiously dignified' Spotted Tail,
which disclose an almost uncanny power to penetrate
even barbarian character.[117]

A writer possessing Schurz's penchant for the un-
equivocal and final judgments may readily gain more
credit for penetration than he actually deserves. But
in his case tests are easily applied. Whoever, for example, is willing to permit himself to be convinced that
there is a Lincoln myth, developed since the assassina-
tion of the great Liberator, needs only to read Schurz's

[116] *Atlantic Monthly,* lx, 556.
[117] New York *Evening Post,* August 9, 1881 and August 19, 1881.

calm, discerning, and just estimate of the living president as he gave it to a personal friend before the election of 1864.[118]	He never subscribed to the view that Lincoln was one of nature's geniuses.	But he saw in him 'a man of profound feeling, just and firm principles, and incorruptible integrity.'	'One can,' he says, 'always rely upon his motives, and the characteristic gift of this people, a sound common sense, is developed in him to a marvelous degree.'	He knew him well, he added, had often criticised him severely and later found that he was right.	His personality fitted him to cope with the crisis the country was undergoing.	'Free from the aspirations of genius,' he would never become dangerous to a free country.	'He is the people personified,' the most 'representative' of rulers; whose name, Schurz prophesied would, in fifty years or less, 'stand written upon the honor roll of the American Republic next to that of Washington, and there it will remain.	The children of those who now disparage him will bless him.' Twenty-six years later, in a formal essay on Lincoln, Schurz completed the sketch but in no way contradicted the judgments here presented.[119]	Lincoln was still 'one of the greatest of Americans and the best of men,' although never one of earth's few geniuses.

One of the best tests of Schurz's ability to discriminate, in his study of character, is found in the eulogy he delivered at New York upon Emperor William I of Germany, March twenty-first, 1881, shortly after that monarch's decease.	His German auditors, when they recalled that the speaker was the very man who thirty-two years before had so narrowly escaped death at the hands of William's firing squad, must have won-

[118] Letter to Petrasch, October 12, 1864.
[119] Abraham Lincoln.	*Atlantic Monthly,* lxvii, 721-750.

dered what kind of 'eulogy' they were to hear. Schurz
satisfied them without pronouncing a eulogy at all, in
the accepted sense, by pointing out the emperor's rather
obvious weaknesses, from the standpoint of liberal
statesmanship, and also his more recondite noble qualities, especially those of generosity, devotion to the duty
of ruling as vice-gerent of God, and his sound judgment in selecting and holding able advisers. One great
act, he said, the unification of Germany, had 'illumined
all his past.' and destined him for a mythical fame like
that of Barbarossa.

Aside from his life of Clay and his sketch of Lincoln.
which was afterwards issued in book form, Schurz wrote
one other book to which frequent allusion has been made
in these pages, the so-called *Reminiscences.* This story,
growing out of his own life and experiences, was left in
a more fragmentary condition than is the lot of memoirs
generally, which in the nature of the case can never be
completed. Schurz's *Reminiscences* cover the first forty
years of his life and occupy two and one-half of the three
stout volumes bearing that title.[120]

It is a remarkable book. Just as Schurz, in his life
of Henry Clay, can be said to have written one of the
most striking and worthy American biographies, he
must be conceded to have produced, in the varied and
dramatic narrative of his own life, one of our subtlest,
most interesting, and educative autobiographies. The
ripe fruit of a ripe and mellowed life, a career tran-
scending the contentious politics which had made so
large a part of his earlier activities, we have a right to expect the book to shed true light upon men and movements with which he was associated as participant or

[120] The McClure Company (New York, 1907-1908). In the second part
of volume three, Frederick Bancroft and William A. Dunning summarize
the career of Mr. Schurz from 1869 to his death in 1906.

observer. In this we are not disappointed. A few moot characters such as Douglas, Andrew Johnson, and General Hooker, Schurz found it hard to treat otherwise than as personal enemies. But on the whole, his purpose to be a just and merciful judge, which though never expressed can be read on every page, was carried out faithfully.

The *Reminiscences,* like the biography of Clay, gave him a partial opportunity to utilize that myriad tentacled complex of knowledge of American political history which he had wished to develop through extended research and present in more systematic form. His theory of biography, as developed in the essay on Lincoln, justified the employment of only so much history as would establish a background for his subject, and yet would not submerge the individual in the historical matrix. Portions of the *Reminiscences* violate that principle, drawing out the historical narrative beyond what would be strictly required for purposes of interpretation; but the principle of interest is never violated. The old stock phrase of literary eulogy: 'This book contains no dull page,' is hardly stronger than the fact warrants. For Schurz was naturally dramatic, and having a clear field without restraining walls, and an exuberant supply of incidents among which to choose, he followed his natural inclination and selected those items which would most surely grip the reader's attention. The blending in this narrative of old and new world interests largely enhances its effectiveness.

The defects of *Reminiscences* are those which inhere in that form of writing, namely diffuseness, a tendency to rationalize episodes under the mood the writer is in when he writes about them, not when they occur, and an unconscious deviation from the historic fact both as regards chronology and as regards the essential content of experience. Memoirs are not history and whatever else they may be, they are not biography. Fundamentally, they are historical sources, of greater or less value, depending upon the writer.

Not infrequently, however, reminiscences constitute a most enticing form of literature which, by reason of artistic seductiveness, is by many intelligent readers accorded a higher historical authority than, in the nature of things, it can possibly possess. For Recollection and Emotion are oath-bound conspirators against the reason and in memoirs they find their opportunity for drugging it and carrying it into captivity. A few examples of how our author, who was a relatively wary writer of memoirs, permitted himself to be deceived by these enemies, are given in the preceding chapters. Many others could be cited; yet when all deductions have been made, Schurz's *Reminiscences* remains one of the great books of the early twentieth century, which no intelligent person can read without palpably experiencing an expansion and enrichment of his life.

The descent from literary production to 'quill driving' seemed to Schurz in his youth to represent a plunge into the abyss. Under the latter head he classified journalism, but this turned out to be precisely the division of the writing field in which he was destined to serve longest and, so far as practical results go, perhaps most effectively. Of course, the influence of his editorials in the *Westliche Post* upon the hundreds of thousands of Germans who read them, directly and indirectly, during a crucial decade in our history cannot be assessed with even an approximation to accuracy. Yet, in imagination, we can see going forward week by week, year after year, the educational process which was to build into the individual lives something of the leader's ideals of citizenship and public service, under the conditions of the new allegiance which he shared with his neophytes. His newspaper instruction, supplementing his speeches, went far toward setting the German population of the country on paths where they would encounter mainly the best class of American citizens.

There were times when Schurz fairly revelled in the joys of journalistic self expression, but those were the unquiet periods when politics were seething. Stagnant intervals in public affairs were apt to be boresome. He developed a most happy faculty of writing short, crisp paragraphs which usually stated some guiding principle and epitomized the facts bearing on the particular question to which the principle applied. But he regretted the necessity of extreme condensation. His habits of preparation and thinking being adapted to the requirements of the speech or lecture, yielded on nearly all topics material adequate for a series of editorials while the exigencies of newspaper appeal justified the use of only one. So he felt that he was being split up into fine kindling wood for merely starting the popular interest, not satisfying it with reasoned argument and with adequate information.

The most satisfying exercise of the editorial office to Schurz was his weekly leader for *Harper's* during several years. Here he was able to say his say with reasonable amplitude, to treat important public questions, like those relating to the war against Spain, with a breadth and dignity which he felt they deserved.

But after all, the speech or lecture was Schurz's favorite instrument for impressing his views upon the public mind, as his readiness to respond to calls of many kinds indicates. He loved to utter his thoughts fully, with the force, fire, and eloquence always generated in him by the presence of the living audience. This is merely to repeat that, fundamentally, whatever else and however many other characters he exemplified, Schurz was a natural orator. If, in the hour of his dissolution some good fairy had vouchsafed him a clairvoyant picture of the 1860 Douglas speech incident, even if all else were blotted out, we could fancy him dying happy. It was true instinct that induced the editor of the Schurz manuscripts to call the work *Speeches, Correspondence, and Political Papers.*

For nearly ten years, from 1892 to 1901, Schurz was president of the National Civil Service Reform League. He took the office after the first president, George William Curtis died. It called for a close and unwearying scrutiny of the departments of government with a view to guard against infringements of the law, and an annual report, or address, showing the moral gains and losses of the year. It entailed correspondence with presidents in office, presidential candidates, and other public men. But this was a type of activity which to him was especially congenial and for which no man in the country was better fitted. Letters which passed between Schurz and Cleveland are particularly abundant and have a high significance for the light they shed on Cleveland's ideals of government.

From a party standpoint, Schurz's last twenty years were a protracted bivouac. But he had now become so accustomed to taking the political weather in the open that he seemed actually to enjoy the experience, particularly since he always had a congenial company of fellow campers about him. Independency became for Schurz the substitute for partyism. In a sense, it was a new kind of partyism, more satisfying in many respects than the old. The company was smaller but more select, and there were in him some very decided aristocratic leanings. The campaigns of 1876 and 1884 had disclosed the power of a compact group of independents and that power was not apt to grow less. On the contrary, the trend toward independence in voting steadily increased as party platforms tended toward uniformity, though after 1884 it never became easy actually to organize any large fraction of the independent voting element.

In 1888 Schurz was in Europe and took no part in the election. In 1892 he favored Cleveland, and wrote an argument in behalf of his candidacy. But an affection of the throat prevented him from speaking. This, however, he did four years later, on the sound money issue, with such good results that he must be called an appreciable factor in the defeat of Bryan. He helped to sustain McKinley's administration so long as there was an honest effort to avert the war with Spain, which he believed to be unnecessary. Schurz, however, was ready, once war had been entered upon, to do everything to bring it swiftly to a successful issue. But when the peace negotiations threatened to saddle upon the United States permanently the tropical Philippine Islands, he revolted and joined the anti-imperialists, continuing to act with this group as long as there was any chance to affect the result. Consequently, his sympathy in 1900 was with Bryan who stood sincerely on an anti-imperialistic platform. But the forces of expansion were too strong and Schurz, to the day of his death, had to lament what he was convinced had been a false step on the nation's part. In 1904, the last presidential election he was destined to see, he voted for Judge Parker.

One of Schurz's last public appearances was as commencement speaker at the University of Wisconsin, in June, 1905. At that time the institution of which forty-five years earlier he had been a regent, conferred upon him the honorary degree of Doctor of Laws. His daughter Agathe accompanied her father and they were entertained at the home of the then governor, afterwards senator, Robert M. La Follette. The address is remembered for the ease, fluency, and eloquence with which it was delivered, a fair sample of the historic Schurz style, despite his seventy-six years. The occasion called for a very different effort from the Madison speech of September, 1857, but of its type it was quite on the same plane of perfection.

The following winter Schurz spent in Georgia, on account of the throat affection which had troubled him intermittently for many years. He came north too early in spring, encountered raw weather in New York, contracted pneumonia, and passed away on the fourteenth of May in his summer cottage on Lake George.

At the time of his death three children were living. They were Agathe Schurz, who had been his secretary, house manager, and confidential aide from the time of her mother's death in 1876; Marianne Schurz, the second daughter, and Carl Lincoln Schurz, who became a prominent lawyer in New York. A younger son, Herbert, said to have been a most promising young man, died in 1900 without issue. Agathe died July eighteenth, 1915; Carl Lincoln, also without issue, May nineteenth, 1924. Marianne, the last member of Carl Schurz's family, died on the twentieth of May, 1929.

Thus the line of Carl Schurz, like the line of Abraham Lincoln, is extinct. Both failed to impress themselves upon the country through children of the body.

But in Schurz's case, as in Lincoln's, the children of the spirit can be depended upon to keep green the memory of a service to the cause of human liberty and welfare, of justice, mercy, and truth, such as in every age of human history has been all too rare.

INDEX

INDEX

ADAM, escape, 52-53, 55.

Adams, Charles Francis, possible presidential nominee, 199; Schurz silent on, 200; aids Schurz, 208; for Tilden, 211.

Adams, Henry, writer, 243.

Adams, W., at New York convention, 209.

Alabama, Schurz sent to, 164.

Albert of Coburg, at Bonn, 21.

Alps, Schurz vacation among, 70.

Althaus, Frederick, letter to, 73, 103, 163.

Althof, ——, at New York convention, 209.

Ann Arbor (Mich.), Schurz speaks at, 148.

Anneke, Fritz, organizes attack, 43; blamed, 47; messenger, 51; Schurz meets, 59.

Anti-Masonic organization, members leave, 101.

Arkansas, reconstruction in, 160; land grant, 235.

Arkansas River, Indians removed to, 219.

Armstrong, Gen. Samuel C., directs Hampton Institute, 220.

Arndt, Ernst M., German scholar, 20-21; prestige of, 28-29; secedes, 48; appreciation of, 240.

Arthur, Chester A., becomes president, 226.

Atlantic Monthly, Schurz contributes to, 174; cited, 245-246.

Auburn (N.Y.), Schurz speaks at, 147.

Auerswald, Gen. von, murdered, 38.

Augusta (Mo.), Schurz visits, 176.

Austria, Catholics favor, 31; reaction under, 37; absolutism of, 37; relations of, 39, 45; compulsion, 59.

BACON, Leonard, at New York convention, 209.

Baden, German state, 41; uprising in, 42-43, 45-46, 48; grand duke of, 48; refugee from, 59; Hecker revolutionist in, 101.

Baltimore (Md.), Kinkel at, 70.

Bancroft, Frederick, author, xvi, 247.

Barclay, Thomas S., *The Liberal Republican Movement in Missouri,* quoted, 185.

Basel (Switzerland), Schurz near, 55.

Bauman, ——, at New York convention, 209.

Bavaria, German state, 41.

Bayard, Thomas F., Schurz favors, 233.

Beard, Frank, illustrated *That Convention,* 199.

Becker's *Universal History,* mentioned, x.

Beer-Zeitung, Schurz edits, 22.

Bell-Everett followers, broke up meeting, 147.

Belleville (Ill.), Hecker at, 82; Schurz speaks at, 137.

Berlin (Germany), resident, xv; Kinkel at, 34; committee at, 39; Spandau near, 62; Schurz at, 63, 175.

Bethlehem (Pa.), Schurzs at, 85.

Bethlehem Philharmonic Society, provides music, 85.

Bismarck, Prince Otto von, Schurz invited to call on, 175; sketch, 245.

Bissenger, ——, at New York convention, 209.

Blaine, James G., Schurz opposes, 123, 207, 211; as cabinet possibility, 213; watches Schurz, 214; on timber question, 216-217; Schurz silent on, 225; Schurz distrusts, 228; unacceptable, 229, 238; dislikes Schurz, 229, 231-232; approves Schurz bill, 230; ambition to be president, 233; Schurz speech against, 234-235; and Mulligan letters, 229, 232, 234-236; Wisconsin Republican vote, 237; defeat, 239.

Blanc, Louis, quoted, 72.

Blanchard, H., at New York convention, 209.